This Bramcost Publications edition is an unabridged republication
of the rare original work first published in 1950.

www.BramcostPublications.com

ISBN 10: 1-934268-91-7
ISBN 13: 978-1-934268-91-9

Library of Congress Control Number: 2009920619

Bramcost
Publications

Hat Tactics

Written and Illustrated

by

BRETT OURS DRAGER

ABOUT THE AUTHOR, BRETT OURS DRAGER . . .

Brett's ambition is to have a permanent picket fence and a fireplace with a fender where she and her husband can rest their feet. Actually, her life is the reality of a dream that to most picket fence owners is a cherished ambition.

She received her degree in Fine Arts at the University of Oklahoma, and also studied with the Art Students League in New York City. This talented young woman is a member of the Oklahoma Artists Association, and has exhibited widely her portraits, landscapes and other paintings. She was invited to show her work at the San Francisco World's Fair in 1939.

Brett has travelled extensively in Europe, and for a number of years has made temporary homes in various far-flung places of the Orient—China, Indo-China, and the Philippines. For three years, she taught art in Honolulu.

During the war, Brett was evacuated from China where she and her husband had lived for several years, but even after such an experience, her unlimited energy did not allow her much rest. With an eager curiosity, she went to New York to study Dress Design at the Traphagen School of Fashion and Millinery at The New York School of Modern Millinery. On returning to her home in Oklahoma City, she taught classes at the Oklahoma City University, and gave demonstrated lectures throughout the State.

By the time Brett rejoined her husband in China on the cessation of hostilities, the fascinating hobby of hat creation had captivated her fancy completely. Determined to share her enjoyment with other women, she decided the best way to make available her knowledge would be through the motion picture medium—a new artistic adventure for Brett. She produced and directed a full length color motion picture, also entitled HAT TACTICS, which illustrates in detail the various processes of planning and making hats. This excitingly different movie, filmed against an authentic Oriental background with lovely models in picturesque native costumes, is available on demand. Brett's wide artistic experience as well as her authoritative handling of subject matter, make this film helpfully instructive as well as enchantingly beautiful.

In writing this book, she has displayed yet another facet of her versatile capabilities. Long painstaking hours have gone into the preparation of the hundreds of concise line drawings, and clearly phrased instructions.

In addition to an already impressive catalog of interests, Brett finds time to keep up with her painting, and collects Oriental screens, sculpture, fabrics, embroideries and costumes.

With confidence, one may assume that the accomplished author of HAT TACTICS is well qualified to present her material in a professional manner. Brett believes that any woman can make her own hats. She hopes her book may lead women everywhere to the realization that by combining up-to-date work room methods and imagination, they may discover an exciting and profitable hobby in the field of hat creation.

A.M.

TO THE BEGINNER, ADVANCED STUDENT, AND THE PROFESSIONAL!

The correct hat is to the ensemble what the maraschino cherry is to an ice-cream sundae! It is the perfect climax to the well-groomed YOU. Lively or lovely, daring or demure, the right hat gives you a delicious sense of poise and well-being for any occasion from your morning marketing to that after-five dinner date. And not only is your head-dress an emphasis to your costume, it is a proclamation of your mood.

Wonderful, you sigh, but how could I afford a hat for each costume? Easily! Make them up, make them over, make them excitingly and exclusively your very own! Your hat, that important center of interest, can be your own creation through the delightful discovery of hat-making.

The success and enthusiasm of my former students in the art of designing and producing their own hats has encouraged me to write this book, HAT TACTICS. It will supply you with a text accompanied by many line drawings which will guide you simply, step by step, to grasp the basic methods and conventional principles of every type of head-dress. A full length movie has also been prepared to further explain through visual demonstration.

Why not convert your sewing club to a Hat Club? You could go over the lessons in HAT TACTICS together, and perhaps see the movie. Many women have found it's fun to exchange inspirations and make suggestions for each other's designs. Of course, after you have carefully studied the book and the movie, observation and experience are your best teachers. Watch the smart hats on the street. Glean ideas from parties and teas. Be an alert window shopper, and examine the better fashion magazines. Then, armed with your own creative imagination, compose YOUR hat within current style trends, most expressive of your personality. Clever handling of style, shape and color can perform astonishing illusions that will flatter both face and figure.

Remember that a beautiful hat in harmony with your costume marks you as a WELL DRESSED WOMAN. Good luck! I hope you will enjoy the fascinating discovery of hat-making as much as I have enjoyed preparing HAT TACTICS for you.

Sincerely,

BRETT OURS DRAGER

A Beautiful Film in Color (16mm), also Called HAT TACTICS Illustrates in Detail Every Step in Hat Making — How to Plan, Design and Make Smart New Hats — How to Renovate and Remodel Old Millinery to New Life

Script, Produced and Directed by

BRETT OURS DRAGER

This unusual movie was filmed in the Orient with models and actresses in native costumes. Brett Ours Drager has lived and travelled extensively in the Far East, and among the beautiful things she has collected on her journeys are silks, brocades and embroideries from Hangchow, Soochow, and Shanghai, China; costumes and hats from Peiping, China; exquisite screens from Shanghai and Foochow, China; fabrics, hats and jewelry from India. HAT TACTICS features many of these exciting treasures, as well as a careful step by step demonstration of making hats. While the exotic background provides entertaining variety, the procedure exhibited is contemporary and the MILLINERY PRINCIPLES ARE BASIC.

It is a graphic illustration of the methods outlined in this book. Although the film does not stress current trends, it explains how styles are inspired, and how they may be adapted to popular fashion.

You will enjoy seeing HAT TACTICS—it is an excellent course integrating instruction with appreciation.

For further details and availability, write

Brett Ours Drager,
P. O. Box No. 3624,
Oklahoma City, Oklahoma

CONTENTS

Patterns

Just imagine the kind of house a carpenter would produce if he had no definite plan before he drove the first nail! You wouldn't want to live in it, would you? When you're "building a hat" you need to plan first, too—if you want a finished hat you'll be proud to wear.

From this chapter you will obtain a very workable knowledge and understanding of hat structure and formation. Therefore, it is very important to study and work out each step as presented. You'll find the old adage "practice makes perfect" applies in this case, and before you know it, you'll be able to plan your Headsize and make your preliminary plans in a breeze!

The first section of this chapter shows how to measure your own head, how to transfer measurements to the headblock, and how to apply those measurements to your patterns. You'll learn, too, how to make flat brims, shaped brims and crowns, and then you'll branch out to copying and designing by drafting and draping. These methods apply to every type of hat.

Keep each pattern you make. Make them in cardboard and mark with ink the Center Front, CF; Center Back, CB; Right Side, RS; and Left Side, LS. From CF and CB points connect a **continuous line through each pattern with ink.** Match this line to true bias or straight thread grain when cutting frames, blocks, bodies or fabric. Mark patterns well. With ink, draw a picture of the finished hat on its pattern.

Make NO SEAM ALLOWANCE on patterns. Allow for seams when you use the pattern.

Soon you'll be making your own patterns and designing your own stunning creations. And won't it be fun, when you are admired not only for your good taste in hats—but your ingenuity in making them!

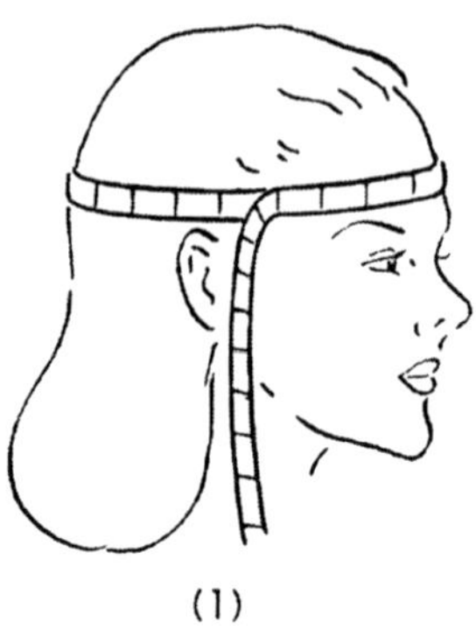

(1)

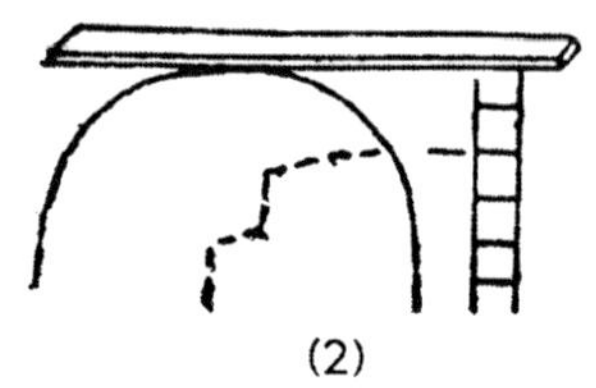

(2)

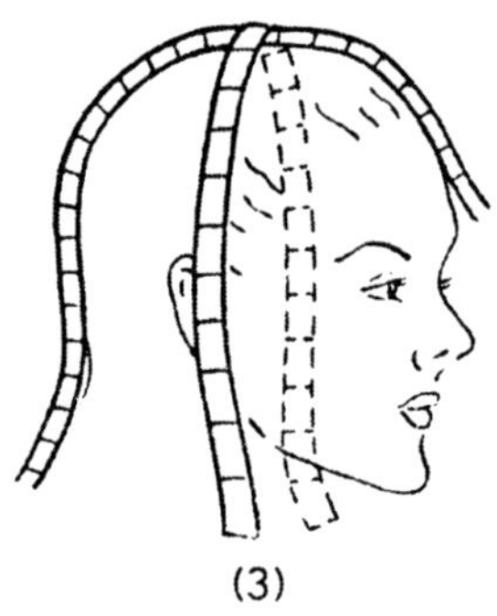

(3)

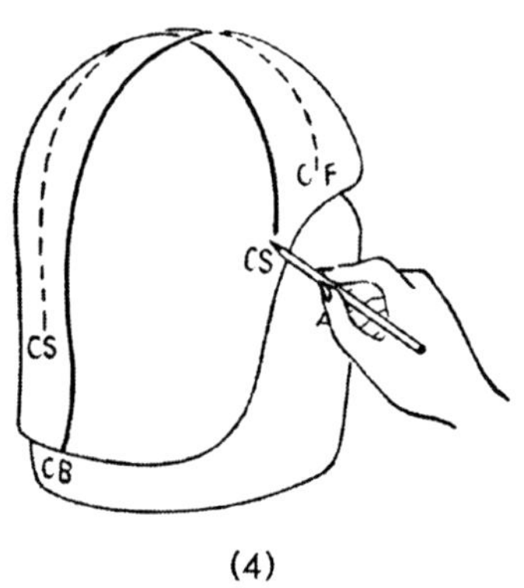

(5)

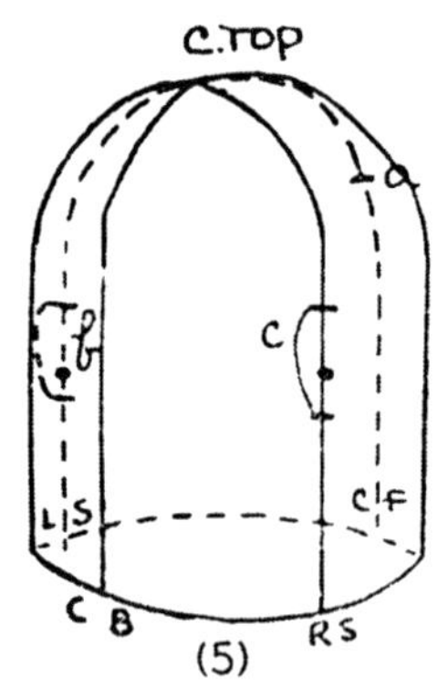

(4)

Patterns

★ **How to Measure the Head . . . and Mark the Headblock**

(1)

The Headsize is measured horizontally above your eyebrows, around the largest part of the head. This is the number of inches around your head and is your Headblock size.

(2)

Head DEPTH, from the top of the head to the hairline, is measured vertically from the hairline to a ruler laid horizontally on the top of the head. Mark this HAIRLINE on the wooden block.

(3)

To find Center Front-Center Back Line of Headblock, put an elastic band around the wooden head. Check, and mark a line from Center Front to Center Back with tailors' chalk. Lay a tape over your own head, from center of one ear across to the center of other ear, and measure distance from front hairline to Center Top of head with measuring tape and mark wooden block. Measure distance from top of one ear to the top of other ear and mark on wooden head. These tapes also show how to lay tapes to measure your own head for desired head depth of hat to be made.

(4)

Figure 4 shows marking Center Front, Center Back and Center Sides.

(5)

On the Center Front line is marked: "a," the hairline, "c," Center Top, and the Center Back. The Right Side-Left Side line is marked. On your own head, measure distance from top of one ear across to top of other ear, "b" and "c." Measure the height of the ear, and locate center. Mark on wooden head.

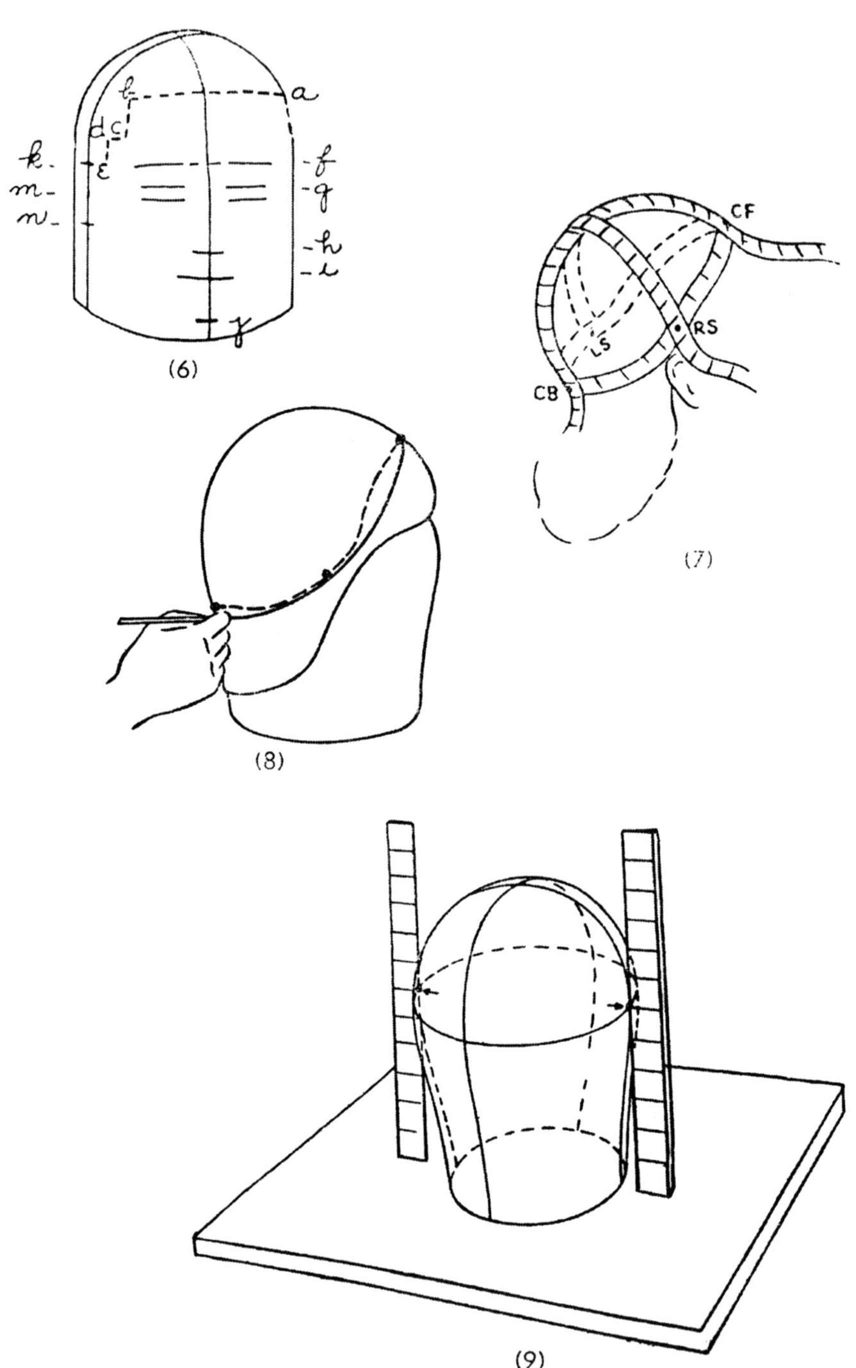

b
a
d
c
k
m
n
ε
f
g
h
i
j
(6)
CF
LS
RS
CB
(7)
(8)
(9)
(12)

(6)

From the front, measure width of your own hairline. Mark on the wooden head, "a-b." Measure and mark "b-c," "d-c" and "d-e." "k," "m" and "n" is the ear measurement. Mark the width from outside end of one brow to outside end of other, and distance down from hairline. Mark distance between eyebrows. When eyes are open, measure and mark distance between upper lashes and brow. Also measure and mark the distances from brow line to nose line, to mouth and to chin line. There is a difference in HEAD DEPTH between a long and short face, even if the Headsize measures the same. Paint all marks with black enamel, then paint the headblock with a clear varnish or shellac so dyes will not remain on the block and spoil later blocking.

(7)

Around your own head, put a measuring tape the depth you wish to wear your hat. Then, from Center Front, on tape, measure to Center Back, and from Right Side to Left Side.

(8)

On wooden block, mark Center Front to Center Back, Right Side to Left Side measurements and headsize of Step 7. Design Headsize. See dotted line in Figure 8.

(9)

After the Crown Depth and Headsize have been drawn, check each side. Is height the same? Is height at equal distances from Center Back the same? And is height the same at equal distances on Headsize line from Center Front?

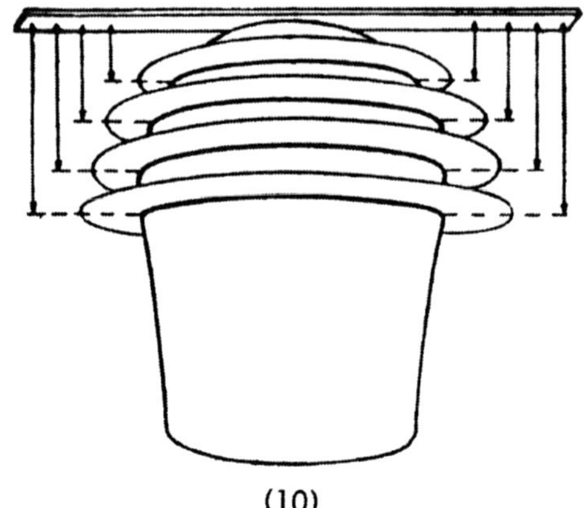

(10)

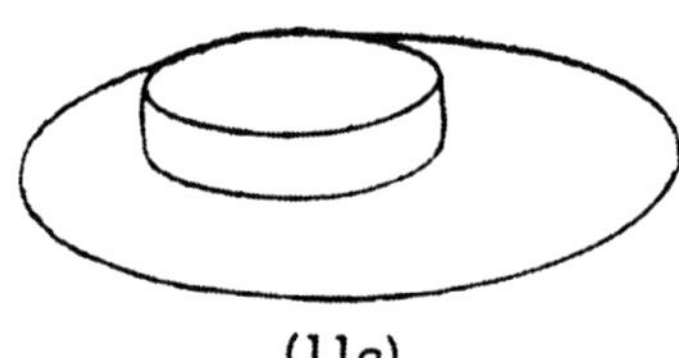

(11a)

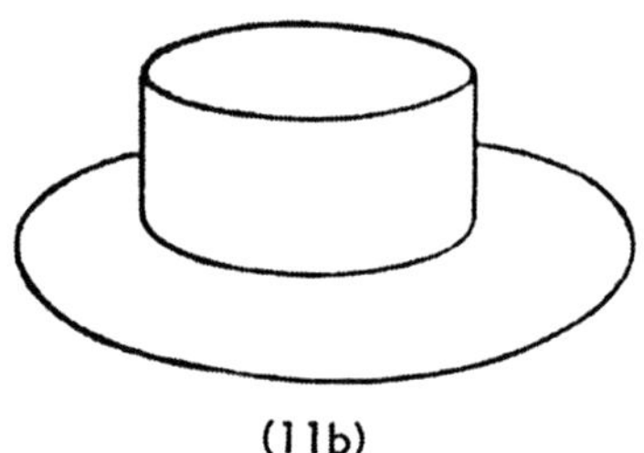

(11b)

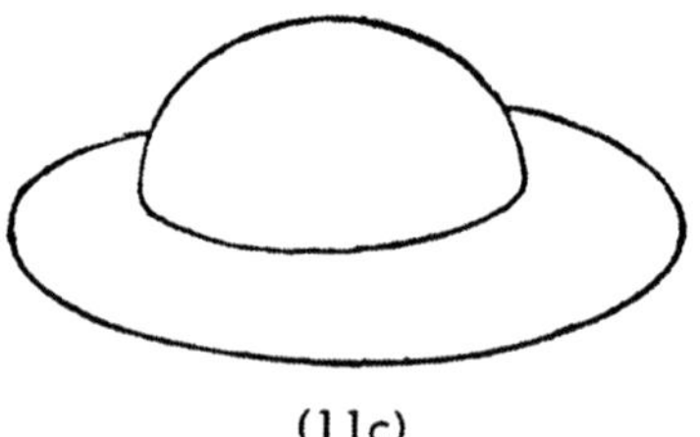

(11c)

(14)

(10)

How deep must crown of hat be if worn at first brim? 2nd? 3rd? 4th? Lay ruler horizontally level at top of head, and measure down to headsize. Study arrows.

(11 a, b & c)

11-a shows a shallow crown and a small headsize. 11-b shows a large head-size and deep crown. It is worn down on the head, so must have a deeper crown. Headsize of 11-c is large with a blocked fitted crown. NOTE: All brims are same circumference.

(12)

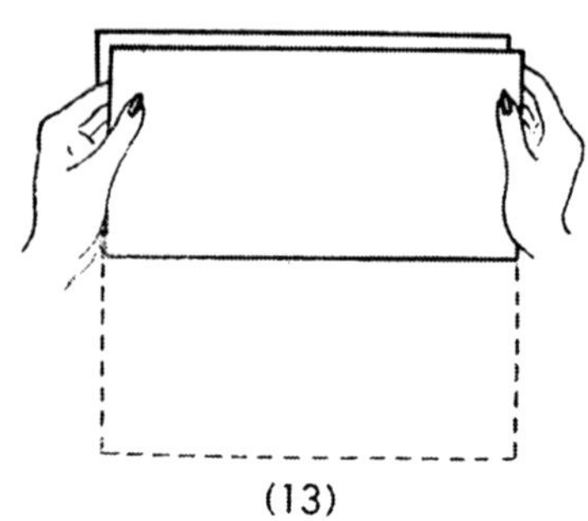

(13)

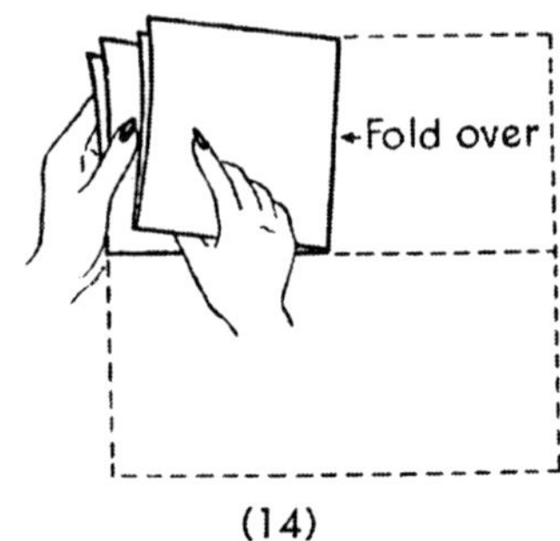

(14)

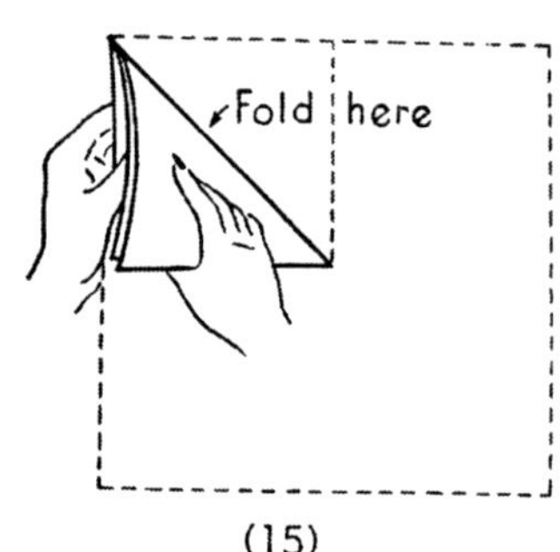

(15)

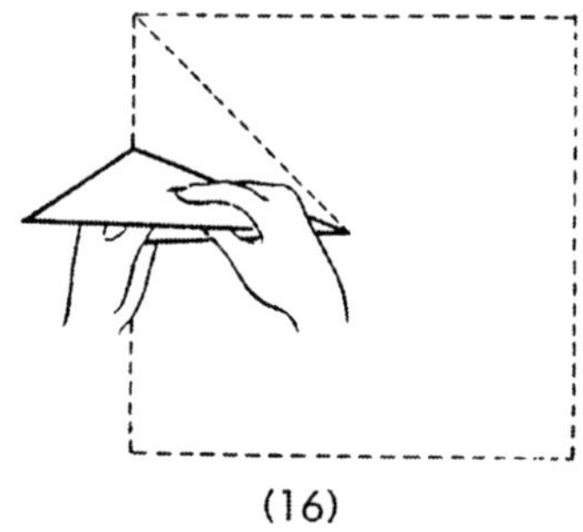

(16)

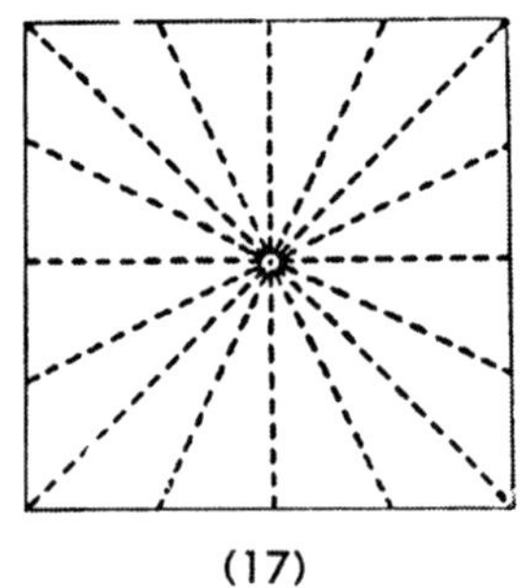

(17)

Starting the Hat

★ **Brims**

The following methods will give you an idea of how to start working. From these methods you can copy or create your own designs.

The FOLDED PAPER method is good, because you can rely on the folds for accuracy in checking the width of one side of the brim against the other side at the same distances from Center Front or Center Back.

(12)

Start with a 20-inch square of paper.

(13)

Fold up once.

(14)

Fold over once to the left.

(15)

Fold over to left again.

(16)

Fold to the left the third time.

(17)

Unfold and mark Center Front at the top of the paper and on the same vertical line, mark Center Back at the bottom. On the middle horizontal line, mark Right Side, and on the left side, mark Left Side. Use these lines as guides when cutting fabric on thread grain or bias.

Headsize Chart

— Above and Below Center —

(See instructions Nos. 18 through 23)

	½ inch	9/16 inch	⅝ inch

HEADSIZES

Radii
(See instruction No. 19)

	½ inch	9/16 inch	⅝ inch
2 15/16			21
3 1/16	21¼	21½	21¾
3 3/16	22	22¼	22½
3 5/16	22¾	23	

The above table in inches represents the closest calculations to EVEN
Headsizes. (With radii and off-centers shown)

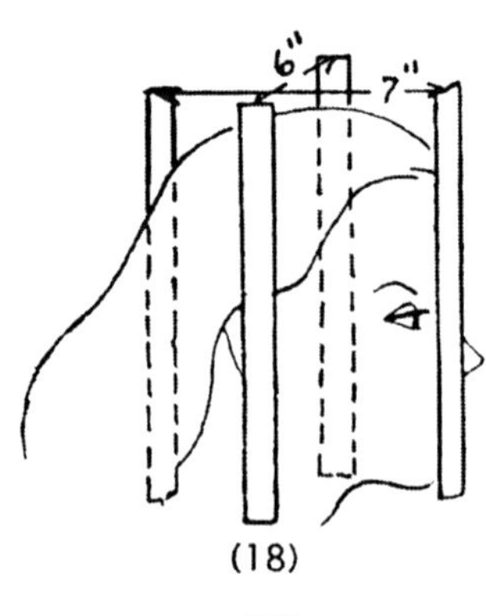

(18)

(18)

The Headsize

The size of the Headsize and the outside size of the hat are determined by hat styles and trends. Over a period of time, skirt lengths go from long to short, and back again to long. Hats also follow a cycle—from very large, bulky hats to petite half hats, and again to the very big hats. Headsizes vary from large (down on the head) to small (setting on top of the head). See Figure 11. The small headsizes have a round Headsize, and the hats which are worn deep on the head have oval Headsizes. HAT TACTICS suggests making a series of cardboard oval and round patterns, for quick tracing in the future.

(18)

To determine your very own Headsize Oval, hold rulers vertically straight at the Right Side and Left Side, measure distance between them. Do same from Center Back to Center Front.

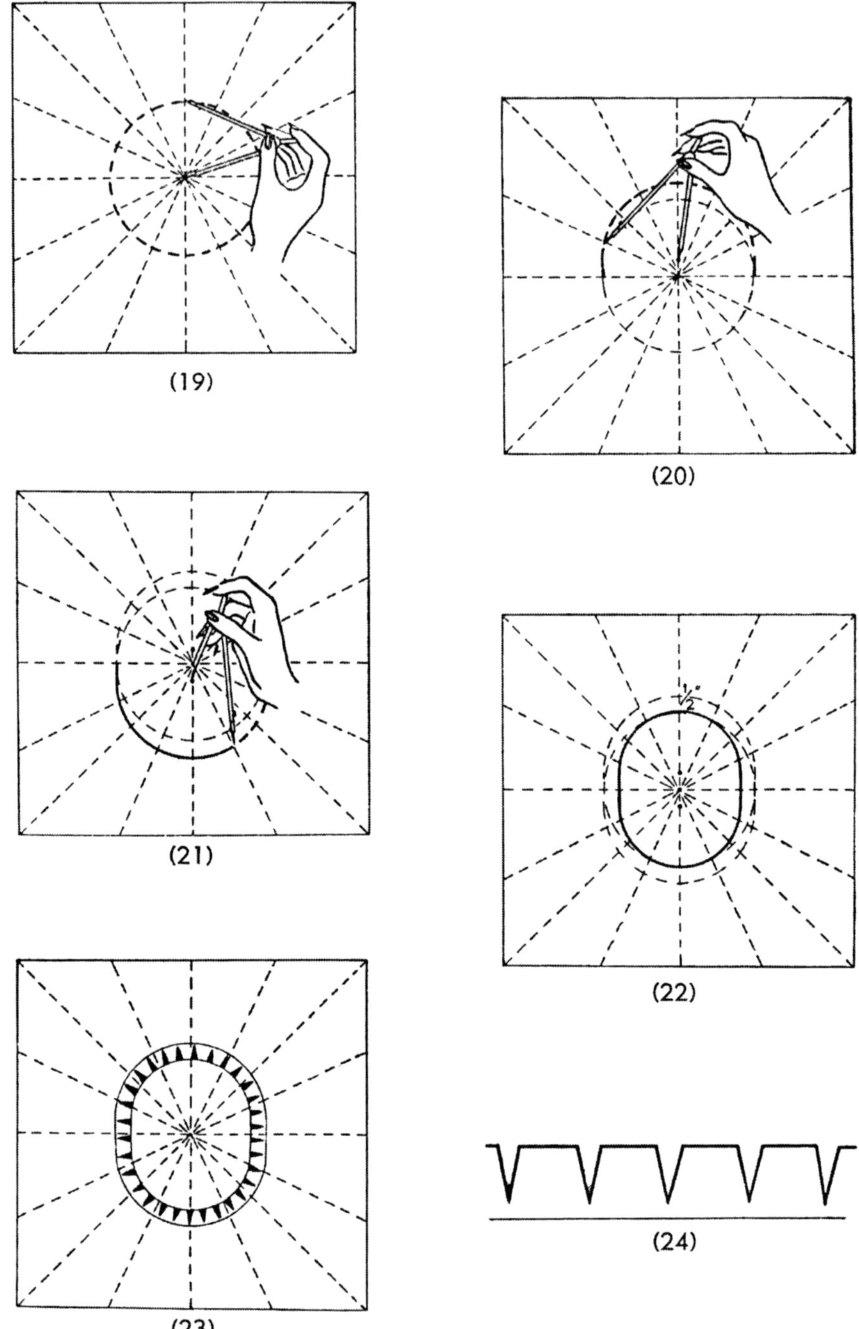

(19)

(20)

(21)

(22)

(23)

(24)

(19)

First, draw a circle with a compass, setting the point at the center of the paper where folds come together. Use a radius ½ the width between Right Side-Left Side measurement. Or consult Headsize Chart.

(20)

Using the same radius as above, set the compass point above the center of the paper, at a distance equal to ½ the difference between Right Side-Left Side and Center Front-Center Back measurements. Swing a half circle from Left Side to Right Side line. Or follow Headsize Chart.

(21)

The same distance from the Center of the paper as in Step 20, swing a half circle at the bottom of the circle.

(22)

If you measured correctly, this oval is the exact oval of your head. The Headsize Chart is a satisfactory guide in making your patterns. Measurements in Step 18 are for only **you.**

(23)

After the oval has been drawn, draw an allowance of ½" to ⅝" on the inside of the oval. On this allowance, draw tabs freehand.

(24)

Actual size of tabs.

C F
5¼″
3¾″
2″
5¼″
3¾″
2⅛″
5⅜″
3⅜″
2¼″
5⅜″
3¼″
2¼″
5⅝″
LS
CARTWHEEL
BERET
SAILOR
5½″
3⅛″
2¼″
3″
RS
5″/8
5″/8
2″
2″
4¾″
2″
3″/4
2″
1½″
3″/4
1¾″
3⅜″
4⅞″
3″/16
3¾″
3¼″
3 1″
C B

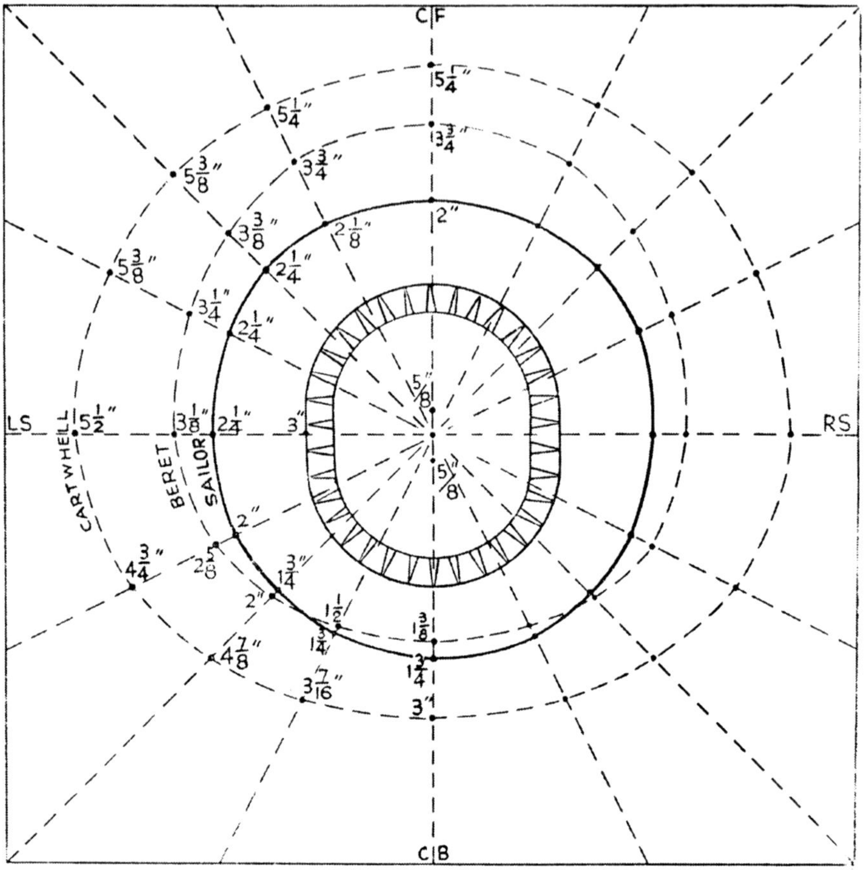

(25a)

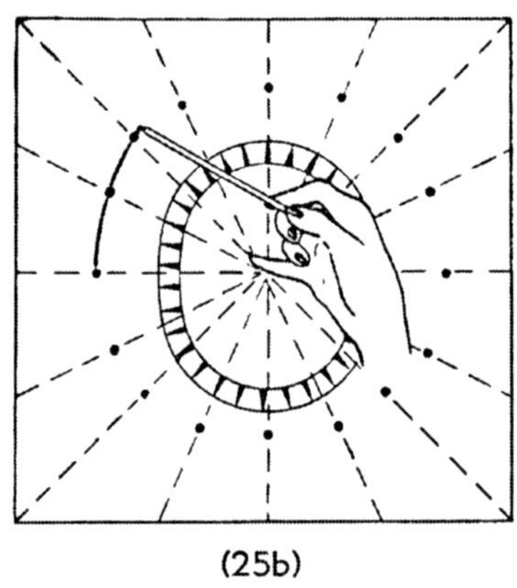

(25b)

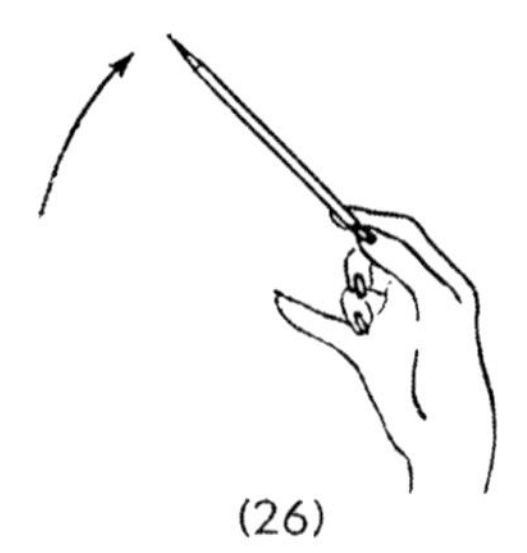

(26)

★ THE DOT METHOD

(25 a & b)

After the Headsize is drawn, for a small brim or sailor brim a little narrower at Center Back, use the DOT METHOD (25a). Start at Center Front and measure up 2'' from Headsize Oval line and dot——(25b). To the left, measure up 2⅛'' from Headsize line, etc., to Center Back. On the Right side mark correspondingly, using the DOT METHOD Brim Chart as a guide. Connect the dots.

(26)

Use little finger as a compass point, and swing a smooth rounded line.

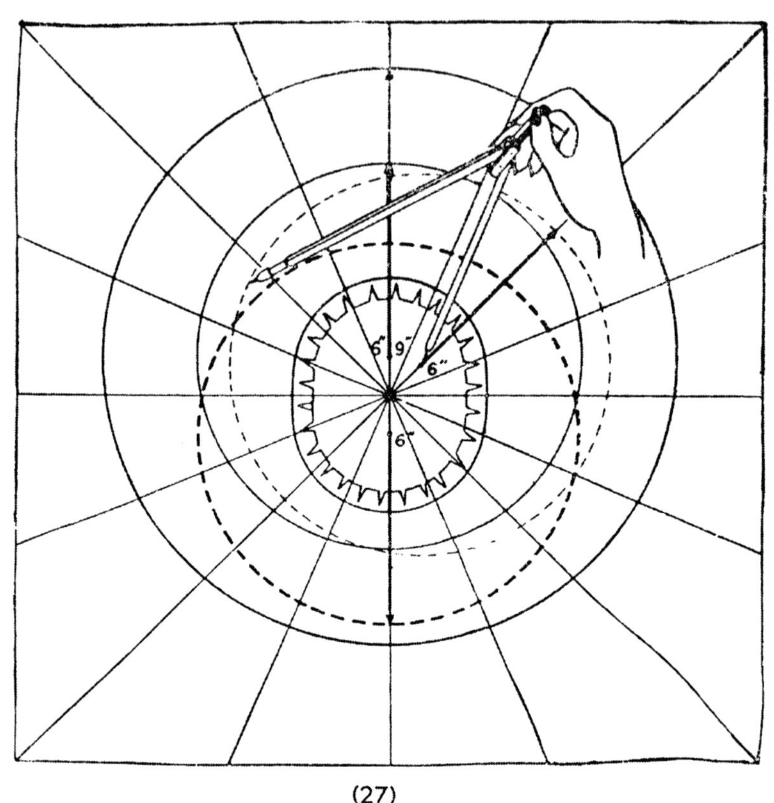

(27)

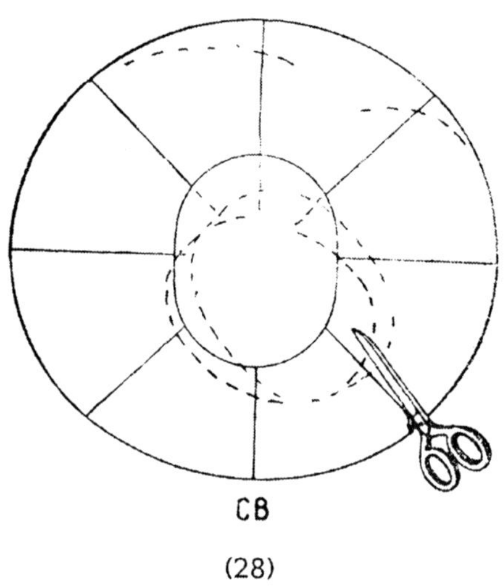

(28)

(24)

★ BRIMS DRAWN WITH COMPASS

(27)

These brims are circular. Before the inside of Headsize is cut away, set compass at any desired point within the Headsize Oval, and swing a circle. If
width is desired at Center Front, set compass point above Center at points
9 or 6, and set compass radius 6" for small circle, 9" for larger circle—
follow arrow. Try for different sizes and shapes by setting the compass
point in positions on or away from Center Line.

★ FREEHAND METHOD

(28)

The outside edge of the brim (see dotted lines) may be changed by freehand drawing. Instead of drawing Headsize each time, use a Headsize pattern. Lay at Center or off-center, and trace around the cardboard pattern.
See dotted lines. If Headsize oval or circle is laid off-center, and away from
Center Front-Center Back line, then the Center Front-Center Back line (fold)
is moved to another fold. If brim is to be shaped, cut at Center Back to
correspond with one of the Headsize dotted lines.

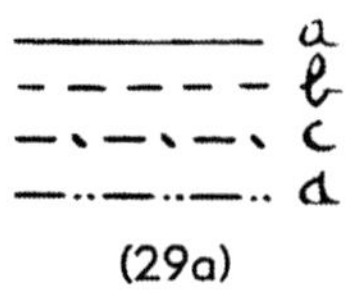

(29a)

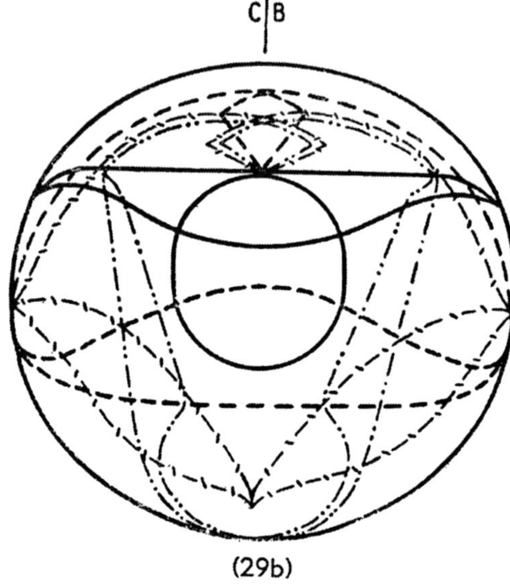

(29b)

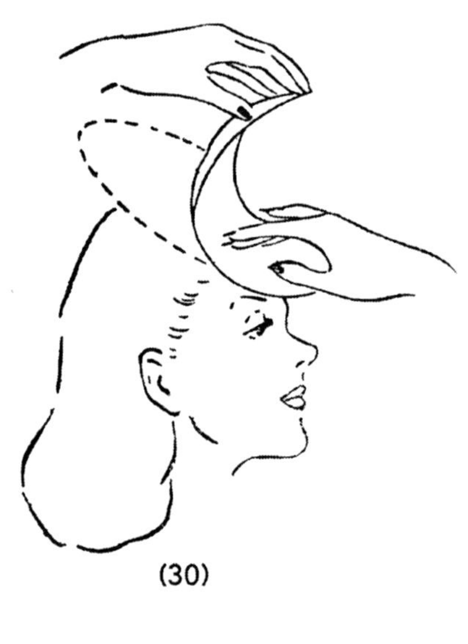

(30)

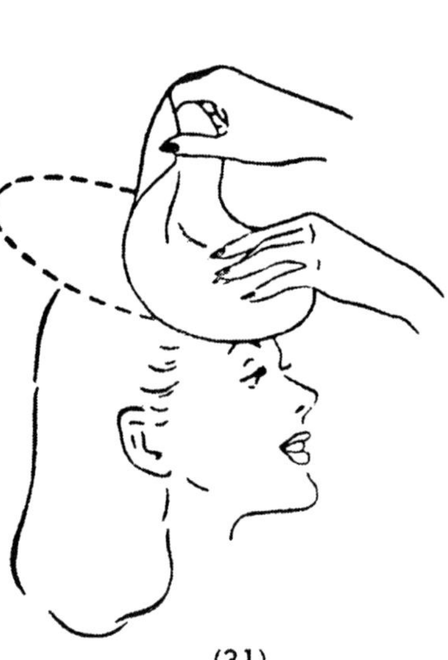

(31)

(26)

Changing the Shape
Of the Flat Brim

★ **The Bend Method**

(29)

Follow line "a" in figure 29b. Only the back of the brim is turned up. With line "b," only the front is up-turned. Line "c" shows the front sides turned toward the Center Front, making the tricorne. "d" shows two sides rolled like the fedora. Notice the Center Back of lines "c," "b" and "d" are cut and lapped, giving brim a curved roll or slant.

(30)

Bend a circle of paper forward, thus shaping the watteau.

(31)

OR dimple the top of the circular paper. After the shape is made in material and wired, the dimple can be bent in the wire.

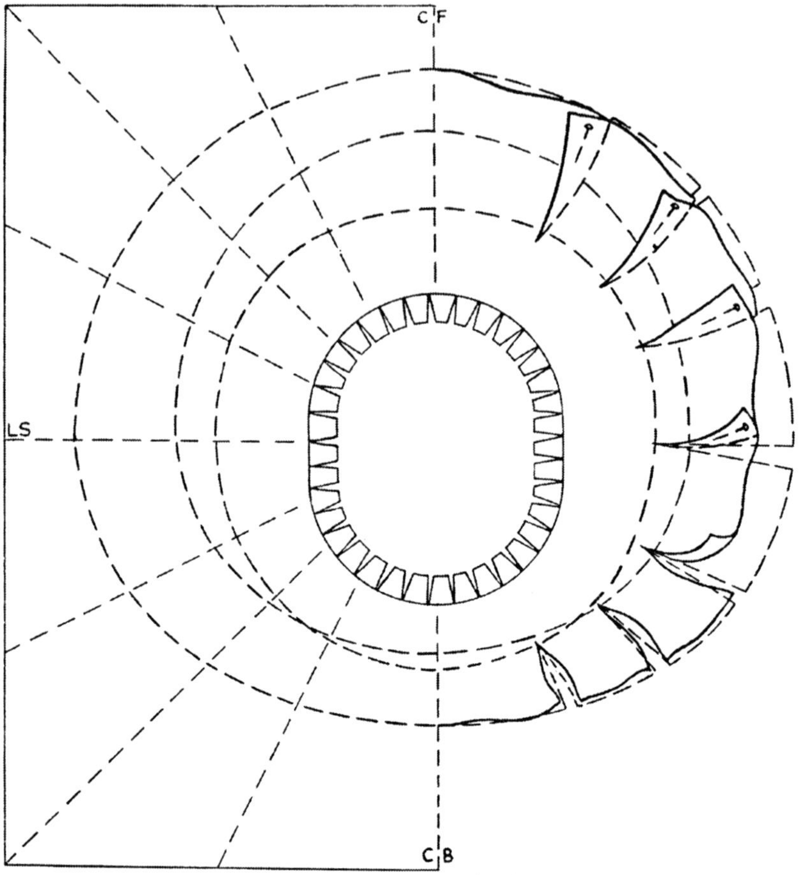

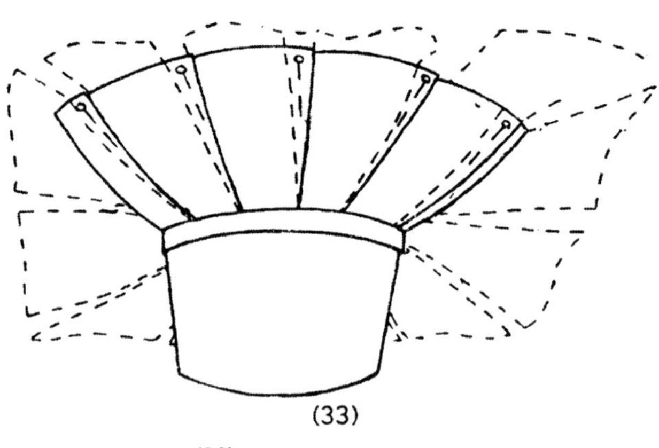

(28)

★ LAPPED EDGE METHOD

(32)

From the folded paper, cut each fold an equal distance in from brim edge. Lap equally at outer edge, and pin. This causes edge to curve, or makes a slanted brim. Cut away inside of Headsize at tabs.

(33)

The cut folds may be cut to the Headsize and lapped to curve, or lapped to extend up or down in a straight slant.

(34)

To make a pattern from one of these shaped brims, cut through the Center Back line. The shape then lays flat on the cardboard. Trace around the lapped brim at Headsize and edges. Mark and ink folds on cardboard pattern, as well as Center Front, Center Back, Right Side and Left Side.

(35)

A straight band of paper may be first folded and lapped to shape for a side crown, or turned-up or turned-down brim. Lay on cardboard and trace for a pattern. Mark Center Front, Center Back. See Figure 11, Frames, for finished side crown.

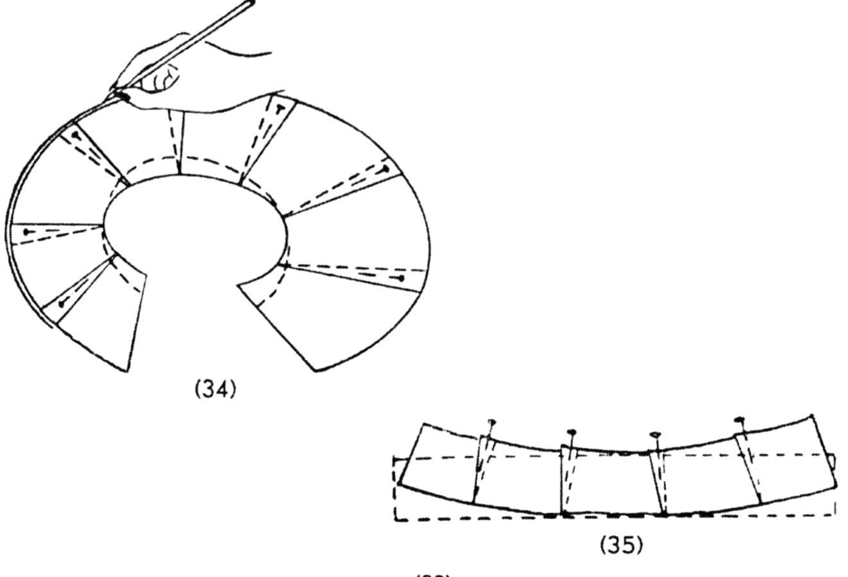

(34)

(35)

Sectional Crown

(36)

A length of paper, as wide as from Center top of head to Headsize and as long as Headsize measurement, is folded at Center and again, in four equal parts.

(37 a & b)

On one section, mark Center at top—37a. From about one-half way down one side, draw a curved line to Center Top. Mark opposite side the same, fold and cut on dotted lines—37b. There will be seams at the top sides and one seam from Center through Center top to back at Headsize.

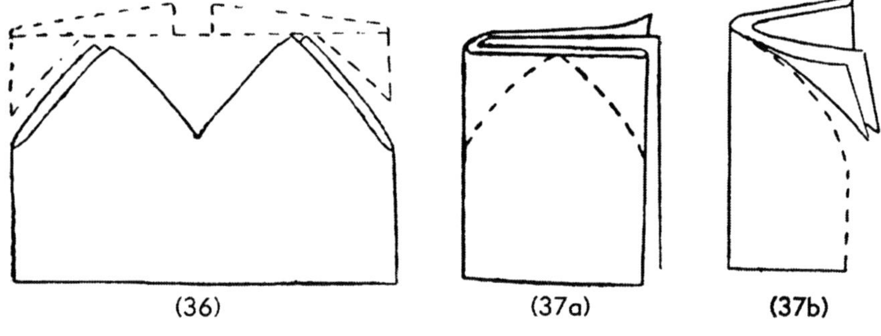

(36)   (37a)   (37b)

(38)

See Figure 28, Frames—set gore in paper brim or crown for ripple.

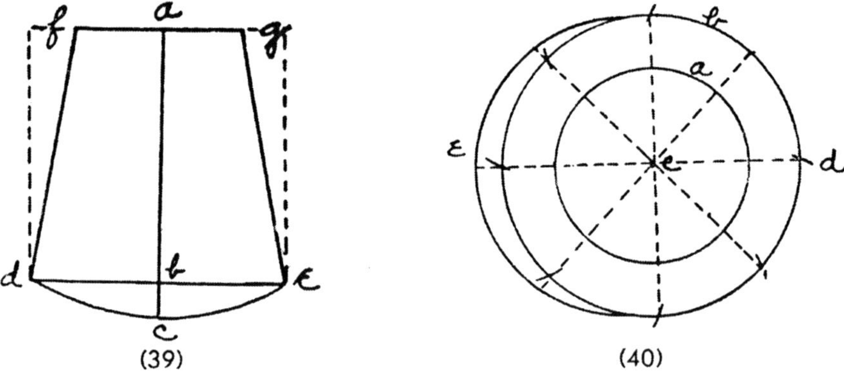

(39)   (40)

$\mathcal{D}rafting$

The drafting methods can be applied to the following chapter on Draping. The principle in both cases is: Vertical and horizontal lines (any length), representing the thread grain or true bias. Carefully mark these lines on the working paper, as well as on the final pattern, for use in matching thread grain or true bias when cutting fabric. Refer to drafting Headsize Oval, Steps 18 through 22, and Brims, Step 27. Patterns can be drafted by measuring a hat in front of you or from a picture by estimating measurements. Copy and originate by drafting.

(39)

Line "a-b-c" represents the vertical line, and "d-e" the horizontal line or the thread grain lines. Line "a-c" is the longest length. Mark the horizontal line the total width of "d-e" (OR half the pattern can be drafted, then folded and marked for the other half). At the top of the vertical line "a," the width is marked at "f," and also from "a" to "g." Connect points "f-d" and "g-e." Set compass point at "a" and swing "d-c-e." "c-d-f-a-g-e" is one section of a crown or pillbox.

(40)

From "c," set radius to point "a" and swing circle. Then set compass to point "b" and swing another circle. For additional width to one side, move radius "c-b" to left of "c" on line "e-c" about ½" to ⅝". Swing additional width "e" at left of circle "b." Divide circle "b" in equal parts and mark off as "d." Connect all marked points to "c" with dotted lines. Cut on dotted lines from outside edge of circle 'b" to circle "a." Lap outside edge until it is Headsize. This makes a pillbox, crown or beret.

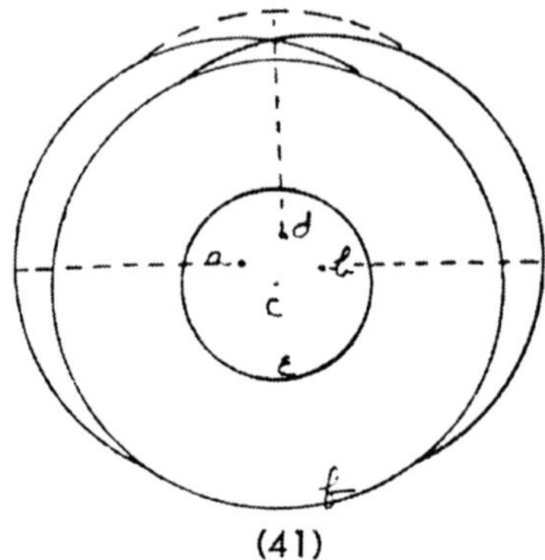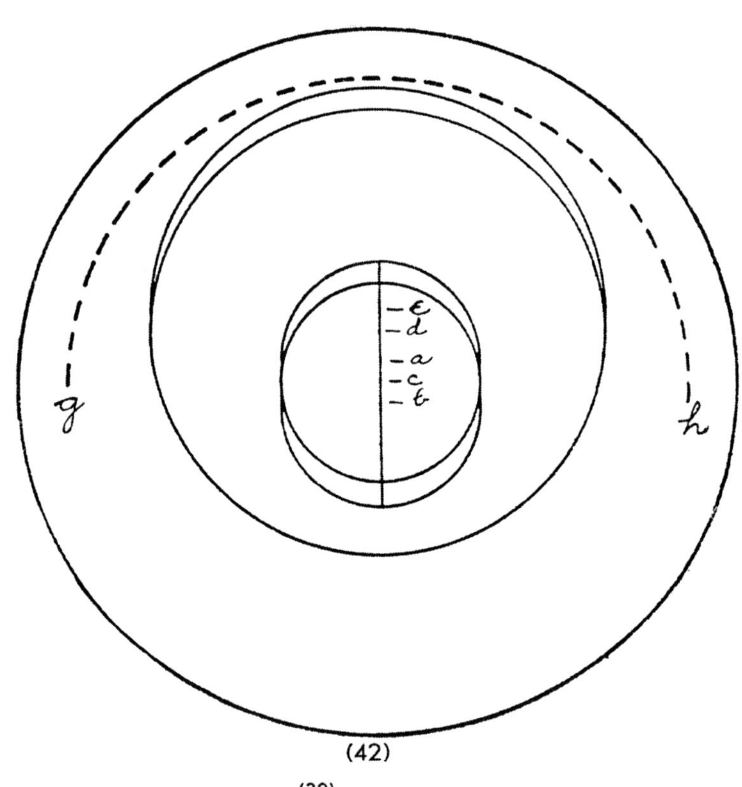

(32)

(41)

From "c," the center of circles "e" and "f," move compass to points "a" and "b," using "f" radius, and swing additional widths. Move to point "d," same radius, and swing a curved dotted line to close top in even circular line.

(42)

The Headsize oval is swung at "c," "a" and "b." The inside brim is swung at "d." "d" radius is moved to "e" for extra width on the brim. The outside circle is swung from the Center, as is partial circle line "g-h."If the line "g-h" and outer edge are cut and lapped at the ends, the brim will slant outwards.

(43)

For a cone-shaped beret or crown, use the necessary radius for desired depth, and swing a circle. The circumference is marked off on the outer edge of the circle. These two points are connected with center. Cut away the wedge and lap at Center Back for the cone shape. See Figure 15, Frames.

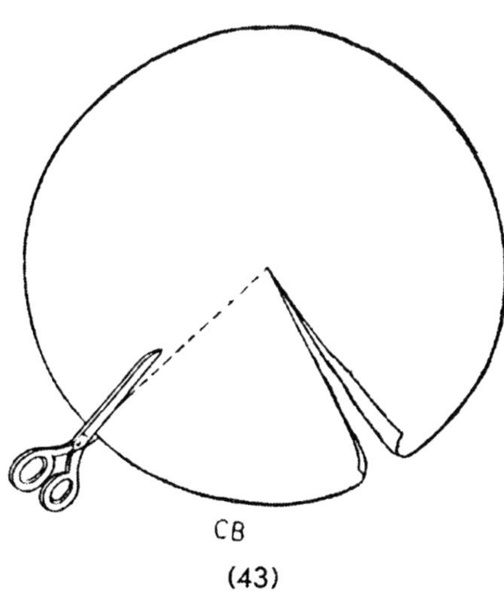

(43)

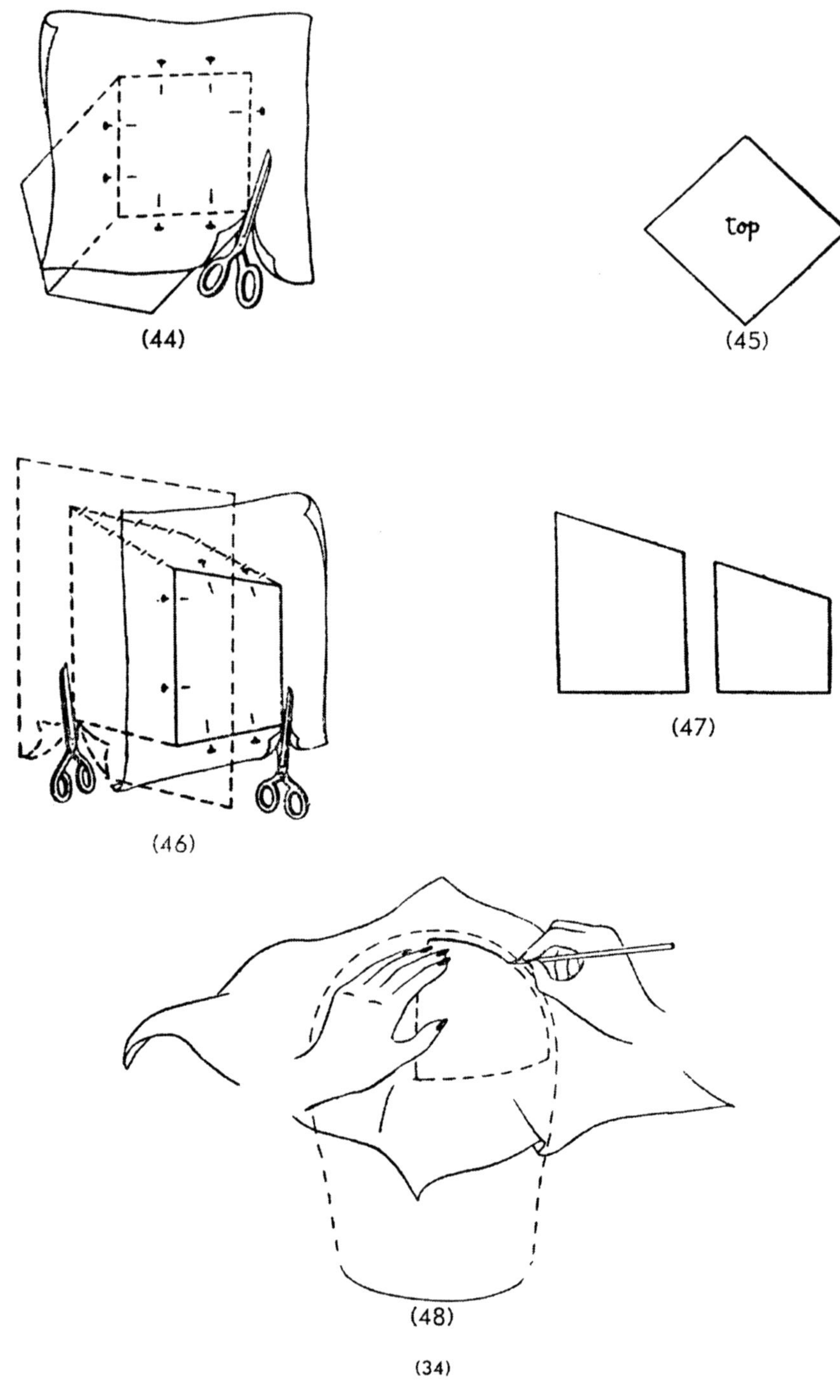

(44)
(45)
top
(46)
(47)
(48)

$\mathcal{D}$raping

Draping is more adaptable to copying. The principle of the vertical and horizontal fold is the same in drafting as in draping. See beginning explanation on Drafting. Draping is done on the hat or object. Draping can also be used in Designing.

(44)

Fold tissue paper vertically and horizontally. Open and lay against top of hat, matching folds with straight thread grain. Pin and trace on edges. Cut on dotted lines.

(45)

Shape of hat-top, as described in Step 44.

(46)

For sides, use folded tissue paper and pin on in same manner as described in Step 44. Pin, trace around edges and cut.

(47)

Drawings show sides of draped hat.

(48)

For a head-shaped sectional crown, first mark the design on a wooden head-block, then lay vertically and horizontally folded paper over the designed section. Match vertical fold with "up and down" of drawing, for a guide to thread grain. The outer edge of this section will be cut on bias, and the up and down and cross will be on vertical and horizontal threads, or straight thread grain. This is a four-sectional crown.

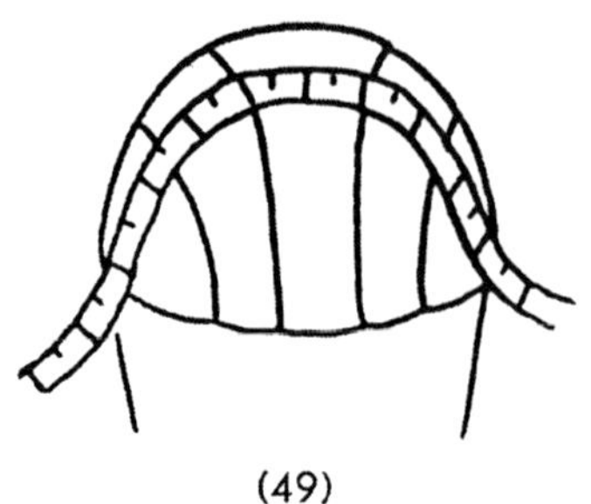

(49)

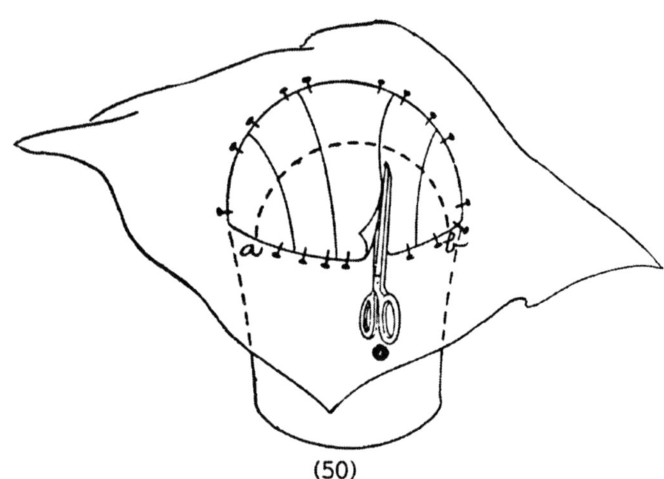

(50)

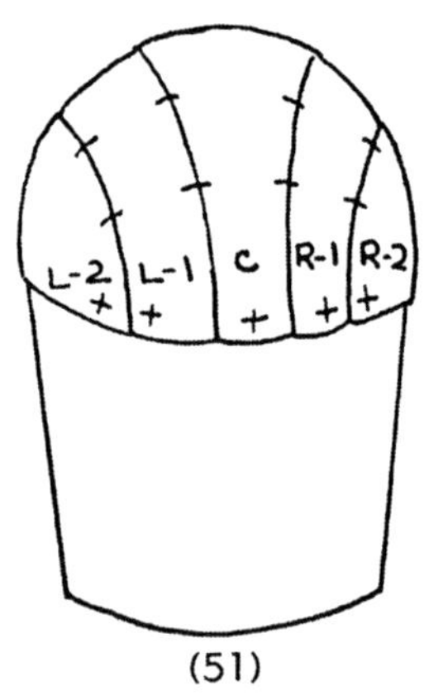

(51)

(49)

Another version of a sectional crown is drawn on headblock, in sections running from front to back. Check measurement of top section to be sure it is
symmetrical. Measure corresponding sections for width and symmetry. Measure up from table to headsize to check.

(50)

After sections are measured and checked, lay tissue paper over one section
at a time, pin and trace. (Follow Step 48.) Cut sections out and trace onto a
cardboard with proper markings. Continue with each section. Line "a-b"
shows how sections can be drawn from side to side.

(51)

Mark sections, as follows: Right-2, R-1, Center Back, L-1, Left-2. Also
make small dash marks on the sectional lines of design on headblock and
trace on tissue paper before making patterns. Copy these dash marks and
section marks on cardboard pattern. In assembling the sections, lay Right-2
and R-1 together at plus marks (Center Back) and match dash marks, etc.
See Figure 9, Pattern Hats.

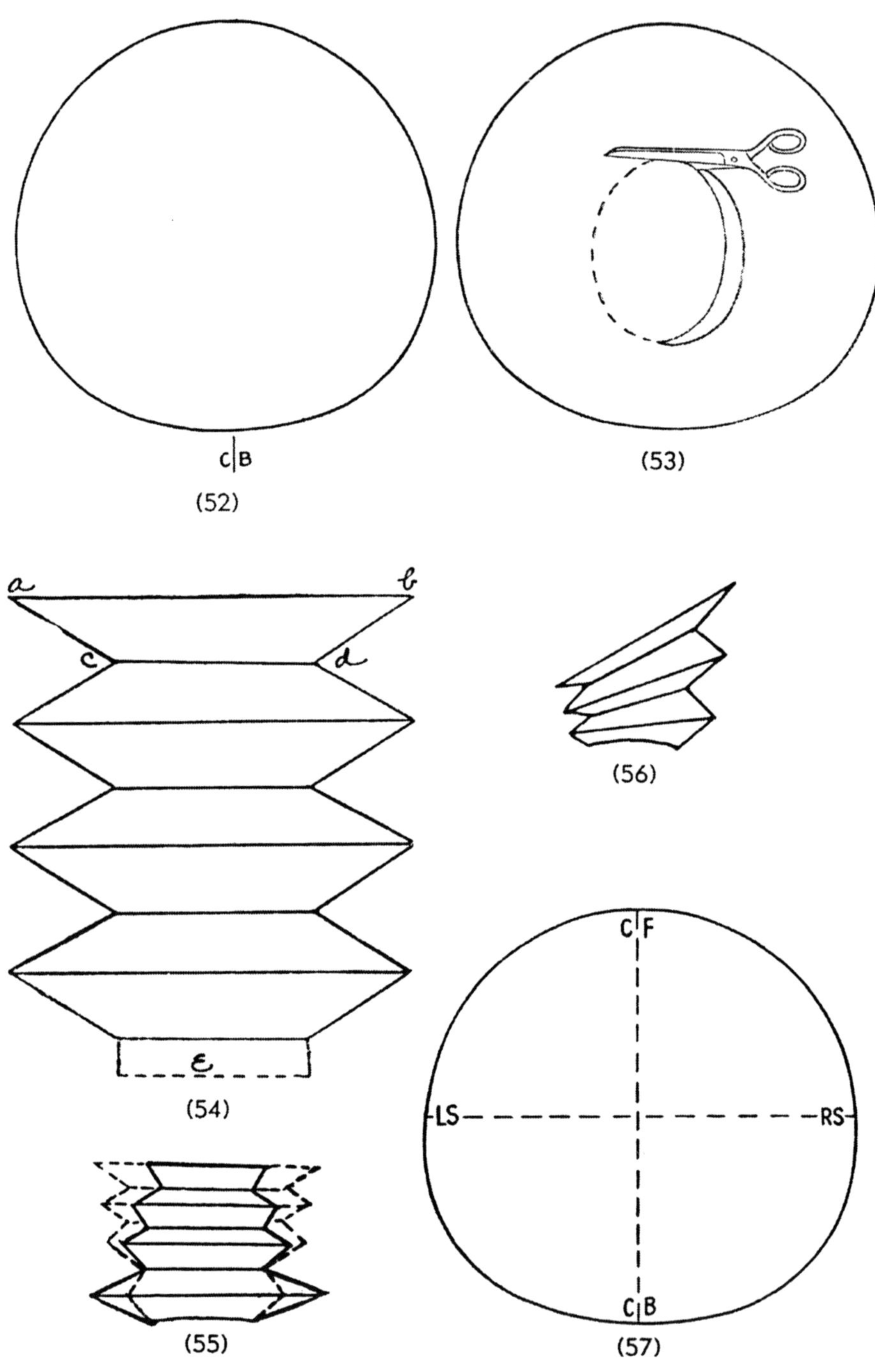

C|B
(52)
(53)
a
b
c
d
(54)
ε
(56)
(55)
C|F
LS
RS
C|B
(57)

Berets

The beret principle is two round discs—one with a Headsize. The outside edges of these two discs are sewed together.

(52)

An irregular shape or a round disc may be used. Mark Center Front and Center Back.

(53)

Trace Headsize pattern at the desired position. Leave an allowance inside the Headsize line for turning up on inside for the Headsize Band. Fabric may be stretched, or tabs cut for Headsize extension.

★ THE ACCORDIAN BERET

(54)

"a-b" represents the tip disc. The under-part has a Headsize at "c-d." The successive circles have Headsizes—so it is actually one disc and seven Headsize discs. "e" is the Headsize Band.

(55)

The straight outline shows the beret discs larger at the Headsize, and smaller at the top. The dotted lines show the reverse.

(56)

This accordion-type beret can be worn straight, to the side, forward or pulled to the back.

★ THE SECTIONAL BERET

(57)

Fold paper at right angles. This locates the Center, as well as Center Front, Center Back, Right Side and Left Side.

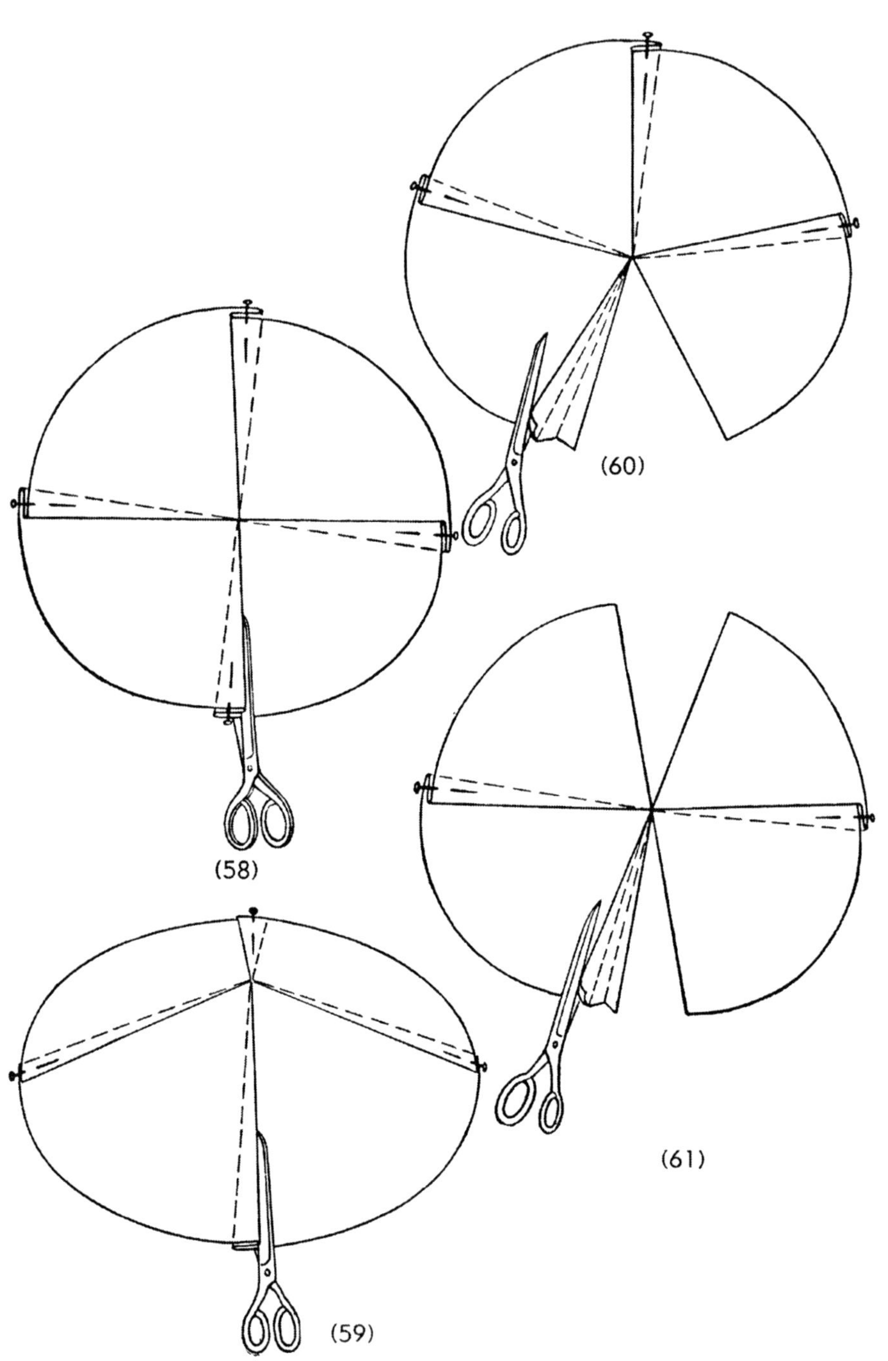

(58)

(59)

(60)

(61)

(40)

(58)

Lap circle at outer edge on folds, pin and cut at the edges of lap to center.

(59)

The disc will be cone-shaped.

(60)

Cut the whole lap away to center. Trace this on cardboard for a pattern.

(61)

Cut away the second lap and trace one of the halves on cardboard. This is a two-sectional beret pattern. Seams may run from Center Front to Center Back, or Right Side to Left Side.

(62)

When half is bisected at "a-b," the pattern is four-sectional. If more shape is desired, cut away the third lap. This makes the fourth section smaller. For eight sections, bisect the quarter section at "a-c." "d-e" is the Headsize of the under quarter-section.

(63)

Figure 63 shows the top and bottom edges of beret together, then the quarter-sections bisected. "g-h" seams can be sewed following the outer curve, or straight from "g" to "h." "a-b" and "e-f" are Headsize marks. "c-d" is the allowance for turn-up at Headsize. This Headsize pattern is laid in and marked before the lapped shape is cut or bisected.

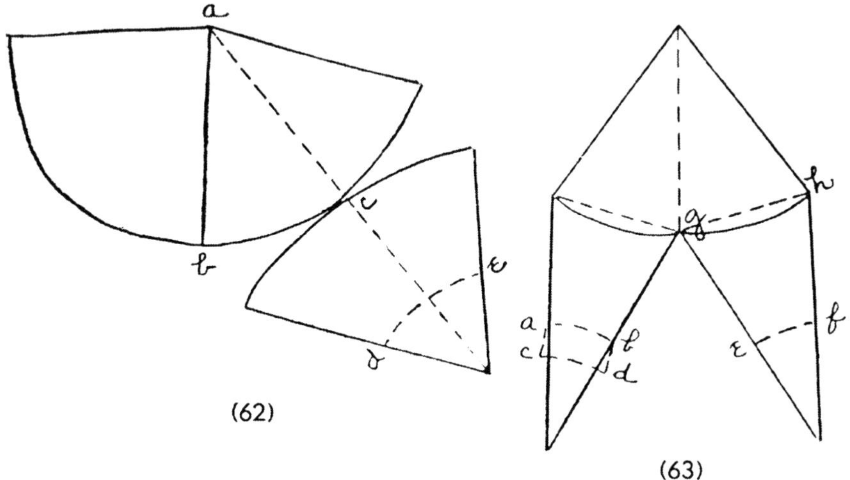

(62)

(63)

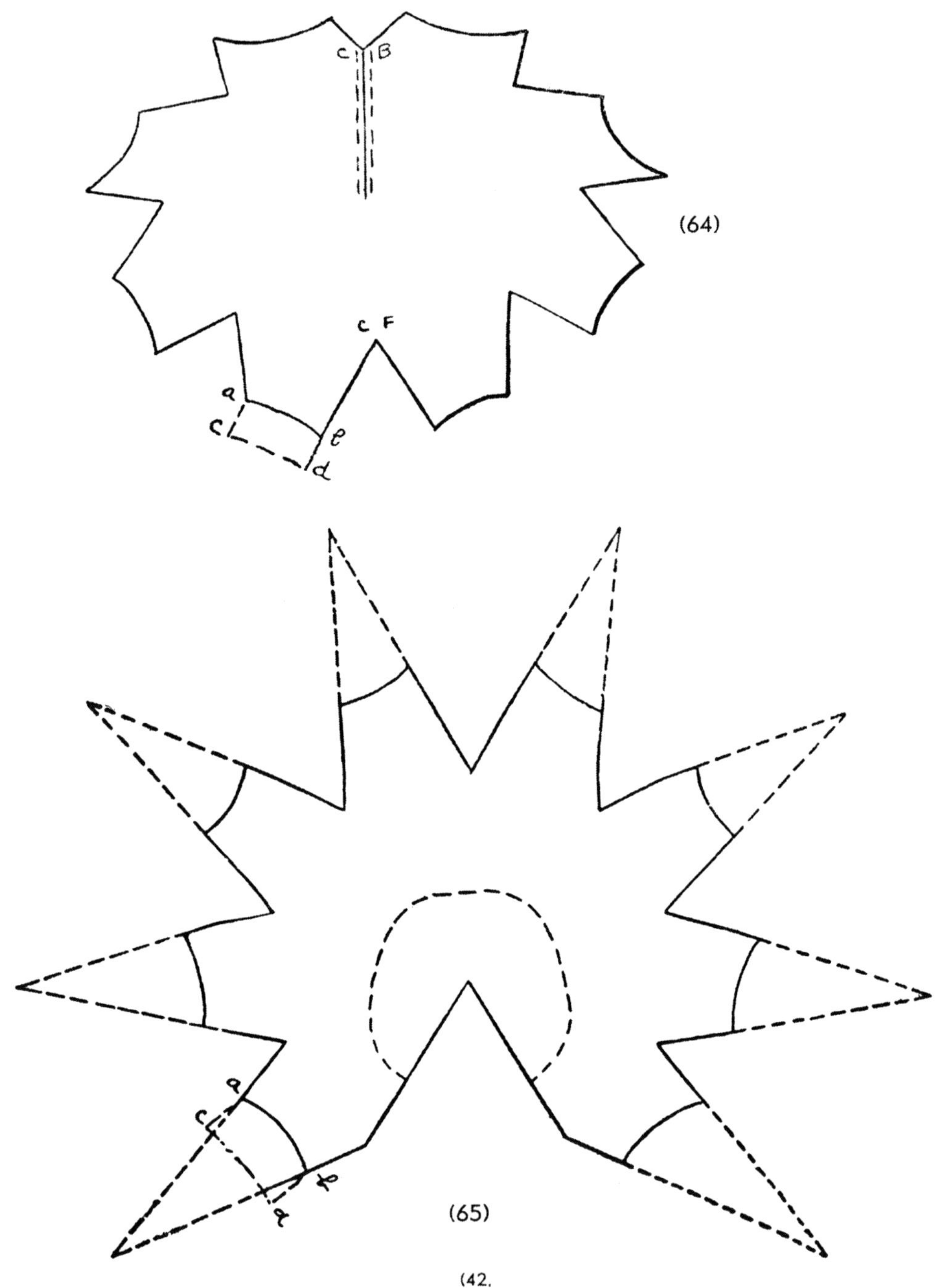
C B
c F
a
c
e
d
(64)
a
c
f
q
(65)

(64)

Step 63 shows top and bottom of an eight-sectional beret. Cut away the Headsize of each of the under-sections. With the Headsizes extending out, place all the points together on a cardboard. Trace and cut pattern. It will look like Figure 64. Seam on the underside and at Center Back up to Center Top. Make allowance on each end for Headsize like "a-c" and "b-d."

(65)

The solid lines of Figure 65 are the same as Step 64. Reverse, and put the points outward (dotted lines), and the Headsize inside. Trace. The seams will then be on top and Center Top to Center Back. There will be no seams on the underside except at the Center Back.

(66)

If an eight-sectional beret, there will be seams from Center Top to Head-size ("c-a-b-c" on each section). If like Step 64, there will be seams on underside sections "a-b-c" and none on top. But if like Step 65, seams will be on the top, "c-a," and none on underside.

(67)
See Headsize Bands, and Figure 38, Pattern Hats.

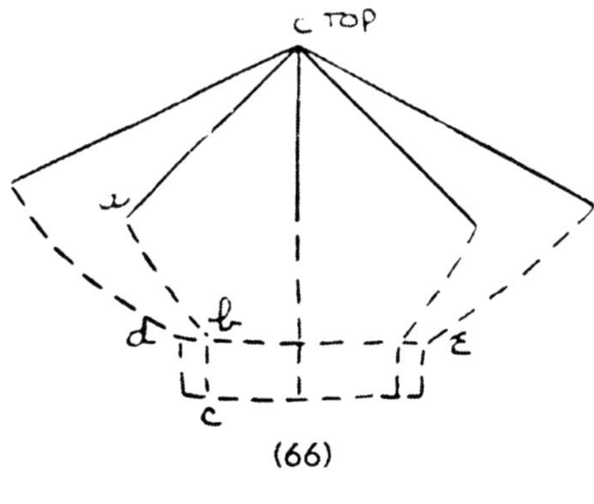

(66)

Stitches, Wire and Tape, and Headsize Bands

This chapter, composed of three short sections, concerns very important details to the finished perfection of your hat. Study the basic stitches, how to Wire, and use Bias Crinoline Tape, and the suggested methods of laying in Headsize Bands, to make your hat look like a professional model.

Certain stitches have been adapted by usage in certain specific steps, and it is well to become familiar with them.

Wire is used on edges, and where additional stiffness or control of hat or trimming is needed. The wire must be covered, either with ribbon, flanges or cut strips of bias crinoline. Bias strips should be pulled and stretched as you work.

Every hat should have a Headsize Band to protect the hat from soil, as well as to hold the Headsize in shape, and cover raw edges and stitches.

TO HELP HOLD ON OUR HAT, at the Center Front sew a narrow grip-tooth comb to the bottom edge of the headsize ribbon, and use a covered hat pin at the back.

If a very shallow crown, on each side across the bottom edge of headsize ribbon sew a small round length of elastic about 1½″ long. Knot the ends and tuck them inside at the bottom edge of headsize ribbon. Overcast these ends to edges of ribbon. Through this elastic, hook a narrow grip-tooth comb. When wearing the hat, pull elastic down and fasten combs into the hair.

OR, knot ends of small round elastic length and tuck ends under headsize ribbon at each side. Overcast to ribbon. When wearing the hat pull the elastic down and under the hair at back.

It's a well-known fact that attention to details is a sign of the true artist—and the following chapter will help you achieve the artistry you're aiming for when making your hat.

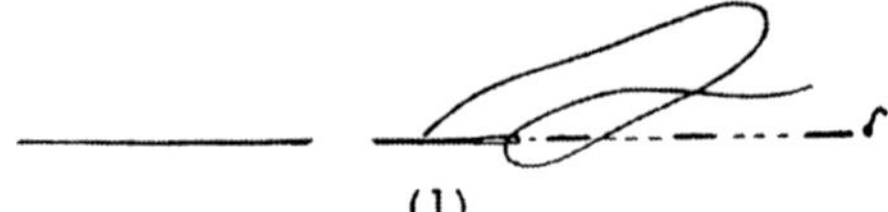

(1)

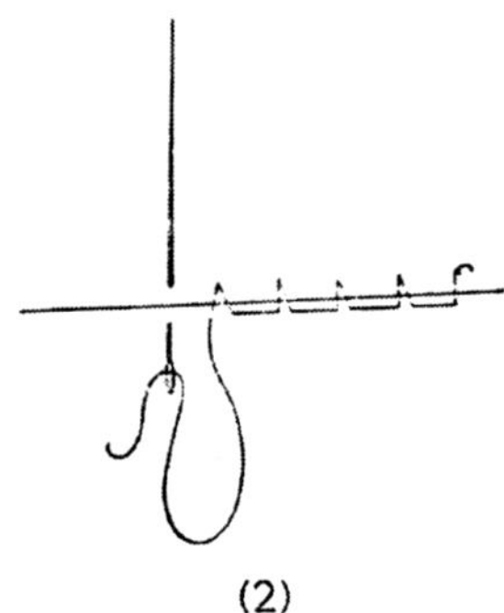

(2)

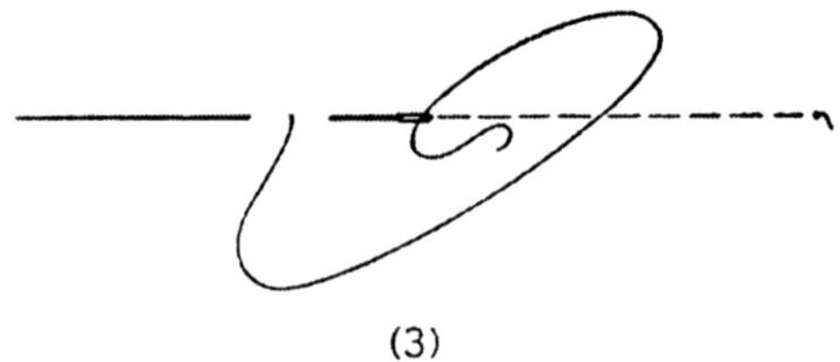

(3)

Stitches

Use millinery thread, or a strong waxed thread. Thread used in quilting comes in a variety of colors, and is very durable.

★ THE RUNNING STITCH

(1)

The running stitch is used on under-work, or when there is no pull or strain—as in tacking.

(2)

This figure shows the running stitch, stabbed. A stitch is stabbed when there are wires, buckram, etc., and the stitch can not be worked easily.

★ THE BACKSTITCH

(3)

The backstitch is a running stitch, then a backstitch. It is a strong stitch, and is used for sewing bias crinoline tape in frame work, joining crown to brim, etc. Sometimes the backstitch is a long stitch, and called the LONG and SHORT BACKSTITCH, and is used on inside or under-work. Other times, it is a running stitch, succeeded by the backstitch, picking up only one thread.

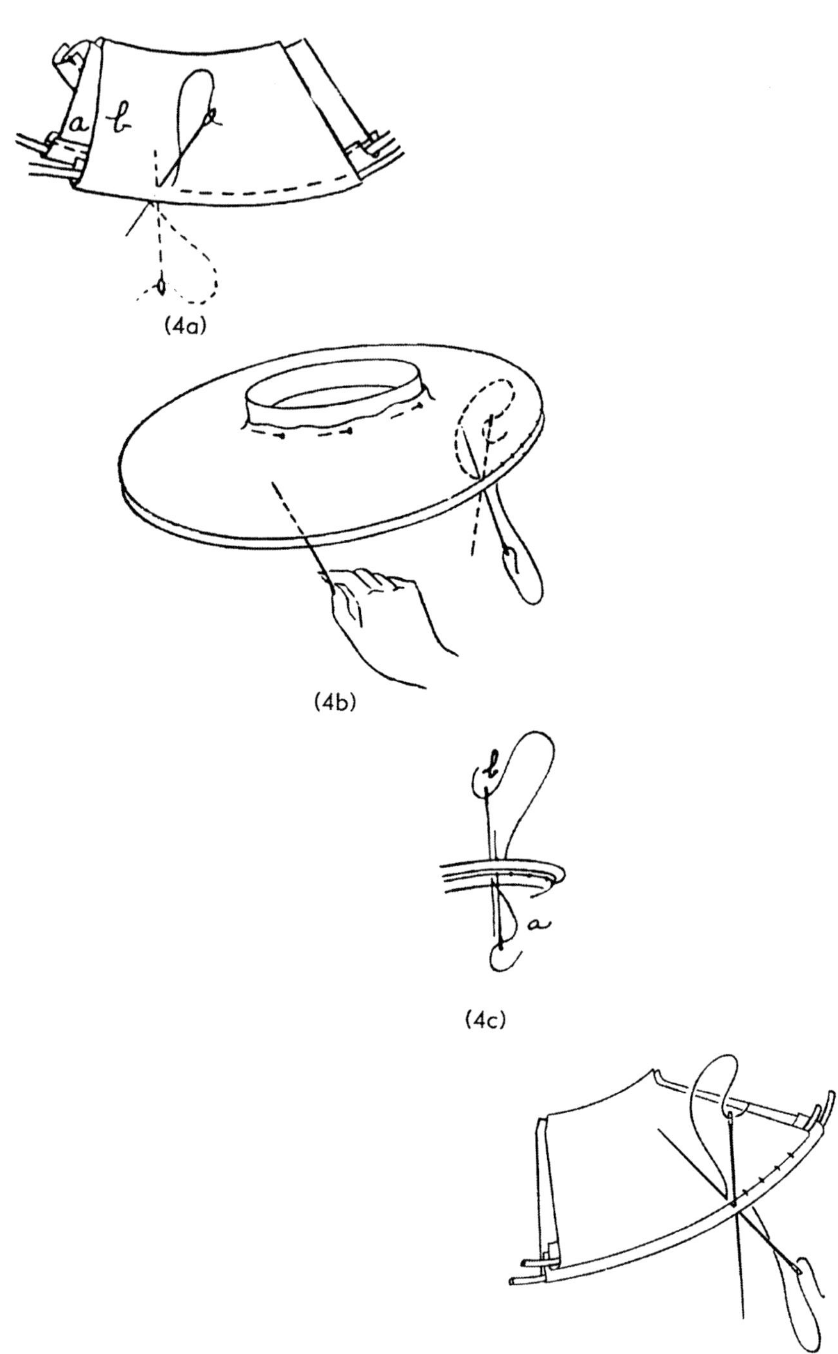

(48)

(4a, b, c & d)

The accompanying four figures show the same stitch. It is a backstitch, stabbed. The backstitch picks up only one thread. This stitch works between two edges. The outer edge is a wire edge. When used in this case, it is called the DOUBLE-EDGE STITCH. In these illustrations, there are wires in each of the two edges. "a" is the covered edge and "b" is the wired edge in Figure 4-a.

To keep edges smooth ,from time to time while sewing, push a needle between the two edges to keep facing edges smooth, as shown in Figure 4-b.

Hold the brim in the position of Figure 4-b. Run the needle under the wire, but not through the fabric, for about an inch, and make stitches in this indentation. Start needle from the top and tuck knot of thread between the two brims. The needle is poised vertically (dotted needle) and thrust through between the edges. Now make a stitch about $\frac{1}{8}$" long in the inden-tation, and pierce vertically between the wires, catching only one thread of the top edge. Repeat, as in Figure 4-c, bringing the needle "a" and "b" again between the two edges.

Figure 4-d shows right side. This may be reversed by putting bottom facing on the top, and top facing on the bottom. As it is shown, the double edge is the right side.

Figure 4-a shows the wrong side of the double edge.

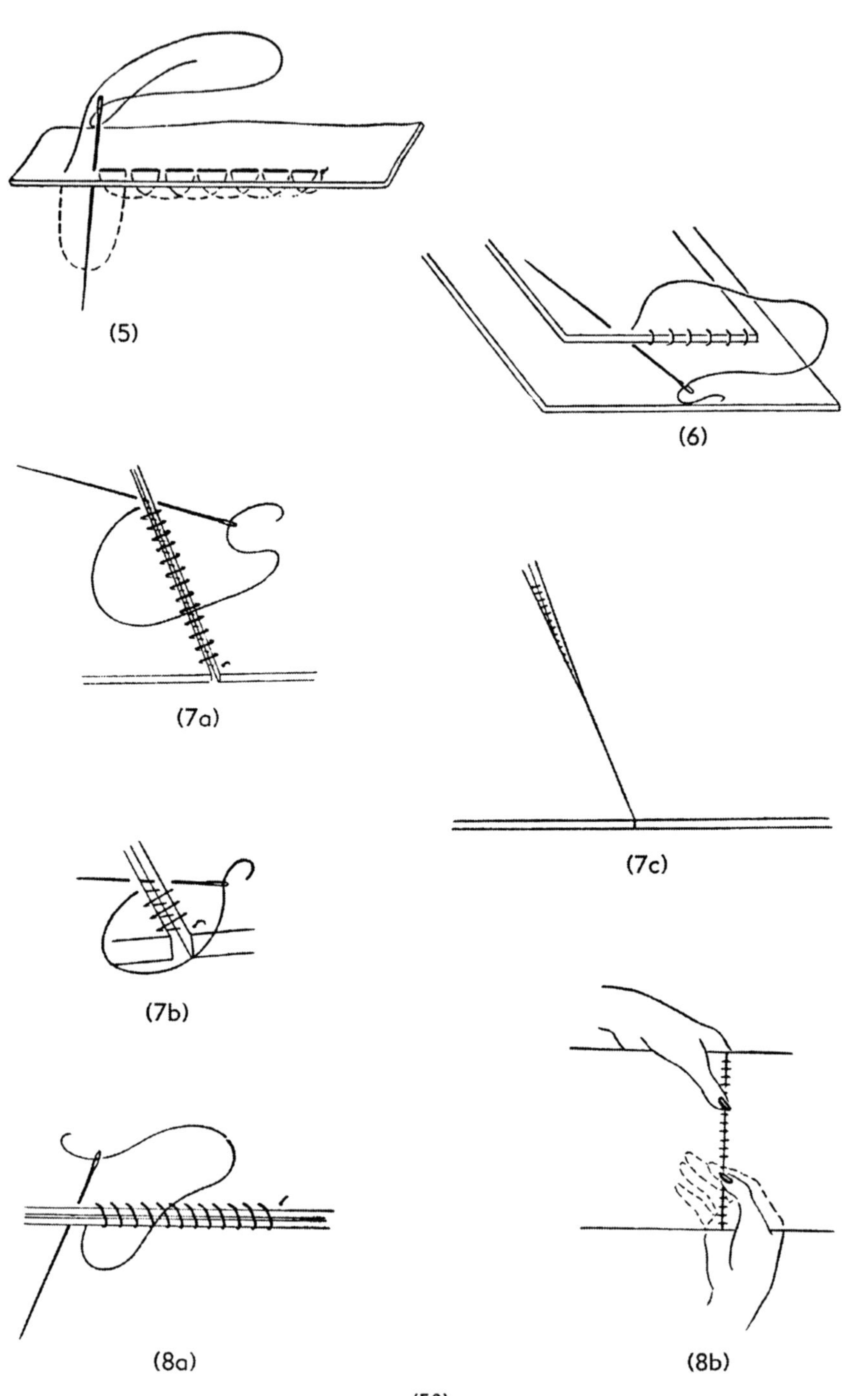

(5)
(6)
(7a)
(7b)
(7c)
(8a)
(8b)

(5)

When there is an obstruction, it is necessary to stab the backstitch. Figure 5 shows the STABBED BACKSTITCH.

(6)

The INVISIBLE BACKSTITCH is primarily a felt stitch. It is used at the hems, joining crown to brim, also at the seams and hems of straw, and Head-size bands. Space the invisible backstitches about 1/4" apart. Use strong milli-nery thread, and pull each stitch so that it cuts into the felt or fabric, and becomes invisible. This stitch is also used in straws, covering frames and wherever adaptable.

(7a)

★ THE OVERCAST STITCH

The accompanying figures show the felt INLAY-OVERCAST STITCH. It is a felt stitch, but is not used very much. It is especially good when one color felt is inlaid into another. It can also be used at seams, although it doesn't hold together as well as Figure 8.

(7b)

The two edges of felt are laid closely side by side and overcast stitches are very close together, picking up only half the felt through the cut. See Figure 7a. Sew from the wrong side.

(7c)

The right-side edges are close together, with no stitches showing.

(8a)

This seam overcast stitch is principally a felt seam stitch. Lay the two edges of felt together, side by side. Overcast stitches very close together, so that the stitches on the right side are at right angles with the seams' length. Pick up very small amount of felt edge. Stay as close as possible to edge, making stitches uniform in depth and length.

(8b)

After edges are overcast, open the two ends, so that the edges butt together, and run thumb and fingers across seam, to be sure it is flat. Repeat opera-tion over steam.

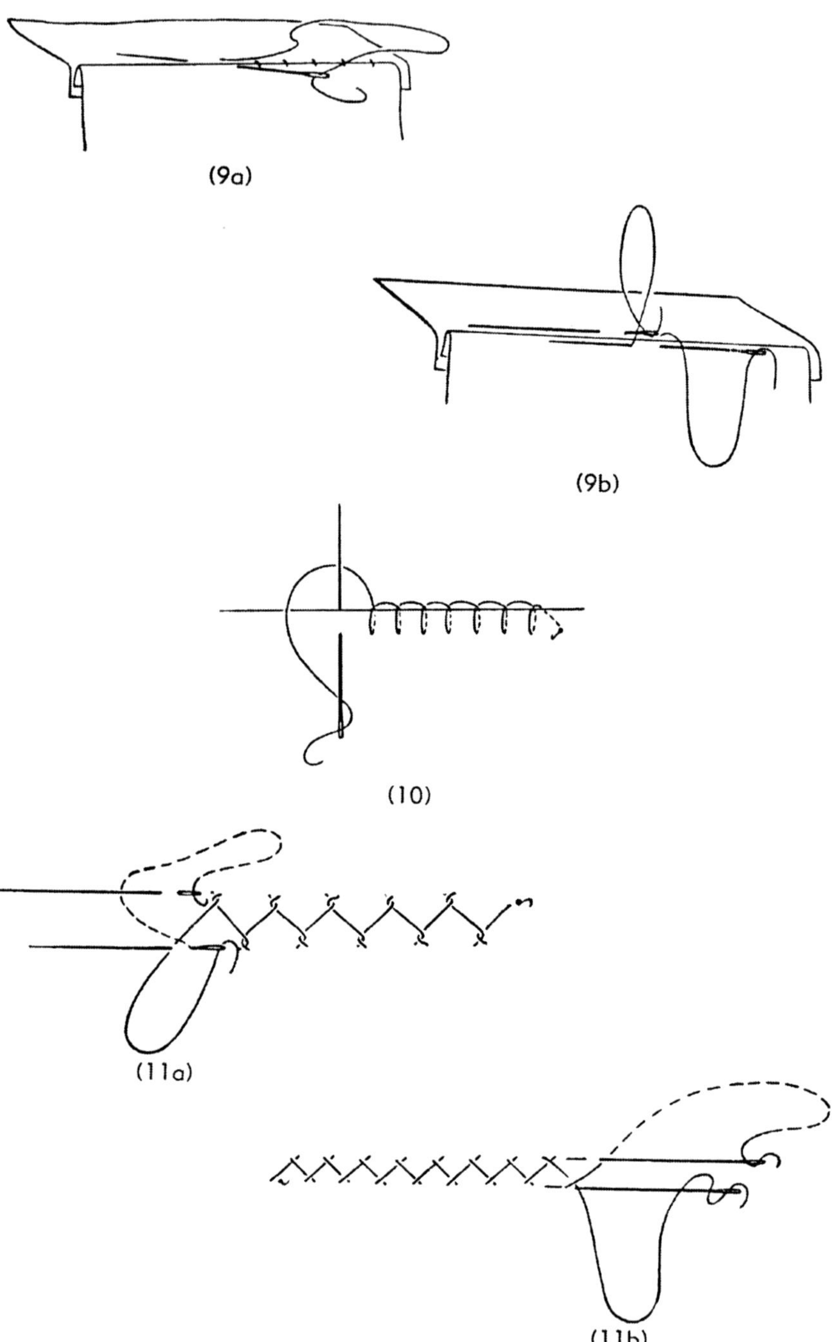

(9a)

(9b)

(10)

(11a)

(11b)

(52)

★ THE SLIPSTITCH

(9a)

The slipstitch is used mostly in covering frames. One fabric is laid over another. Run the needle through the folded edge about ¼". At the point where
the needle comes out, pick up the same amount of fabric on the adjoining
piece.

(9b)

Follow the sequence of the stitch, starting with the needle on the side and
through the folded fabric.

★ THE BUTTONHOLE STITCH

(10)

We think of the Buttonhole stitch as a WIRE STITCH. Although wire can be
sewed on with the overcast stitch, the buttonhole stitch holds it in place more
firmly.

★ THE LABEL STITCHES

(11a)

A label is usually sewed in upside down.

(11b)

11a and b are suggested label stitches.

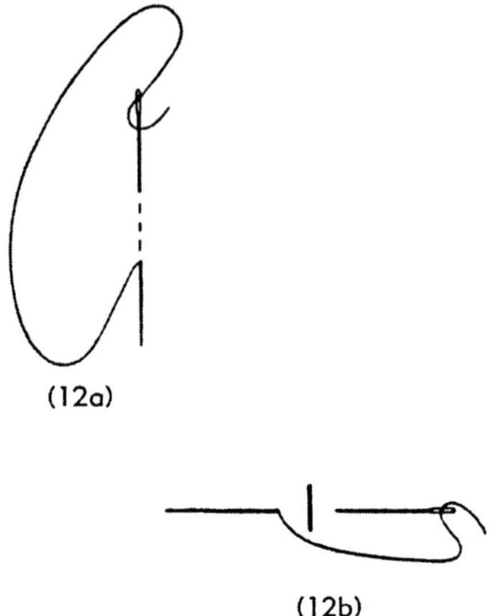

(12a)

(12b)

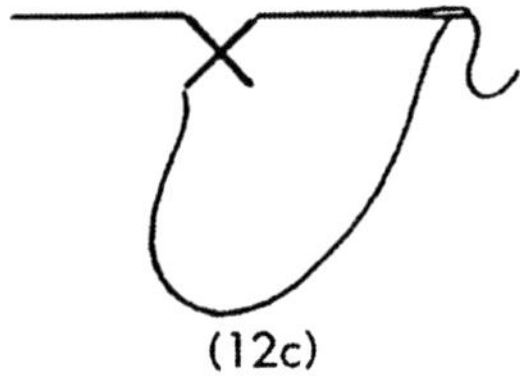

(12c)

(12d)

★ THE CENTER FRONT MARK.

On the Headsize band or ribbon, mark the Center Front with a contrasting thread, so the Center can easily be located when putting on the hat. This may be indicated in several ways—an X, V, vertical mark, horizontal mark, dot, etc.

(12a)

A Vertical Center Front mark.

(12b)

A Cross Center Front mark.

(12c)

An X Center Front Mark.

(12d)

Another version of a Center Front Headsize mark.

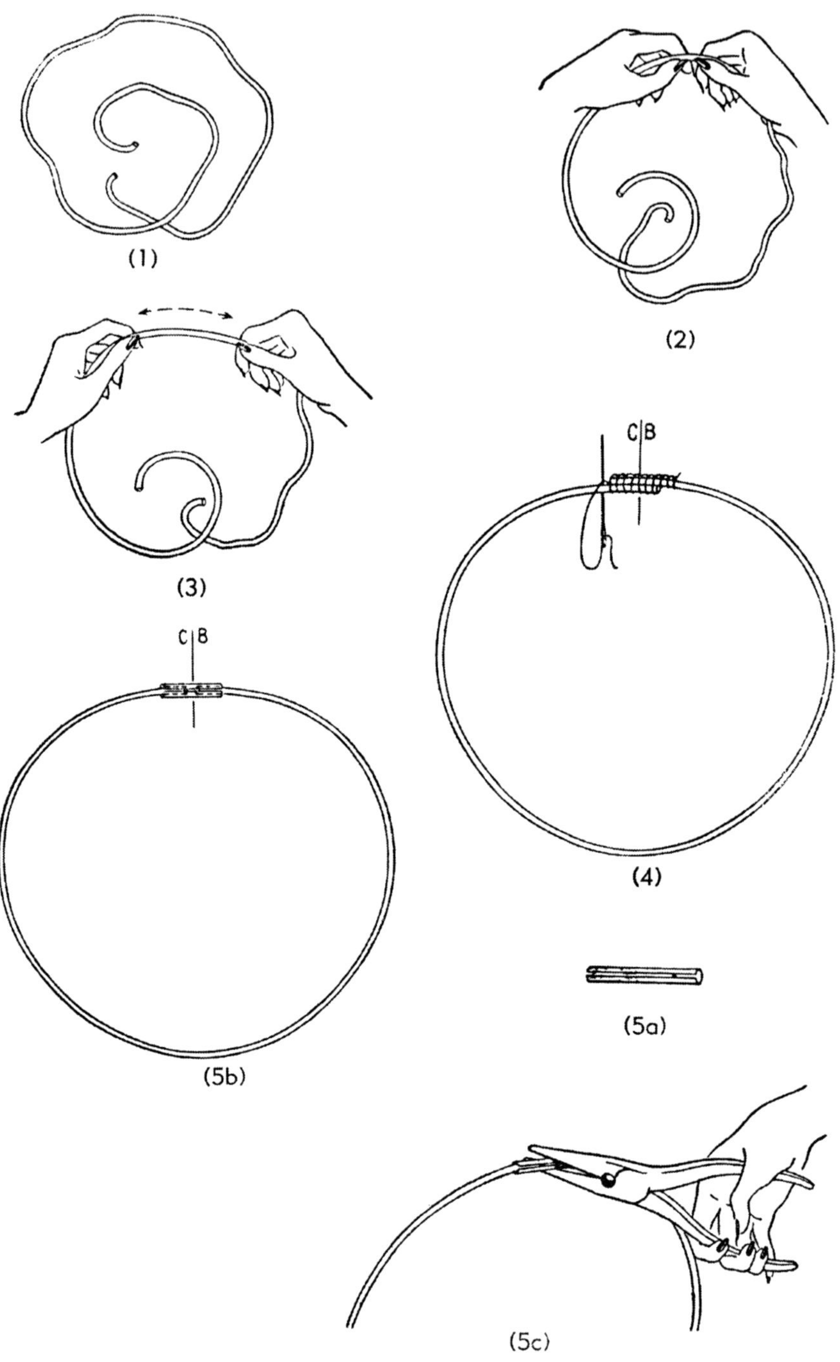
(1)
(2)
(3)
C|B
(4)
C|B
(5a)
(5b)
(5c)
(56)

Wire and Tape

Wire is available from the Millinery Supply Stores. There are two kinds of wire—pliable and steel. Pliable wire is wrapped with cotton threads, or un·wrapped, and comes in three weights: Heavy and Medium for brim edges, and a Light-weight wire used in trimmings, called "Ribbon Wire." There is a still lighter wire, which is covered with crinoline for use in trimmings.
Steel wire is springy and will not bend. It is very good for round-edge brims. Bias flanges are stretched over steel wire hoops.

(1)
If wire is not straight . . . .

(2)
. . . with cushions of thumbs against the wire . . .

(3)
. . . pull outward.

(4)
Wire may be prepared before using on brim edge or tip of crown, or prepare on the hat as it is sewed. The ends are lapped 1½" and buttonhole stitched firmly, or . . .

(5a)
A wire fastener may be used.

(5b)
Slip one end of the wire halfway into the wire fastener, and the other end into the other half. The two ends meet at the Center of the fastener.

(5c)
With a pair of pliers, press each side of wire fastener against the seam. If this doesn't hold fastener over wire, hit each side with a small hammer.

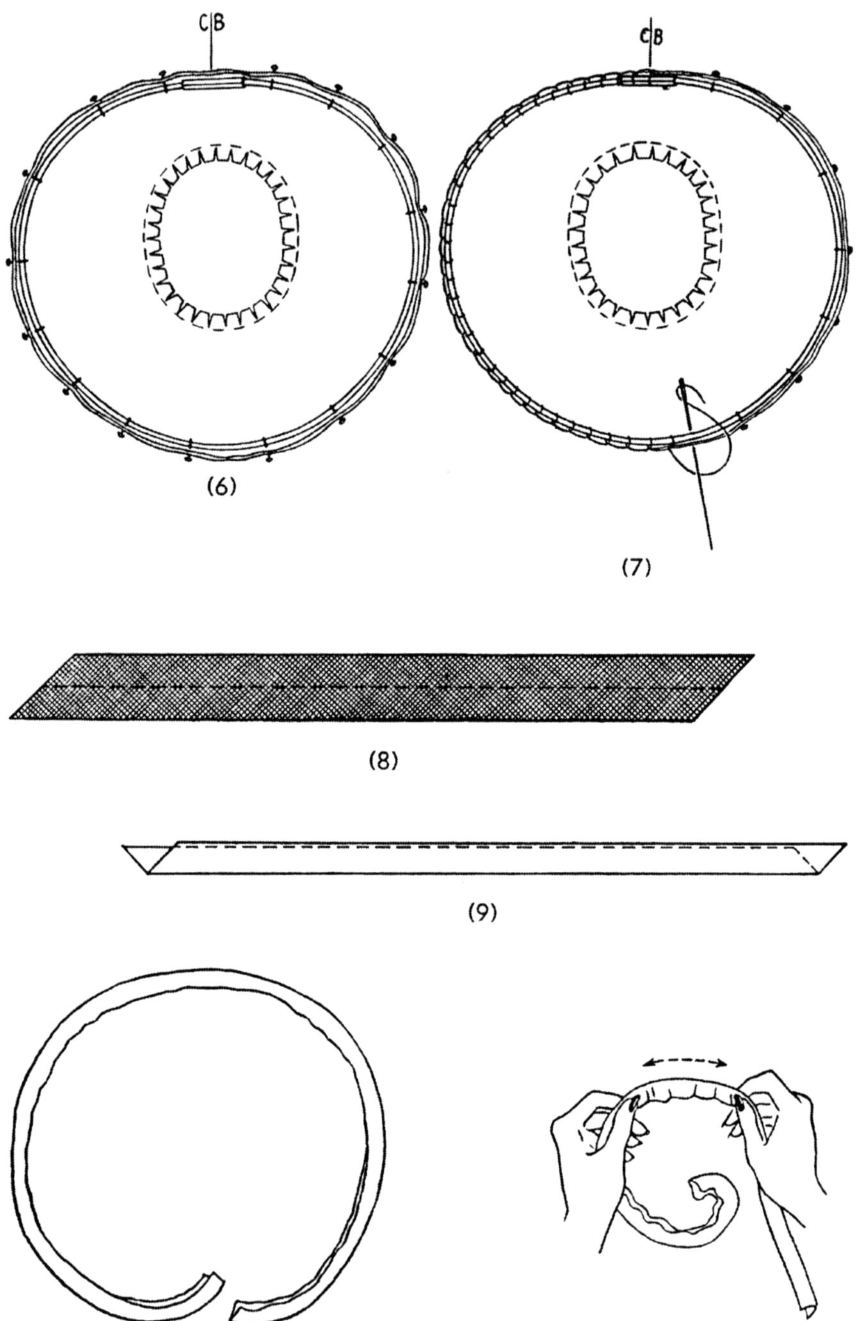

C|B
(6)
C|B
(7)
(8)
(9)
(10)
(11)

(6)

Pin wire to edge. Note position of pins. Wire lays just a little back of the raw edge, perhaps 1/32."

(7)

Sew through brim edge, back of the wire, using buttonhole stitch.

(8)

Cut a bias crinoline strip ¾" to 1" wide.

(9)

Fold crinoline strip at Center, lengthwise.

(10)

The bias crinoline strip is then stretched.

(11)

Pull folded bias crinoline strip on the fold if it is to swirl larger at that side. If the reverse is desired, pull folded bias crinoline strip at the raw edges. It will be wider at the raw edges and swirl with the fold at the inside.

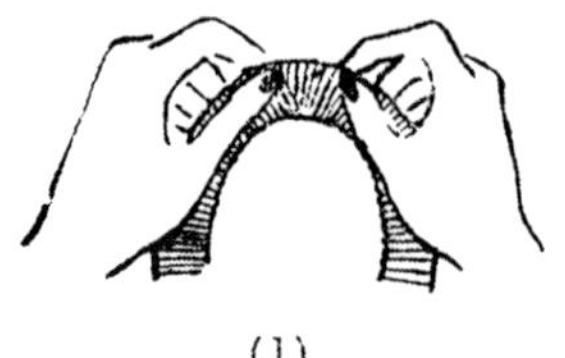

(1)

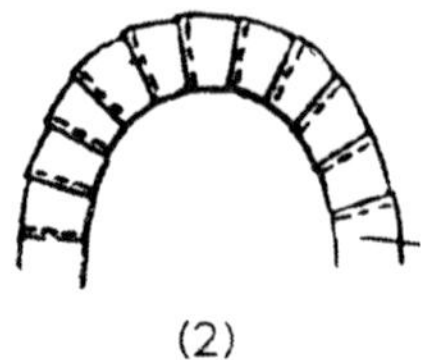

(2)

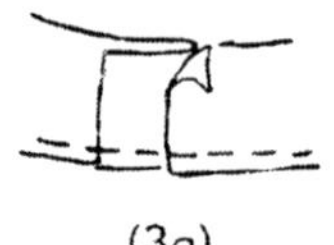

(3a)

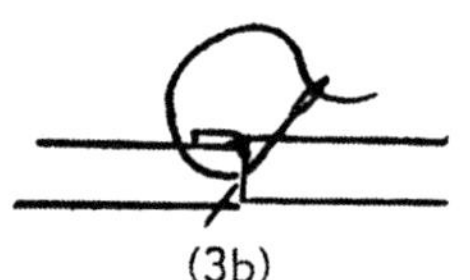

(3b)

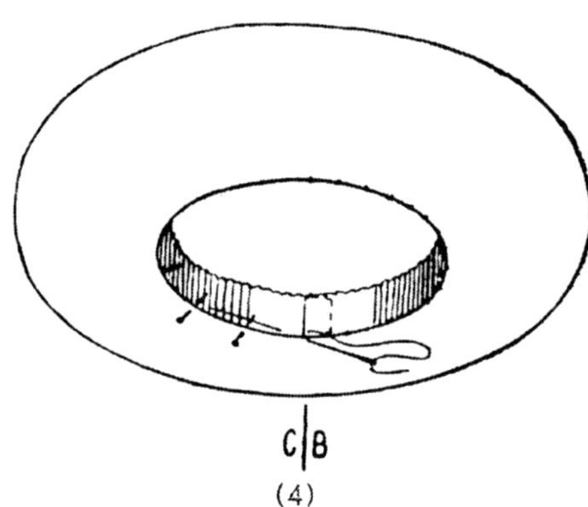

C|B

(4)

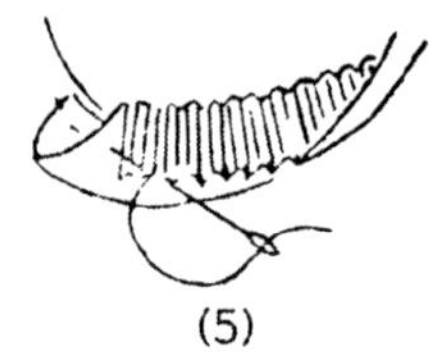

(5)

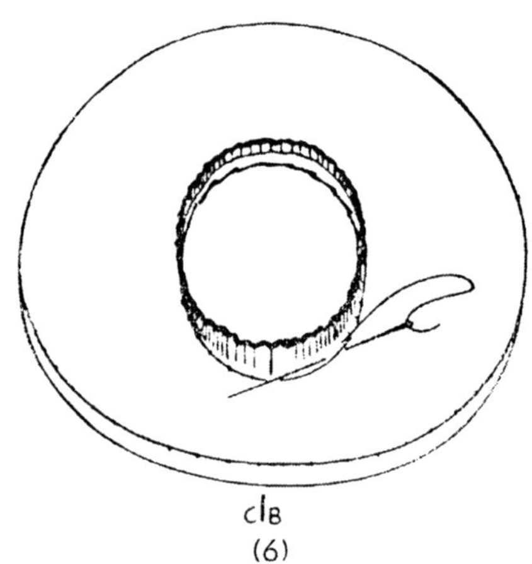

c|B

(6)

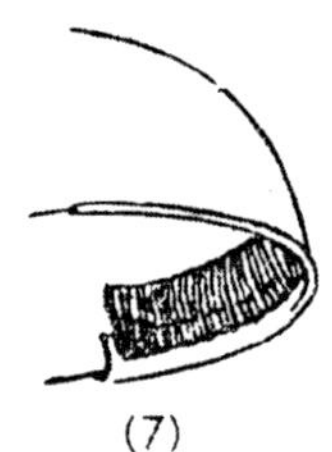

(7)

Headsize Bands

A Headsize Band may be made of grosgrain belting ribbon (loops at edge give more spread when swirled), or of bias fabric. A Headsize Band is to protect the hat from soil, keep the Headsize from stretching, cover raw edges and stitches, as well as allowing the hat to slip off and on the head more easily. The swirled, or wider edge of the ribbon is placed in the hat at the bottom, where the circumference of the head is largest.

★ THE BELTING RIBBON HEADSIZE BAND

(1)

To swirl or stretch one side only, hold dry ribbon over steam from kettle spout and pull one side only. Careful not to burn your fingers!

(2)

If the turn of the Headsize ribbon is too sharp to swirl by steam or iron, make small tucks and sew with running stitch.

(3a & b)

At Center Back, if no label is used ,turn under top end and sew to first end with invisible backstitch. If a label is used, one raw end lays flat over the other—lapped about ¼".

(4)

Headsize ribbon or band is pinned about ¼" or less on the inside from the edge of the Headsize. Sew, using the invisible backstitch.

(5)

Close-up of sewing the band. It is sewed on only one edge of the ribbon at the edge of the headsize.

(6)

In this picture the Headsize ribbon is turned up so that we can see the Headsize of the hat and the underside of the invisible backstitch. The loops on the edge of belting ribbon offer a convenient place for catching thread.

(7)

Figure 7 shows the position of the finished Headsize ribbon.

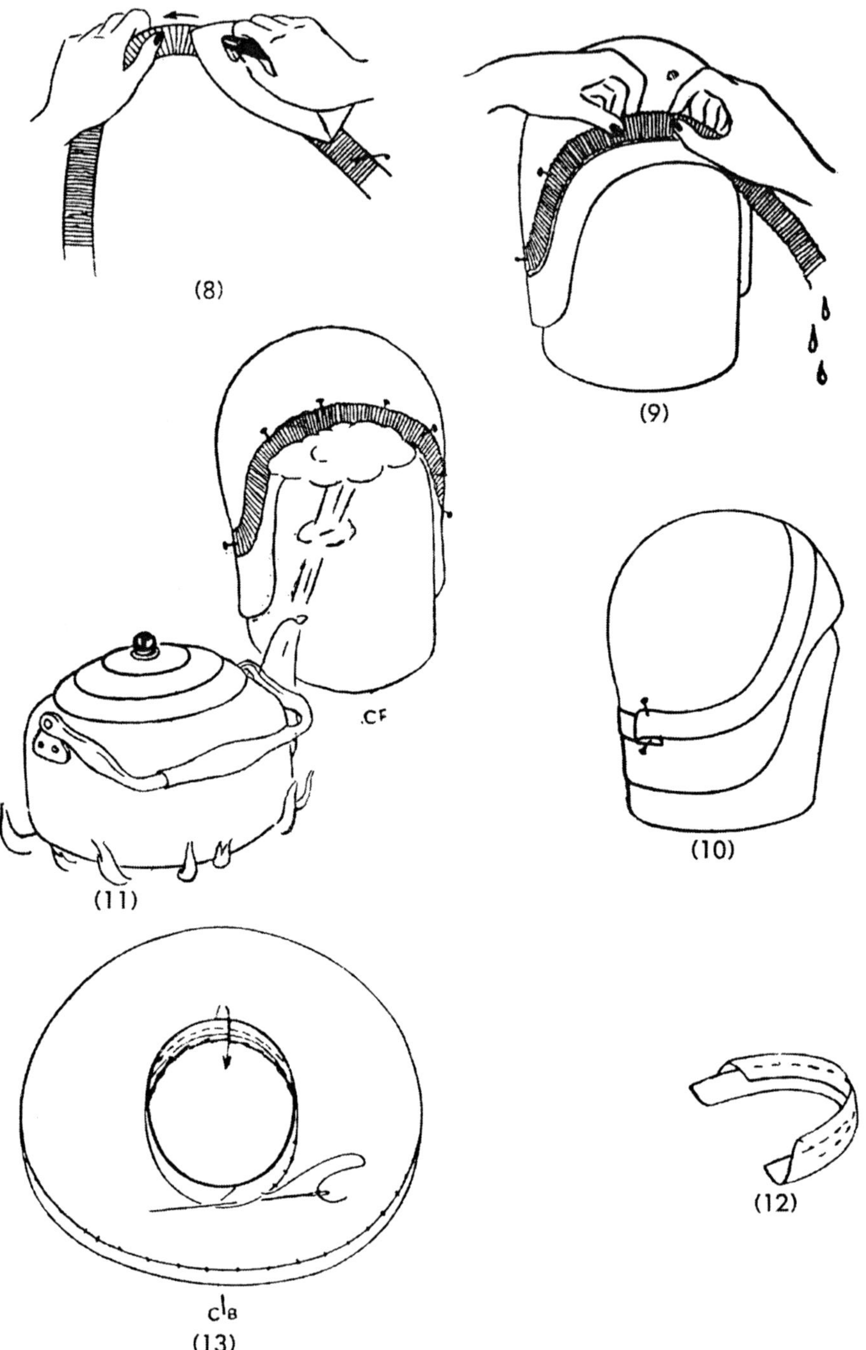

(8)
(9)
.CF
(10)
(11)
(12)
C B
(13)

(8)

OR a Headsize ribbon may be swirled dry. Pull downward with left hand. With right hand twist iron, and work in a circular motion toward you.

(9)

OR if Headsize ribbon is wet and stretched on the headblock, the head depth should be marked on the head. Wet ribbon is stretched and pinned with lower edge above the Headsize depth mark.

(10)

OR, as stated in Step 3, the ends of the ribbon are lapped end over end if a label is used over ends. If no label, the top ribbon is turned under and lays over first end.

(11)

OR a dry Headsize ribbon may be stretched above the marked Headsize depth, pinned and lapped at the Center Back. Hold over steam. Allow to dry.

★ THE BIAS FABRIC HEADSIZE BAND

(12)

If a hat is a covered frame, the covering fabric is often folded in a bias strip and used in place of the Headsize belting ribbon. Cut a bias strip about 1¼" wide. Fold one edge over ¾" and the other edge ¼". With the raw edges laying against the inside of the hat, see Figure 12 for position of folds. The bottom of folded edge lays at edge of hat headsize.

(13)

Before laying in the Headsize folded bias band, sew a bias seam by machine on the thread grain and place seam at Center Back. Sew at hat Headsize, using the invisible backstitch or slipstitch. The band can be extended upward until sewing is finished, then (arrow) turned inside.

For further discussion of Headsize Bands, see Figure 38, Pattern Hats.

Blocks

In hat-making, the block to hats is like the mold to a bowl of jello!
Your block gives your hat its shape, so it has a very important part in making
your hat turn out the way you want it. You can make your own block or
buy it, whichever you prefer. In this chapter, you'll learn how to make
your own blocks—and how to care for them.

Blocks are made from wood—solid or collapsible, paper, buckram,
willow, willowette, crinoline, fiber cloth and many other types of material.
Regardless of the material, blocks must be built up with a water repellent
hardening agent, such as "U BLOCK IT," shallac, clear varnish, clear
lacquer, enamel, or covered with glued tape or plaster of paris, then sized
or painted. If the block is hardened with plaster of paris, build it up from
the non-blocking side and then paint. Your headblock and wooden blocks
should be coated with shellac, a clear lacquer or varnish. **Be sure the lacquer
or shellac is dry** before using block. Buckram, willow, crinoline, fiber cloth,
etc., may be shaped, as in Figures 29-35, Patterns and Figures 12, 16, 17,
19 and 20, 23-30 Frames, or from a pattern.

A block must be adequately wired and reinforced. Remember always
to wire on the inside and block on the outside. A hat should never be blocked
over wire.

A crinoline frame bought from a millinery supply house may be hardened
and used satisfactorily as a block.

A hat blocked over a wooden block may be dried at **very** low tempera-
ture in an oven—but don't try hand-made blocks in the oven, because they
may shrink.

Over a headblock, use adhesive tape to tape an inverted bowl or square
dish on the top of the block, for an unusual or odd-shaped crown. An
example of this is shown in Figures 6 and 7, on Felts. You can use your
imagination and search the kitchen for other possible utensils lending them-
selves to block shapes—a large jello mold, a large wooden salad bowl or
cake tin for a brim.

After your block has been used, repair it. Or if it is made of wood, fill
holes with plastic wood and re-varnish.

Keep all your old blocks, even if they are out of style. For instance, if
the block is a deep crown, a shallow crown can be blocked down the desired
depth. A narrow brim can be blocked over a wide brim block.

Blocks are usually in two pieces—crown and brim—and are blocked
separately.

Always block over the smooth side of a block. If the block is rough,
stretch a cheesecloth over the blocking side and fasten firmly. Willow has
a cheesecloth surface, which is the right, or blocking side.

You'll find it's exciting to make your own blocks and invent your own
hat shapes. Be one of those much-envied women who **make** fashion, instead
of merely following it!

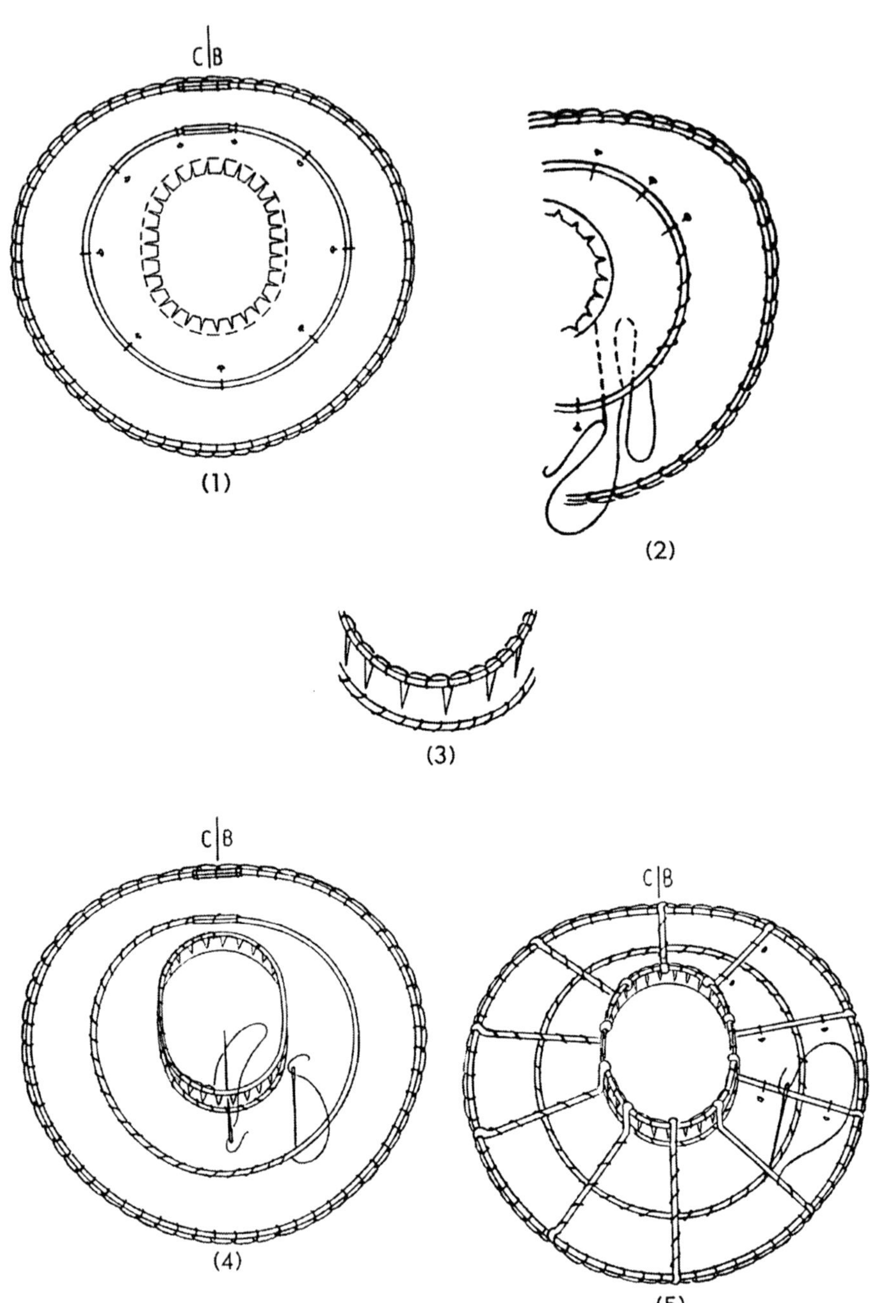

C|B
(1)
(2)
(3)
C|B
(4)
C|B
(5)

Blocks

(1)

Wire the brim at the edge, sew with buttonhole stitch. Reinforce with additional wire. Pin. (Use buckram or willow, etc.)

(2)

Sew additional wire with the stab overcast stitch.

(3)

Wire the top edge of the Headsize extension.

(4)

Also wire Headsize turn at brim. Stab overcast stitch.

(5)

Additional wires are added for more reinforcement.

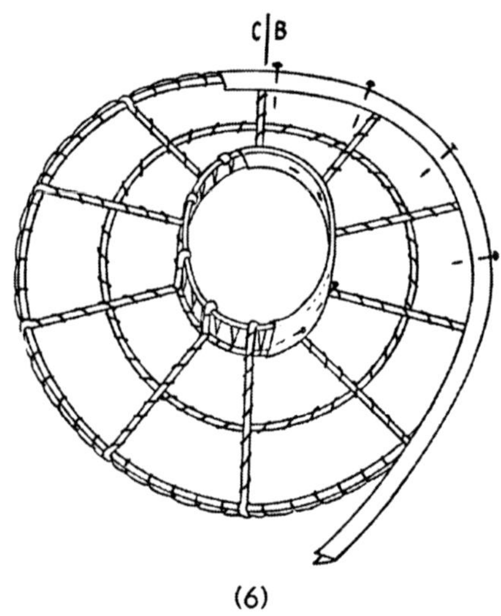

(6)

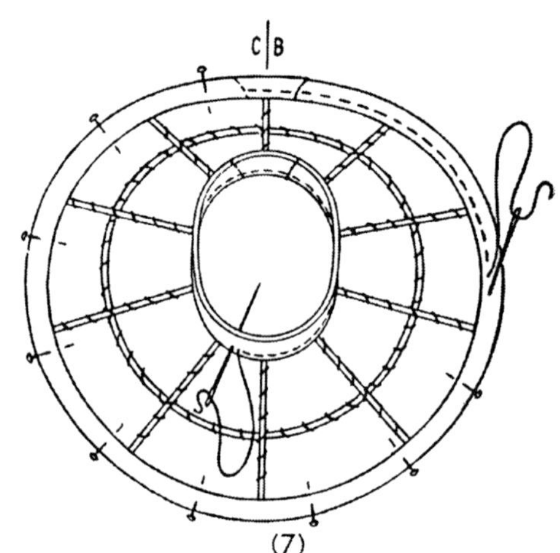

(7)

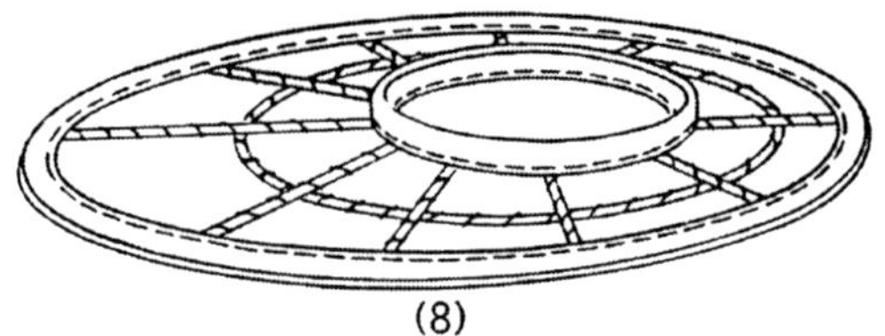

(8)

(6)

Cover brim edge with a folded bias crinoline band. Pin.

(7)

Sew folded bias cinoline band with the backstitch, or running stitch, **near raw edges** at headsize and brim edge.

(8)

A finished straight brim block.

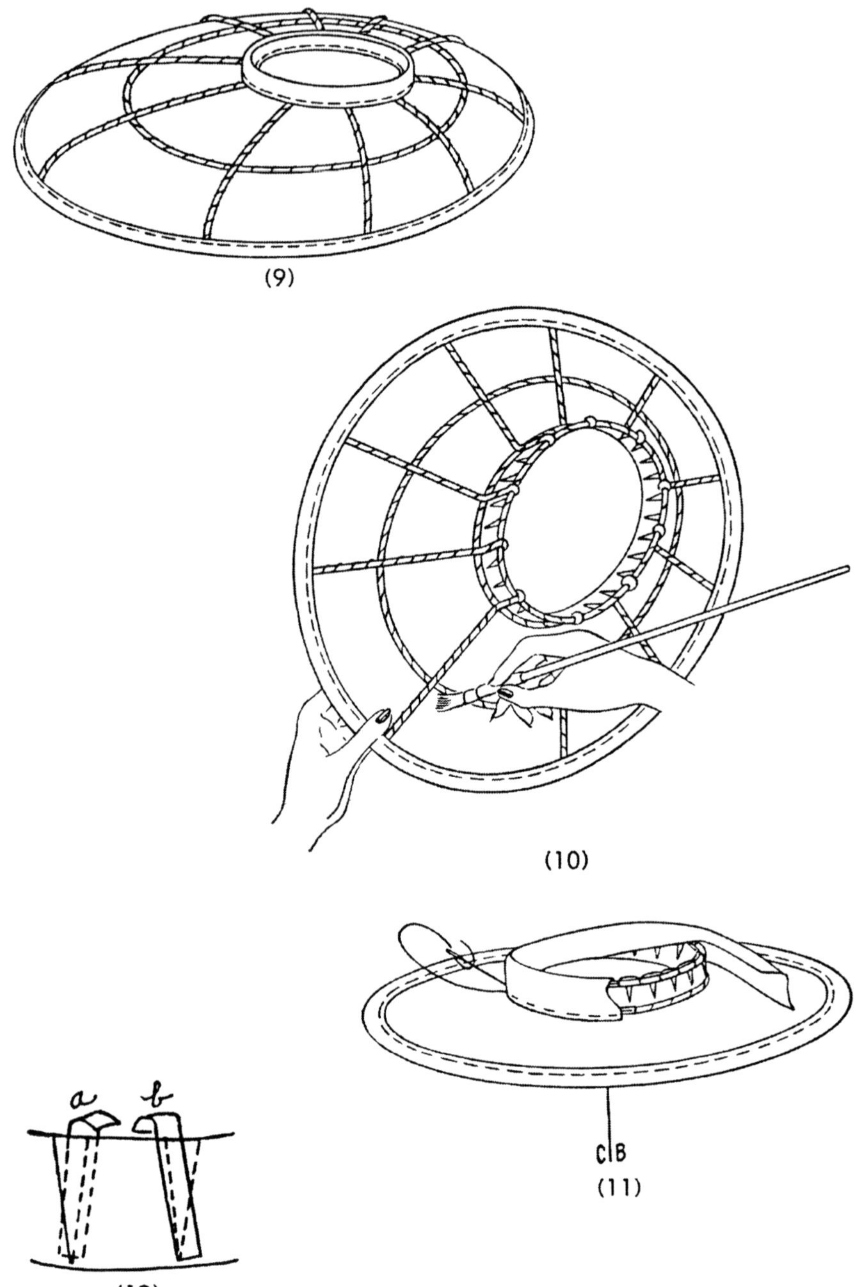

(9)
(10)
a b
(12)
CB
(11)

(9)

Block over the top or convex side of this block. **The wires are on the non-blocking side.**

(10)

The finished block is hardened by painting many times with "U BLOCK IT," clear varnish, clear lacquer, shellac or enamel. Allow to dry completely.

(11)

Harden a crinoline or buckram frame with shaped or straight brim with hardening agent bought from a millinery supply store. Clear varnish, lacquer, "U BLOCK IT," shellac, enamel, or glued tape may be used. If the crinoline shape is factory-made, separate it at the crown for a two-piece block, reinforce with wire and harden.

(12)

OR cover a wired frame with glued tape 1" or less wide. First paint small area with a strong glue and wet short length of tape slightly. Lap ends "a" and "b" over edges.

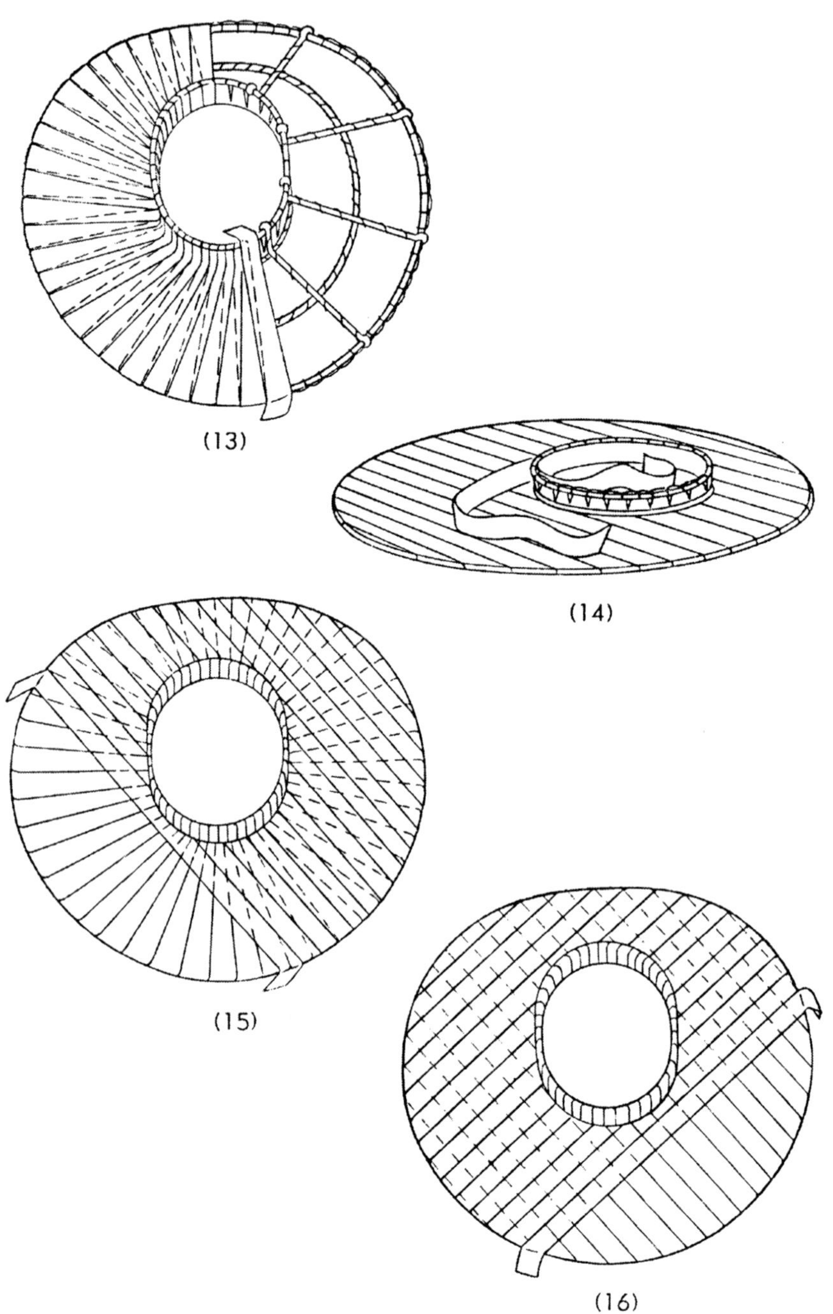

(13)

(14)

(15)

(16)

(13)

Lay dampened-glued tape over painted-glue area. Turn ends of tape over edges of frame block made of buckram, willow or paper, etc.

(14)

Cover Headsize extension with the glued tape.

(15)

Continue covering block, but in a different direction for each layer of tape.

(16)

Cover many times on the wrong side. Use one or two layers on the right side. Keep right side smooth. When glue and tape are dry, paint with a water repellent hardening agent.

Stretch crinoline, willow or willowette over a frame, to get identical shape for additional block.

A paper shape, as in Patterns, may be wired and covered with glued-paper tape, as in Steps 12, 13, 14, 15 and 16, and in the section on Frames, Steps 23-30, "Shaping a Circle of Buckram." This can be done in paper, wired and taped, or done in buckram, wired, painted with glue and glue taped, or hardened with "U BLOCK IT" to make block.

Frames

If you have a skeleton in your closet, you're lucky! That is, if it's the skeleton, or frame of a hat. Don't worry, though, if you don't find one, because in this chapter you'll learn how to make your own Frames—and then go on to cover them in the next chapter.

Frames are like blocks, except that they are not reinforced as heavily, and are usually in one piece. They can be made from buckram, crinoline, willow, willowette, wire or cotton felt, which is usually known as Hat Felt. Hat Felt is desirable in damp climates because it holds its shape well.

There are many types and shapes of Frames, including the calot, pillbox, sailor, mushroom, bonnet, cloche and their variations. You can vary the brim shape by lapping for a curved brim, or setting in gores for a ripple.

If you're making your own frame, you may cut it from a pattern, or dry or wet block it. Remember always to keep your frames light in appearance. Do not use wire at the Headsize, unless absolutely necessary. It may hurt your head.

Factory-made or ready-made frames can be purchased as a time-saver, but you will probably prefer, as you gain experience, to make your own frames, using your own ideas as to shape and type.

When your Frame is complete, cover it as described in the chapter on Covered Frames.

Follow each step in this chapter when making your frame—and you'll be pleasantly surprised at the professional-looking hat that will be your result.

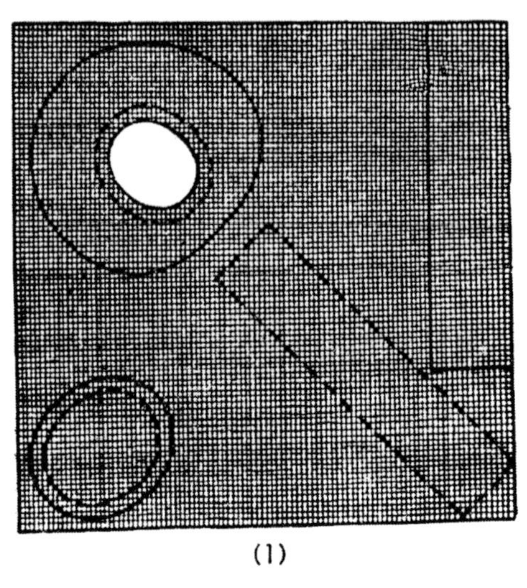

(1)

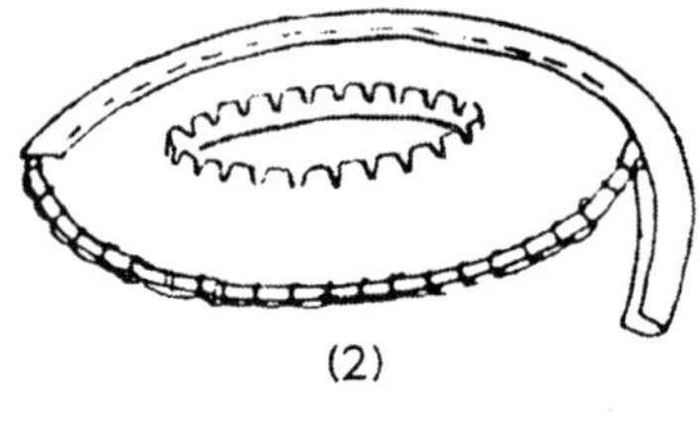

(2)

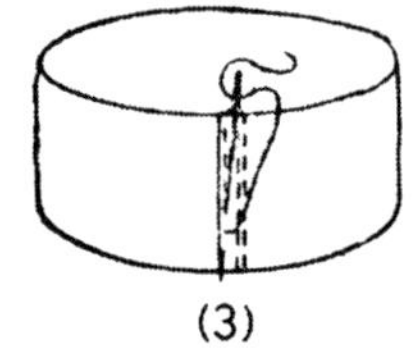

(3)

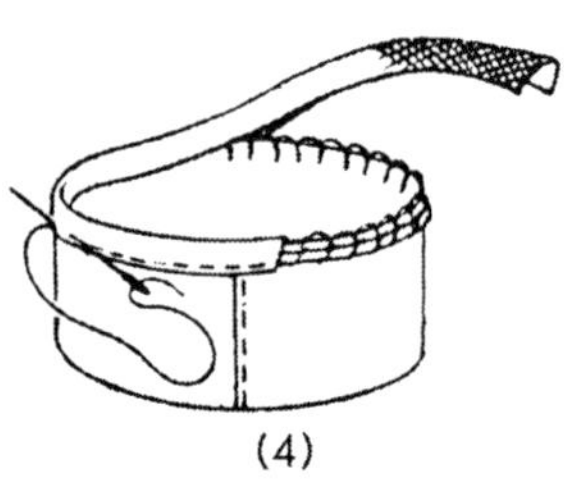

(4)

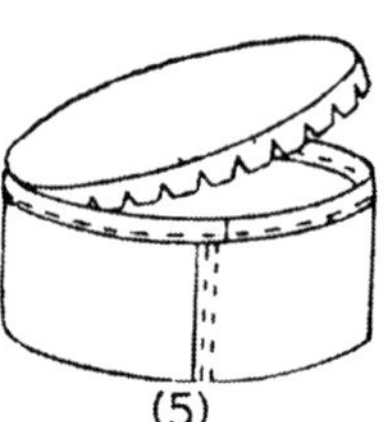

(5)

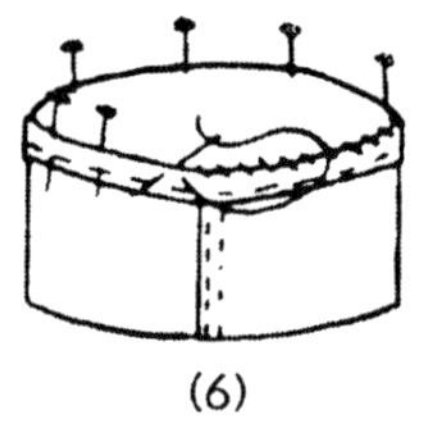

(6)

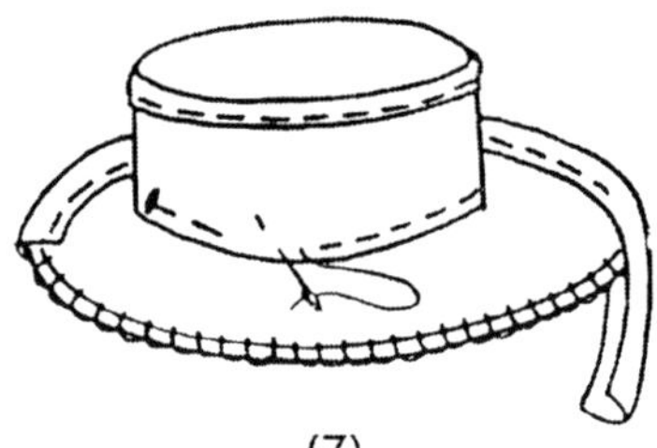

(7)

Frames

THE CONVENTIONAL SAILOR

(1)

Select one of the sailor cardboard brim patterns from Patterns, and lay Center Front, Center Back in line with opposite corners of the square of buckram. Leave an allowance of about 5/8" **inside** the Headsize for Headsize extension. Cut brim **on** outer edge of tracing. At the same time, cut a side crown, leaving 1/2" allowance at both ends for lap. Cut a tip, leaving an allowance of about 5/8" on the **outside** for tabs.

(2)

Wire edge of brim **on right side** and cover with bias crinoline fold, using backstitch. Backstitch **near edge** of folded-crinoline-bias fold.

(3)

The Headsize circumference of the side crown is the same as Headsize of the brim. Lap the two ends. Sew each edge of each end from the right side, using the backstitch or long-and-short backstitch.

(4)

Wire the top edge of the side crown from the **outside** and cover the wire with folded-bias-crinoline strip. Stab backstitch.

(5)

Turn tip tabs down and set tip **into** side crown. Pin, matching Center Front, Center Back and sides of tip to Center Front, Center Back and sides of crown.

(6)

Sew tip to side crown at side top, using overcast stitch, cross stitch or backstitch.

(7)

The crinoline-bias fold is lapped at Center Back and backstitched to the brim edge and finished. Set the finished crown over the tabs of brim Headsize extension. Pin and stab backstitch, stab long-and-short backstitch, or running stitch.

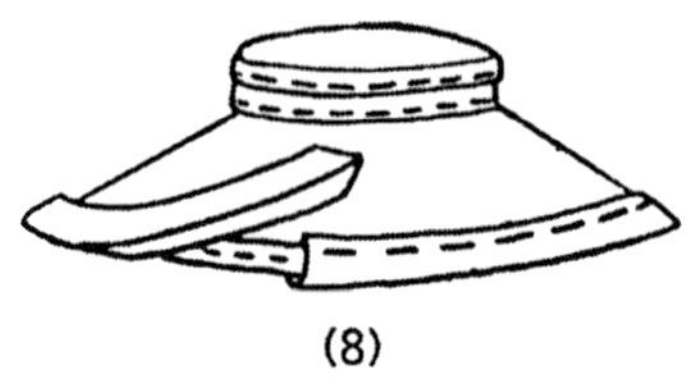

(8)

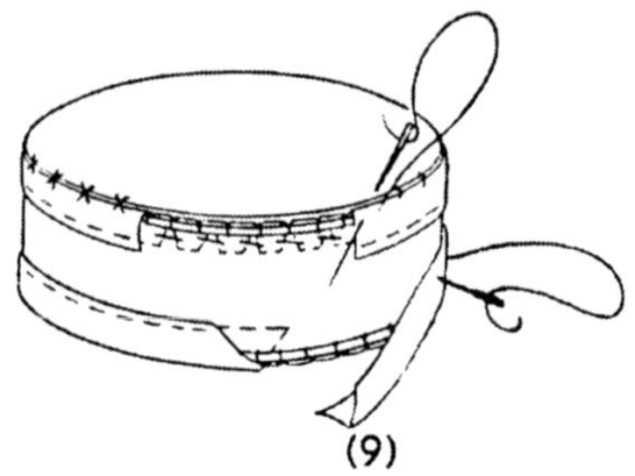

(9)

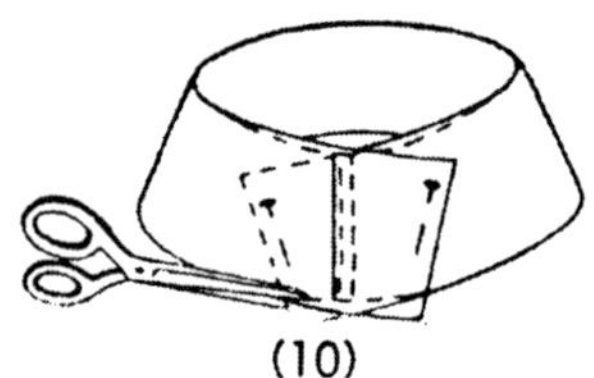

(10)

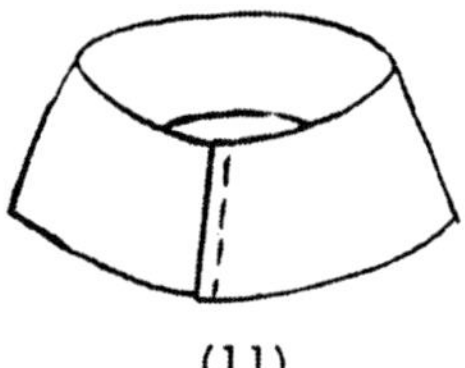

(11)

(12)

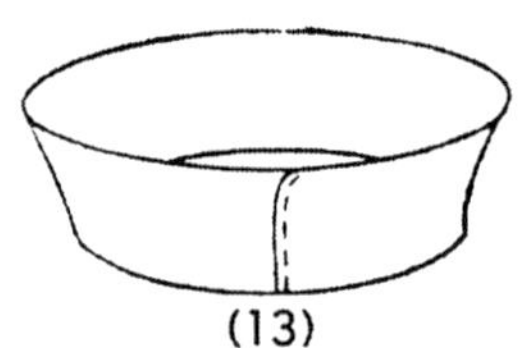

(13)

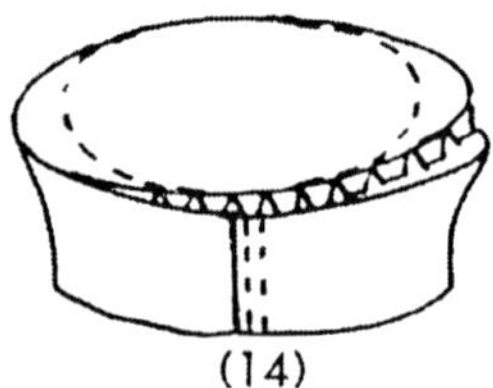

(14)

VARIATIONS OF CROWNS AND BRIMS

★ BRIMS

(8)

Brims may be straight, slanted or rolled. The edge is wired and taped in the same method as the conventional sailor. Note the Headsize extension of this brim. Lay a narrow side crown, wired and covered at the top, over the brim Headsize. There is no tip. It will be covered as an open crown.

★ CROWNS

(9)

A crown may be fastened to a brim as a unit, or the crown shape may be used alone——becoming a pillbox. This shape shows an alternate of the overcast stitch or the cross stitch at the top, or the sides can be backstitched. If the crown fits over a brim headsize, the crown edge is not covered. If it is to be a separate unit, cover edge with bias fold of crinoline and backstitch. The bottom edge can be wired, but it is usually not necessary. If the pillbox or crown fits the Headsize the head will hold the hat in shape. Wire at Headsize may hurt the head, so unless necessary, **do not wire Headsize.**

(10)

For a slanted-side crown, lap two ends of a straight side crown width until it is the correct Headsize. Pin, cut off ends at Headsize, and round off top edges. Trim ends at Center Back seam. To test the evenness of the top, turn upside down and lay on table. If the edge does not touch all the way around, trim until it does, unless it is intended to be uneven.

(11)

Reverse the side crown and the small top can be used as the Headsize and the larger for the tip or top.

(12)

Try a bias-cut buckram and pull one edge only. It will flare.

(13)

Lap ends at back. Use flared edge either at tip or at Headsize.

(14)

The tip may be ovaled from Center Front to Center Back or may be set in with wide sides at Right Side and Left Side. The tip might be wide at only one side and the side crown stretched only at one side, etc.

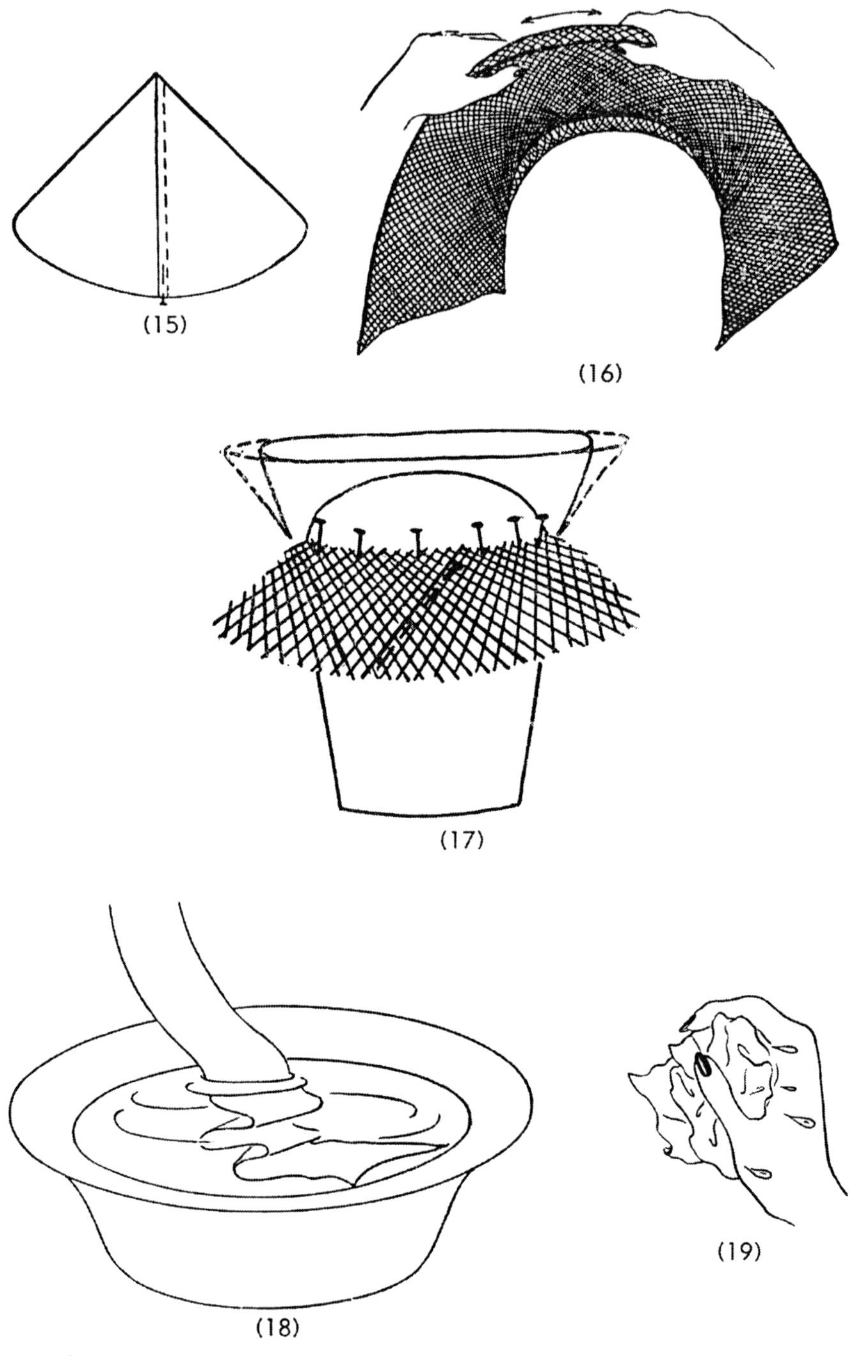

(15)

(16)

(17)

(18)

(19)

(15)

This is a circular shape from Patterns, with a pie-shaped wedge cut away. Leave an allowance for lapping at Center Back. The lap is sewed with the backstitch. If it is to be used as a crown, don't cover Headsize edge. If for a pillbox or toque, cover edges with crinoline, and wire if needed.

Blocking a Frame

★ DRY BLOCKING

(16)

Frame fabric may be blocked DRY. Pull midway of a bias strip until desired roll is achieved. Lap at Center Back. Pull midway of edge again. Hold in at the Headsize and hold in outside brim edge when wiring. Cover brim edge with bias folded crinoline.

(17)

For a flared brim, hold a DRY bias-strip-brim width (of buckram, willow, willowette, crinoline, etc.) in at the Headsize. Pin. Lap at the Center Back and pull the outside-brim edge. Backstitch at Headsize to hold the shape. Brim is in downward position. After it is the correct size, slant or flare, pull upward on outside edges to top dotted position, or leave down. Wire outer brim edge and cover with crinoline.

★ WET BLOCKING

(18)

Submerge frame fabric (buckram, willow, willowette, crinoline, etc.) into water.

(19)

Squeeze out most of water.

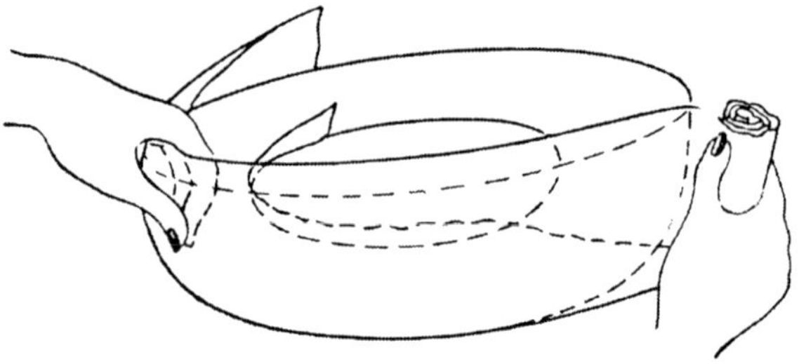

(20)

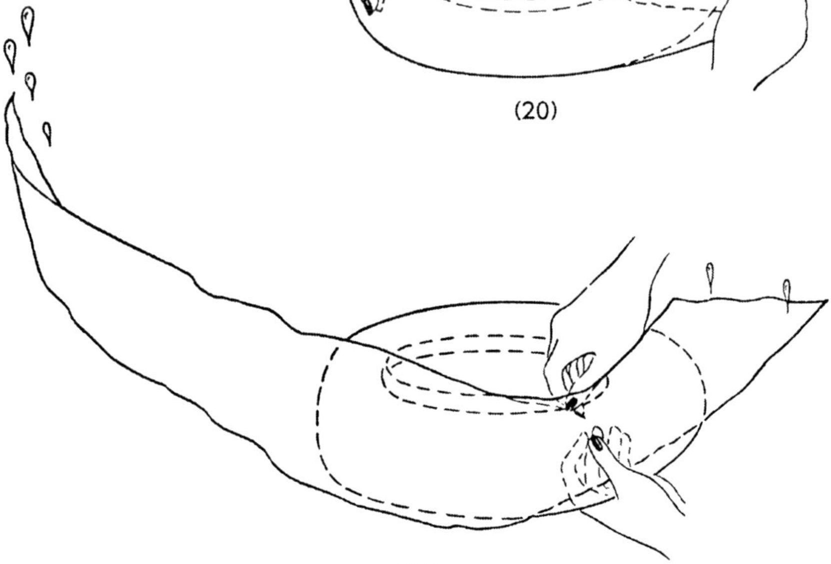

(21)

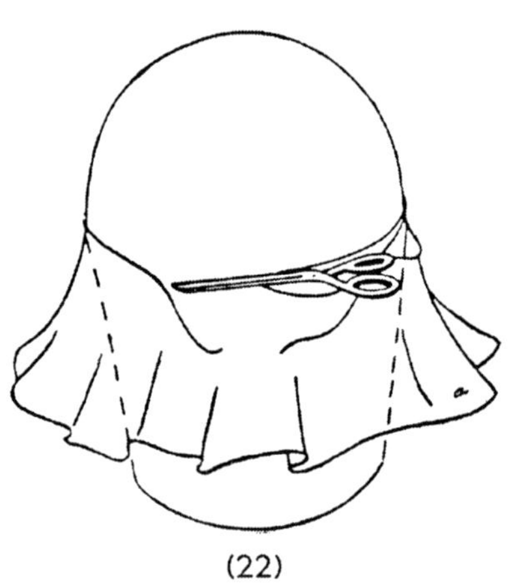

(22)

(20)

Find center of the strip and start at Center Front of brim. Pin. Pull horizontally toward the Center Back of block. Pin and pull from Center Front
toward Center Back with other end. Pin at Center Back.

(21)

Also pull the blocking fabric vertically. Pin at Headsize and at brim edge.
Lap at Center Back and sew when dry, using backstitch. Wire and cover
with bias-crinoline tape.

(22)

Pull wet frame fabric over a headblock. Pin at bottom edges. Pin, and tie with
string below Headsize depth. Mark Headsize depth. Backstitch over mark and
allow to dry. Remove by method described in Blocking the Foundation, in the
section on Turbans.

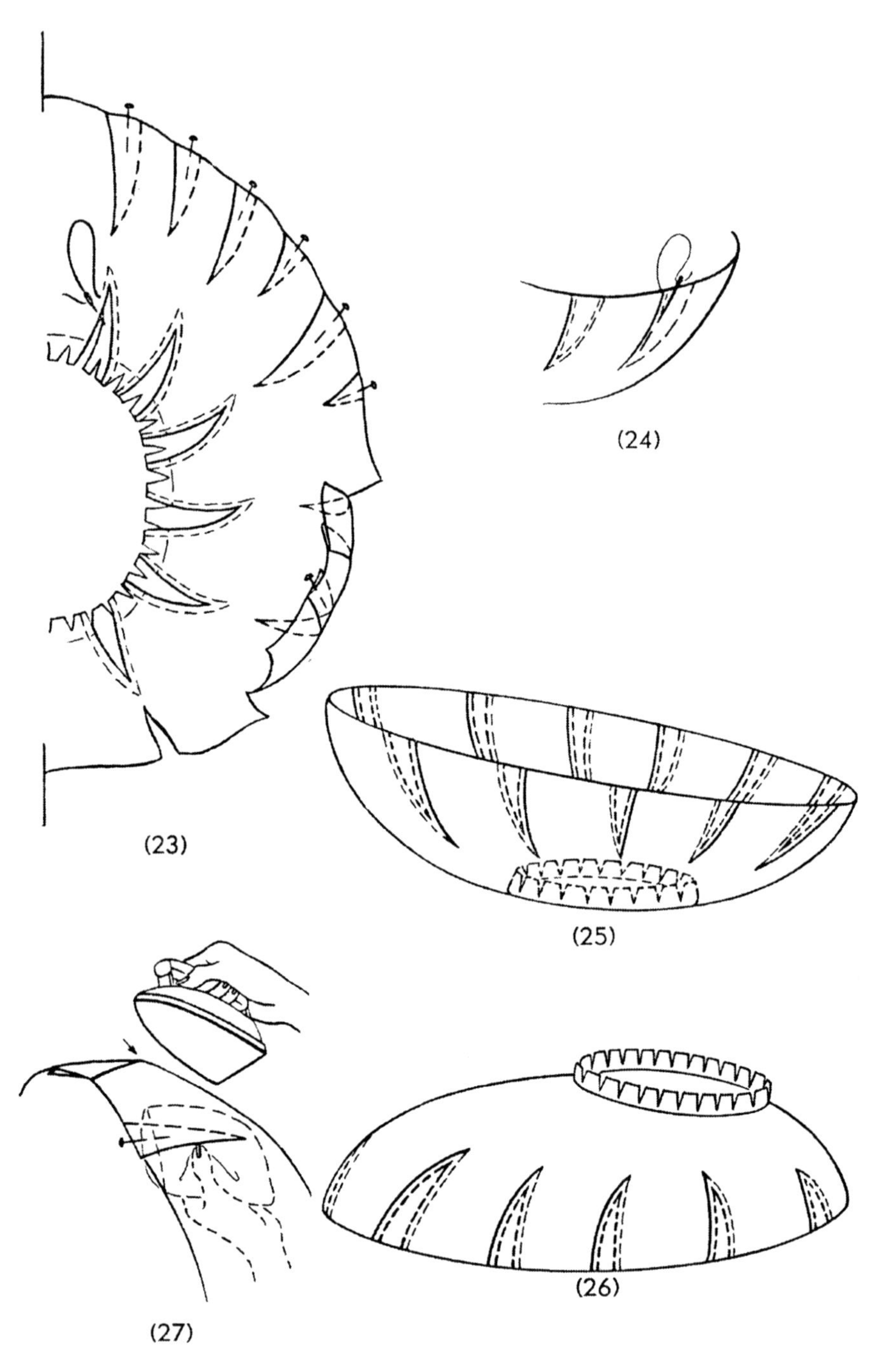

(23)

(24)

(25)

(26)

(27)

Shaping a Circle

★ **LAPPED SLASHES**

(23)

Cut a circle or rounded shape of Buckram, and following the guide fold lines of pattern, slash, curve laps and pin. If this isn't enough curve, slash between laps and curve the shorter laps. Pin. Cut and arrange until curve is right. If slashed to Headsize and lapped straight, the brim will have a straight contour.

(24)

Sew edges of laps with a small invisible backstitch. If there is not too much curve, you may use sewing machine. **Cut away one part of the lap** so that it is **not double** at the lap when finished.

(25)

The Headsize tabs are turned up in the same direction as the brim.

(26)

Headsize tabs are **always** up, but this brim rolls down.

(27)

If the ends of the laps are bumpy place a press pillow under the brim and iron over the bump from the top.

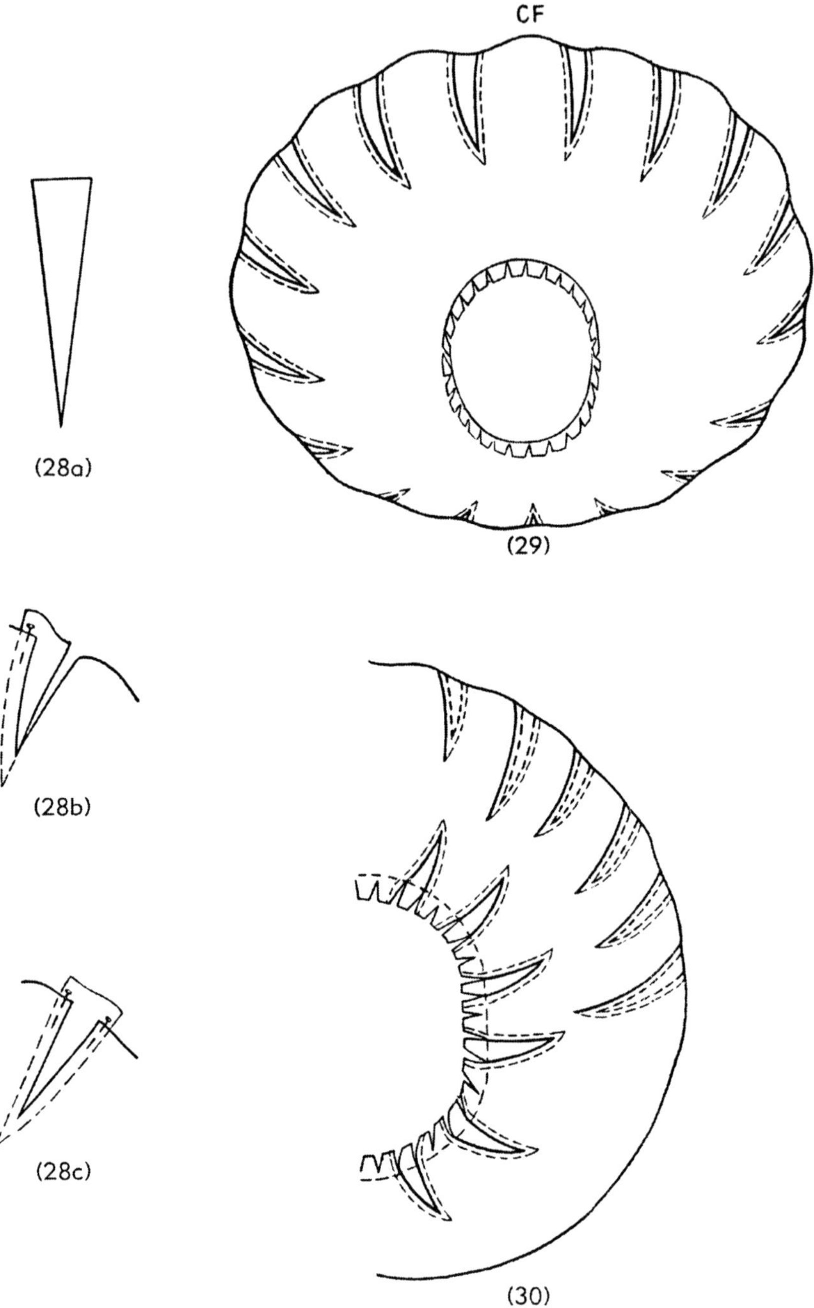

CF
(28a)
(28b)
(28c)
(29)
(30)

★ GORE SET-IN SLASHES

(28a, b & c)
Set in a gore between the slits for a RIPPLED brim or crown.

(29)
Sew gores close to the edge with a small backstitch, or by sewing machine.
Work with the edges to keep them smooth before sewing. If rippled all
around, cut gores narrow. If rippled only at the front, gores may be wider.
Wire and tape outside edge.

(30)
In this figure, laps are at the outer edge and small gores at Headsize. Don't
use too many gores at Headsize. Gores at Headsize are to help buckram
spread for a curve at midbrim and turn up for a rounded Headsize.

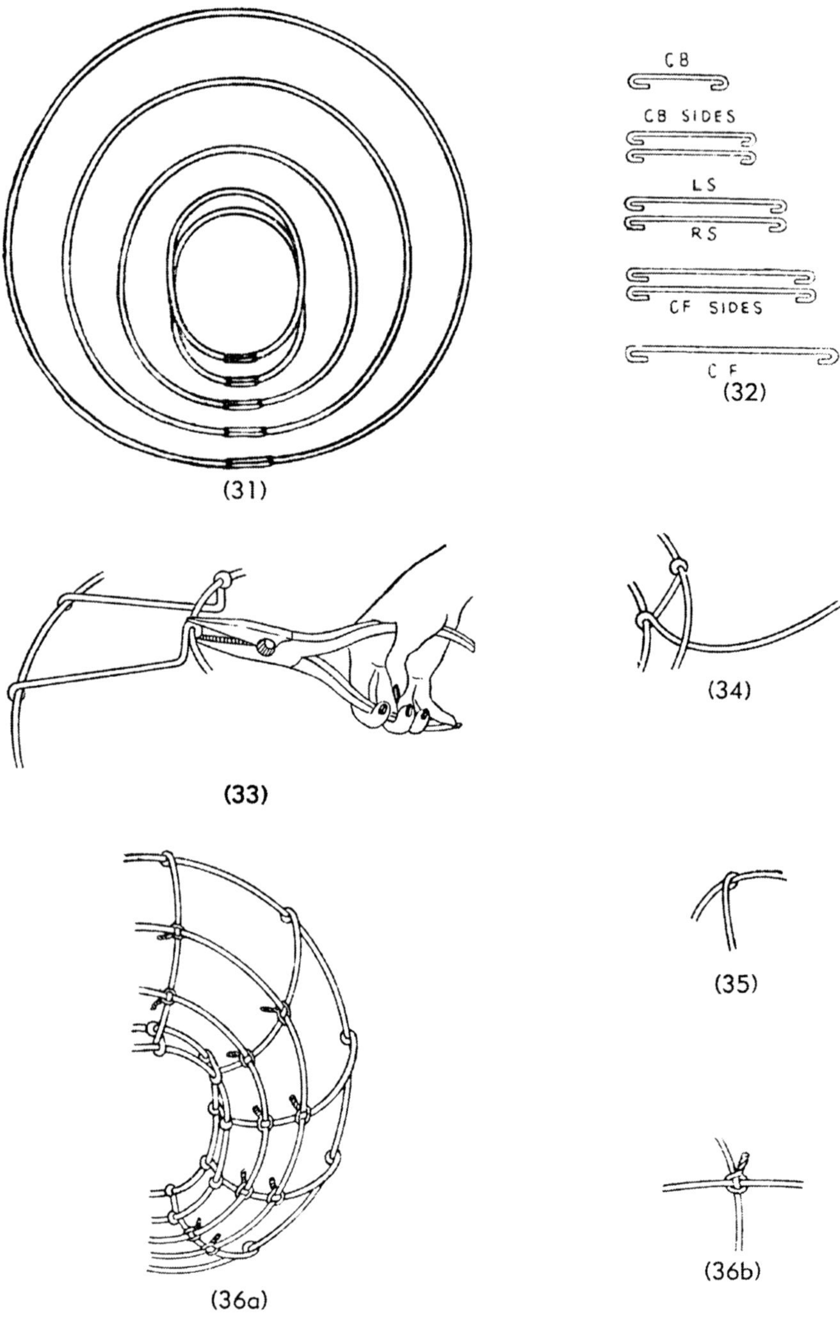

(31)

(32)

(33)

(34)

(35)

(36a)

(36b)

(88)

The Wire Frame

(31)

Cut a wire length the circumference of the outside brim. Use a wire fastener. Cut Headsize wire, tip-Headsize-wire extension, and wires between outer edge and Headsize. Fasten ends of these wires. Lay in their places. Use only the necessary minimum number of wires.

(32)

Measure length of Center Back to Top of Side Crown. Cut lengths of wire allowing for turn at ends—about $\frac{1}{8}''$ or a little more. Prepare a Center Front wire, Side wires and in-between wires if needed.

(33)

Bend these ends over tip of side crown and brim edge.

(34)

Turn wire over the Headsize wire. If it is to be a curved brim, bend wire.

(35)

Turn end of wire over outside-edge of wire.

(36a & b)

In-between wires are laid over the Center Front, Center Back and Side wires. Fasten together with fine wire. Twist. Picture-hanging wire is ideal for this. Carefully notice the wrap before it is twisted.

Covered Frames

Here's another place where you can let your imagination be your guide. You have your frame—now you'll learn how to cover it for a finished hat. The style is up to you—and the fabric you use is a matter of your choice. In summer, you'll want a flattering "garden hat," of cucumber-cool organdie. For winter wear there are glamorous woolens, and a score of other materials to pick from.

The general principle in covering frames is consistency in the thread grain. The fabric may be placed at Center Front and Center Back on the true bias. The true bias will therefore fall at Right Side and Left Side, and the top will be placed similarly. This is the CONVENTIONAL BASIC PRINCIPLE. However, it is **by no means a law** or a rule. If you wish, you may decide to use the straight thread grain at the Center Front. In that case, the straight threads will also fall at Center Back, Right Side and Left Side. Then be consistent and cover the tip and side crown in a like manner. BE SURE TO STRETCH ALL FABRIC IN EACH STEP.

Follow your cardboard patterns, carefully mark Center Front, Center Back, Right Side and Left Side of the fabric as you work, regardless of the thread grain you choose.

Your pattern has NO SEAM ALLOWANCE. As the pattern is placed on the fabric, make your seam allowance—generally ½" to ⅝". Try tailor's chalk on a sample. If it removes easily, mark around the pattern lightly and leave the seam allowance.

To RENOVATE covered frame hats, brush well and rub gently with a cloth dampened with cleaning fluid. If the covering is soiled too much, remove it from the frame, dip into cleaning fluid or wash in sudsy lukewarm water. Replacing the frame cover necessitates RE-MAKING the hat.

So why not use another fabric, and have a brand new hat? A scrap from your newest dress or suit would be perfect, adding the complement to your outfit that brings compliments to you!

(1)   Refer to Fig. 1—in Frames.

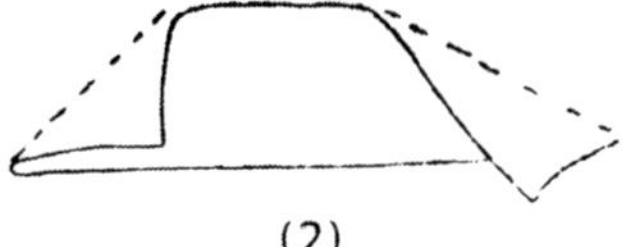

(2)

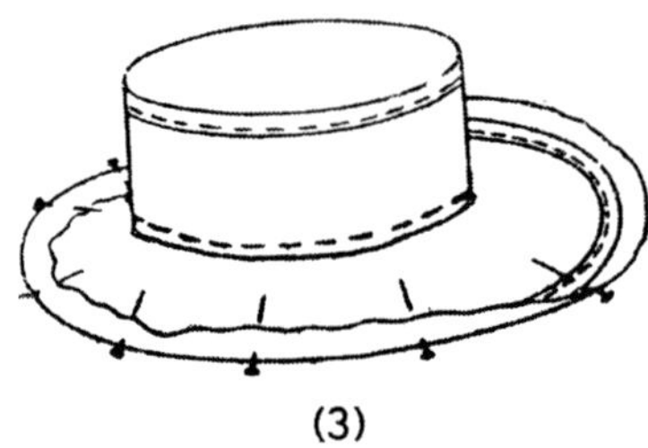

(3)

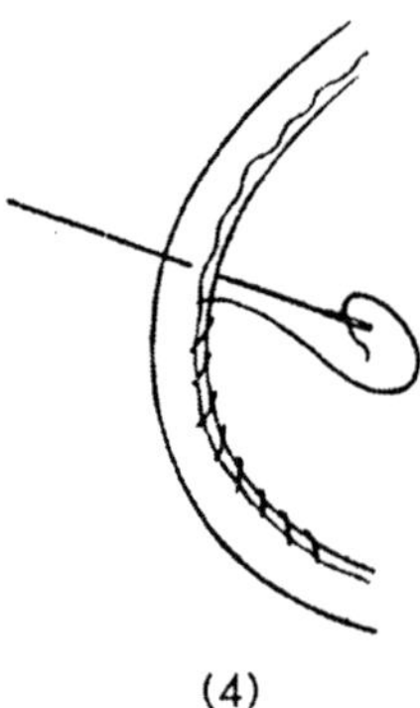

(4)

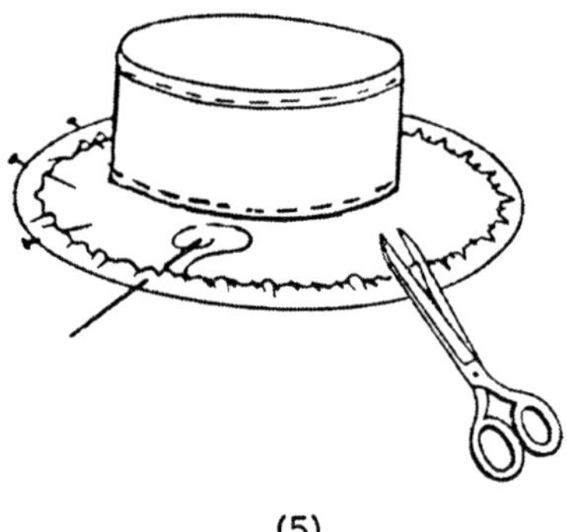

(5)

Covered Frames

(1)

When a square of fabric is folded at opposite corners, the fold represents the TRUE BIAS of the fabric. HAT TACTICS follows basic method of true bias at Center Front, Center Back, Right Side and Left Side. Center Front, Center Back, Right Side and Left Side of Brim pattern are marked. Lay this pattern, matching these marks to bias from corner to corner, and lay tip at corner, true bias matching Center Front and Center Back marks. The side-crown length is shown cut on bias (dotted lines). The side crown on the top right of Figure 1, Frames, is on the straight-thread grain.

(2)

This straight-grain band shows how to find true bias and off-bias. The folded corner at the left shows true bias. The right is folded on the off-bias.

★ BASIC METHOD IN COVERING A SAILOR FRAME

(3)

If worn "off-the-face," cover the underside of brim first. If worn forward, cover top first. Two of these cover facings are cut at one time. Fold fabric corner to corner, allowing ⅝" to 1" on outside edge and inside at Headsize. One with right side up and one with right side down. The thread grain is the same on each. Pin or mark Center Front and Center Back on each. The Center Front, Center Back, Right Side and Left Side of the under facing are matched with those of brim. Pin, turning outside edge of fabric over edge of frame. Pin Headsize allowance of cover to Headsize of frame.

(4)

Overcast turned-over edge of fabric to folded-bias-crinoline-edge cover of frame.

(5)

After outside edge has been overcast to folded-crinoline cover of frame edge, snip off any bumpy places, so that surface will be flat and smooth. Proceed with choice of edge finishes. See Step 24 for continuation of basic sailor.

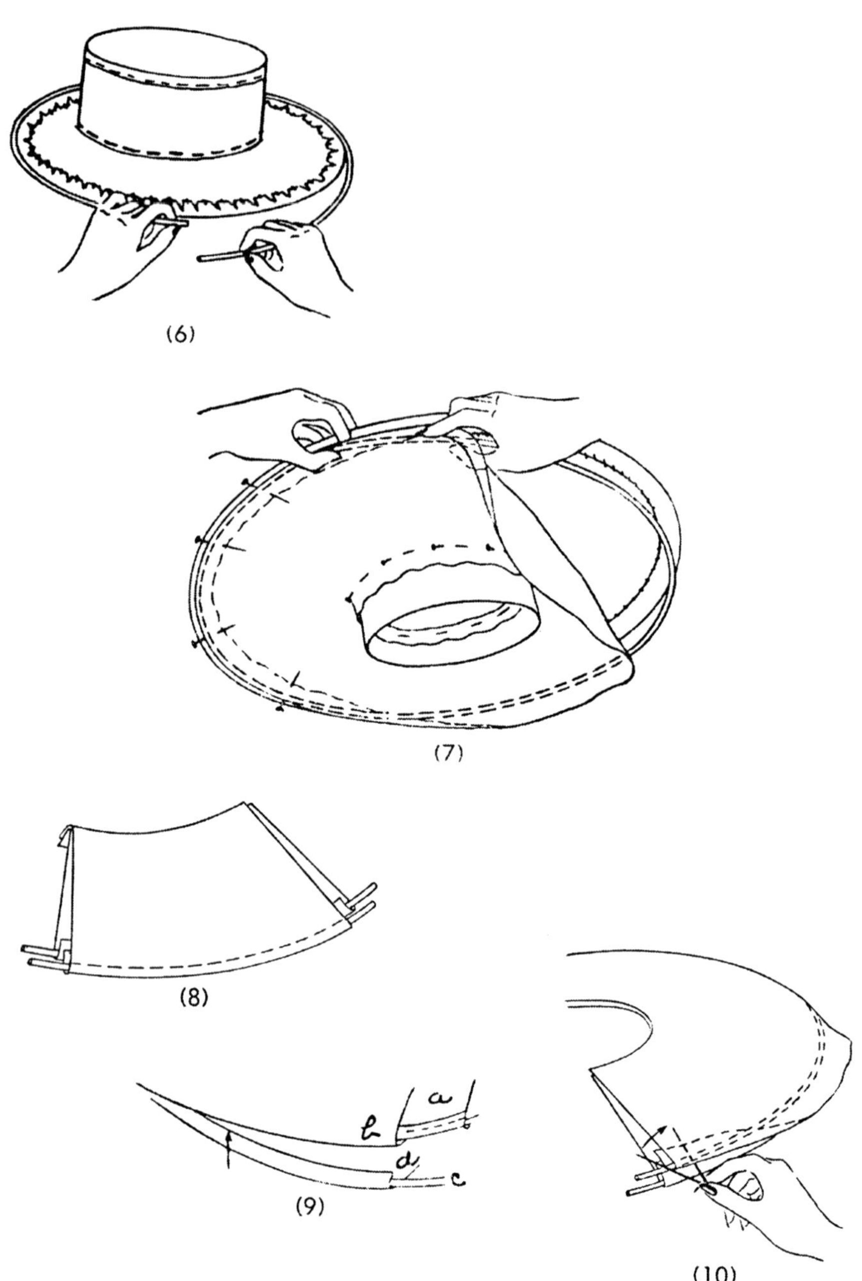

(6)

(7)

(8)

(9)

(10)

(11)
Refer to figures 4a, 4b, 4c, 4d, in STITCHES.

★ BASIC METHOD OF FINISHING BRIM EDGE—No. 1

(6)

This edge has TWO WIRES. The first wire is already sewed on the frame edge and covered. The second wire is measured on the outside edge of the frame. It fits snugly, **just to the edge.** Fasten with a Wire Fastener.

(7)

Place the top facing over the frame, turning up at Headsize. Match Center Front, Center Back, Right Side and Left Side of fabric cover to corresponding points of frame. Pin. At the outside edge, start at Center Back, turn top cover over wire. **Remember** this cover extends over edge of frame. Move to Center Front and turn top cover over wire and fit over edge of frame. Pin. Fit over edge of Right Side, pin. Fit Left Side, pin, matching front to front, side to side, etc., each time. Now, with top cover smooth and in place, work between Center Back and Left Side, Left Side to Center Front, from Center Back to Right Side and Right Side to Center Front. **Be sure the surfaces are very smooth** on the top and on the bottom. If necessary, remove pins and re-do.

(8)

Notice position of two wires at edge and extension of one over the other.

(9)

"a" is frame. "b" first cover. "d" is second cover over wire "c."

(10)

As the facing in Step 7 is being pinned and arranged, to aid in placing edge under wire and facing, continually run long needle under second wire to keep edge smooth under covering.

(11)

Follow carefully the stitches described in Figures 4a, b, c, d, Stitches.

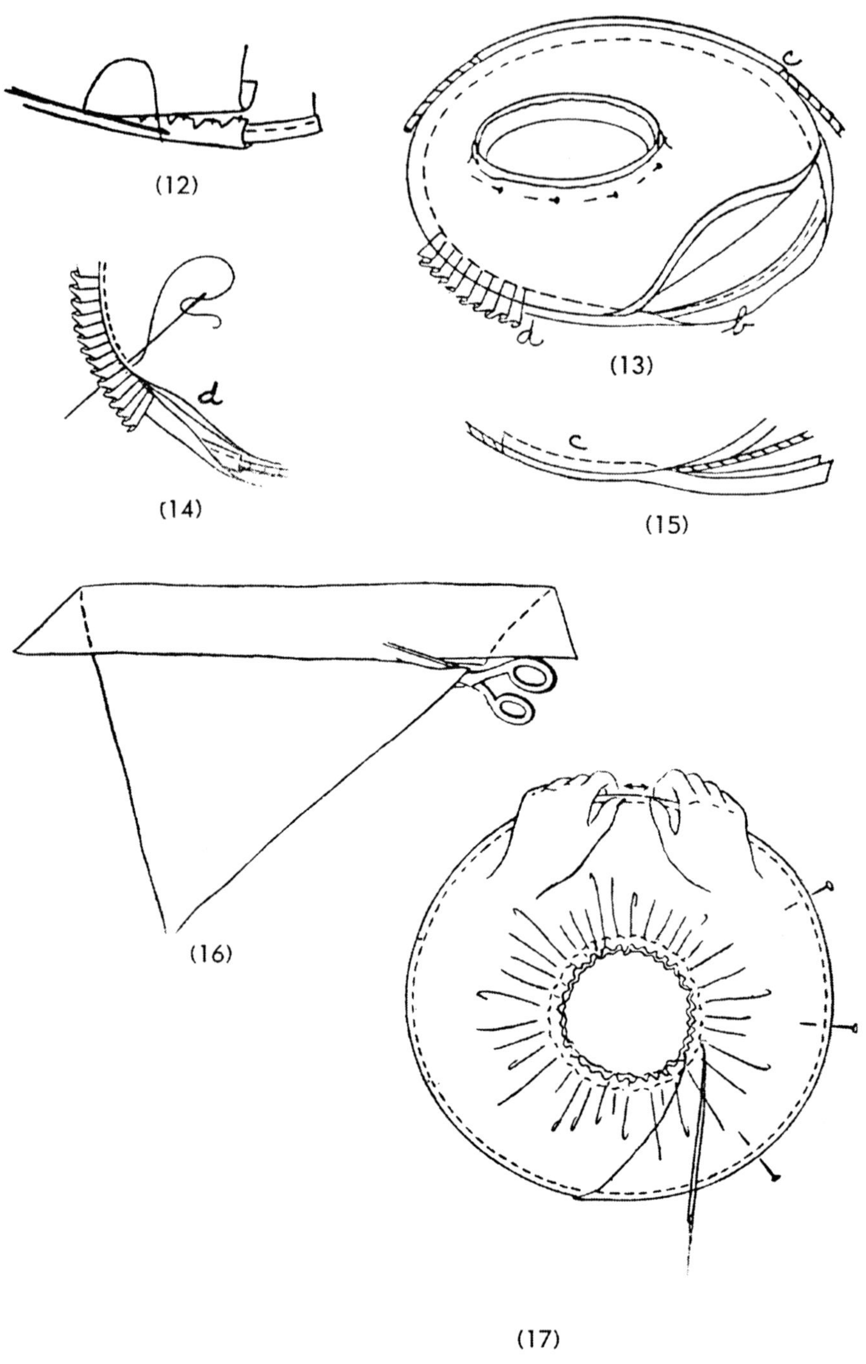

(12)
(13)
c
d
b
(14)
d
(15)
c
(16)
(17)

★ BASIC METHOD OF FINISHING BRIM EDGE—No. 2

(12)

The bottom facing "b," Figure 13, has been matched to Center Front, Center Back and sides, pinned and sewed. The top, or second facing, is matched to Center Front, Center Back and Sides, pinned at Headsize, as in Figure 13. The outside edge of cover is turned under. This top turned-under edge comes not to the outside edge, but **on the edge at the top,** so that when looking at the right side, the first facing looks as if it continues on to the other side. The second facing-edge is seen from the second side. Sew, using slipstitch.

(13)

Between first facing "b" and second facing, interesting edges may be inserted, as edge "c" and edge "d." See Figures 48a, b, c, d, Straw, for other suggestions.

(14)

For stitching top facing, use slipstitch, invisible backstitch, or backstitch.

(15)

Shows insertion of edge "c" in Figure 13.

★ BASIC METHOD OF FINISHING BRIM EDGE—No. 3

(16)

Fold fabric on true bias, double the width of the brim to be covered plus a generous allowance of two inches. The bias length should be as long at the folded edge as the circumference of the brim edge.

(17)

Prepare a strong steel wire exactly the circumference of the frame edge, with fastener at back. Over this steel wire, place the folded bias. Stretch and pin the fold toward ends of bias length. Pin at ends, remove and sew a bias seam (see Glossary) by machine. Replace over steel wire and run a separate drawstring (use very strong thread) in each edge at the Headsize. Pin outside edge and pull drawstring. Hold over steam as you pull drawstrings, remove pins. Allow to dry. Don't remove strings, but remove flange.

(18)
Refer to Figures 7, 25, and 31, this chapter.

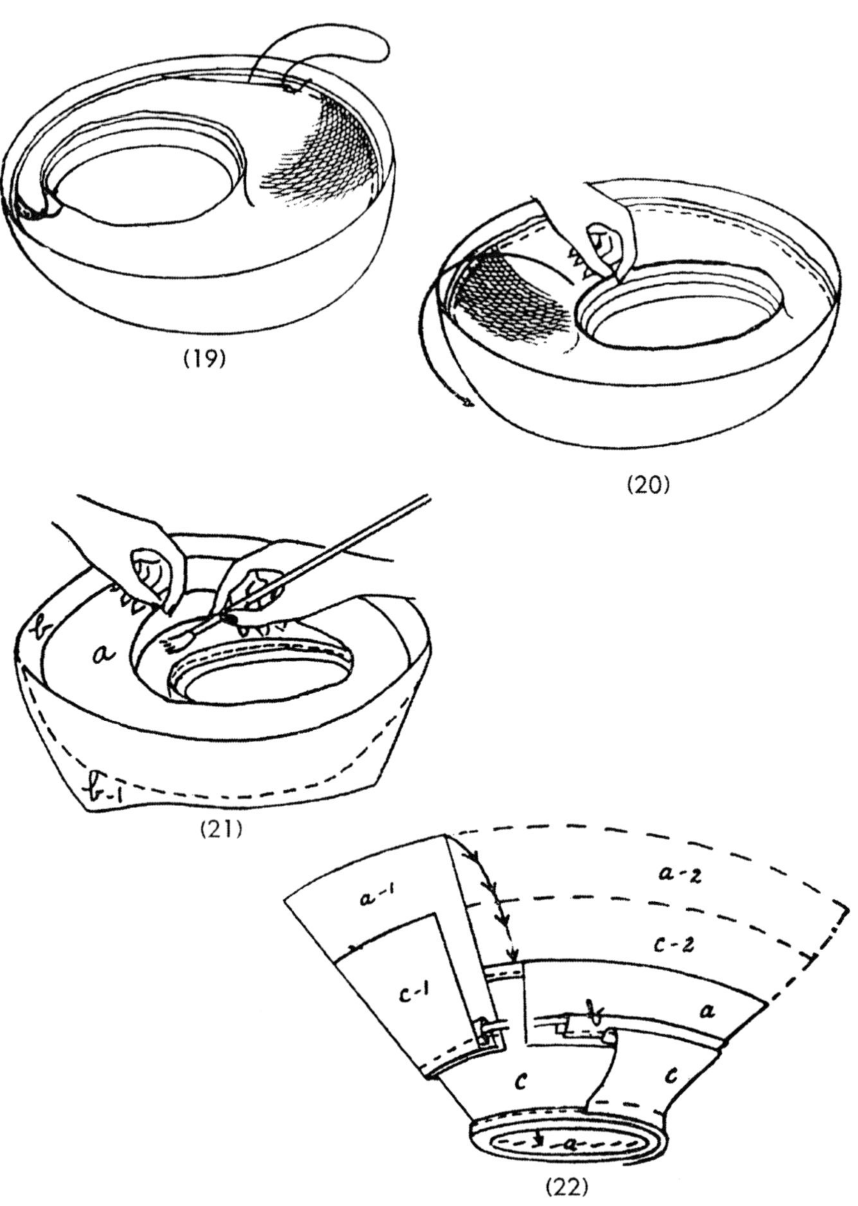

(23)
Refer to figures 37-48, STRAW.

(18)

Slip this round flange without seams at edge, over frame. Pin at Headsize as in Step 7. Run new drawstring if necessary. Pull in until smooth at Headsize on top and bottom. Sew through two facing edges and through frame at Headsize turn, Figure 25. See Figure 31, this section, with bias seam at Center Back. Find straight Center Back line, and place bias seam diagonally across this line.

★ VARIATIONS OF BRIM COVERINGS

(19)

This brim is shaped and rounded. A bias outer facing is easier to stretch over the convex side than concave side. This type facing should be blocked over a block having same shape as frame to be covered. If using a purchased frame, buy two and use one for block. See Step 11, Blocks. OR block facings and buckram shape over same block.

(20)

Lay both blocked facings on the concave side of frame, down from edge. Sew with backstitch. The top facing is wider, because it must turn over top edge of frame. Leave the underfacing, and lift top facing as it lies on concave side, over top edge of frame to other side.

(21)

Cover "b-1" has been turned from concave side. "b" extends over into concave side. "a" is the underfacing, as described in Step 20. If "a" does not lie snugly to frame, paint frame slightly with millinery glue, and press cover "a" lightly to frame.

(22)

"a-2" and "c-2" represent width of bias lengths from corded wire "b." Over the straight shaped brim, the bias strip facings "c-1" and "a-1" are laid and pinned at equal distances from the brim edge. Note bias covered cord between "c-1" and "a-1." Seam will be at Center Back. The seam may be a vertical seam. See Figure 30. Sew brim edges through the brim frame, using the backstitch. After it has been sewed, pull and stretch "c-1" up to Headsize of "c." "a-1" is pulled and stretched toward inside brim up to Headsize. Facings "c-1" and "a-1" are pinned to Headsize and sewed, using long and short backstitch, "a."

(23)

For other variations in covering a Brim Frame, see Figures 37-48, Straw.

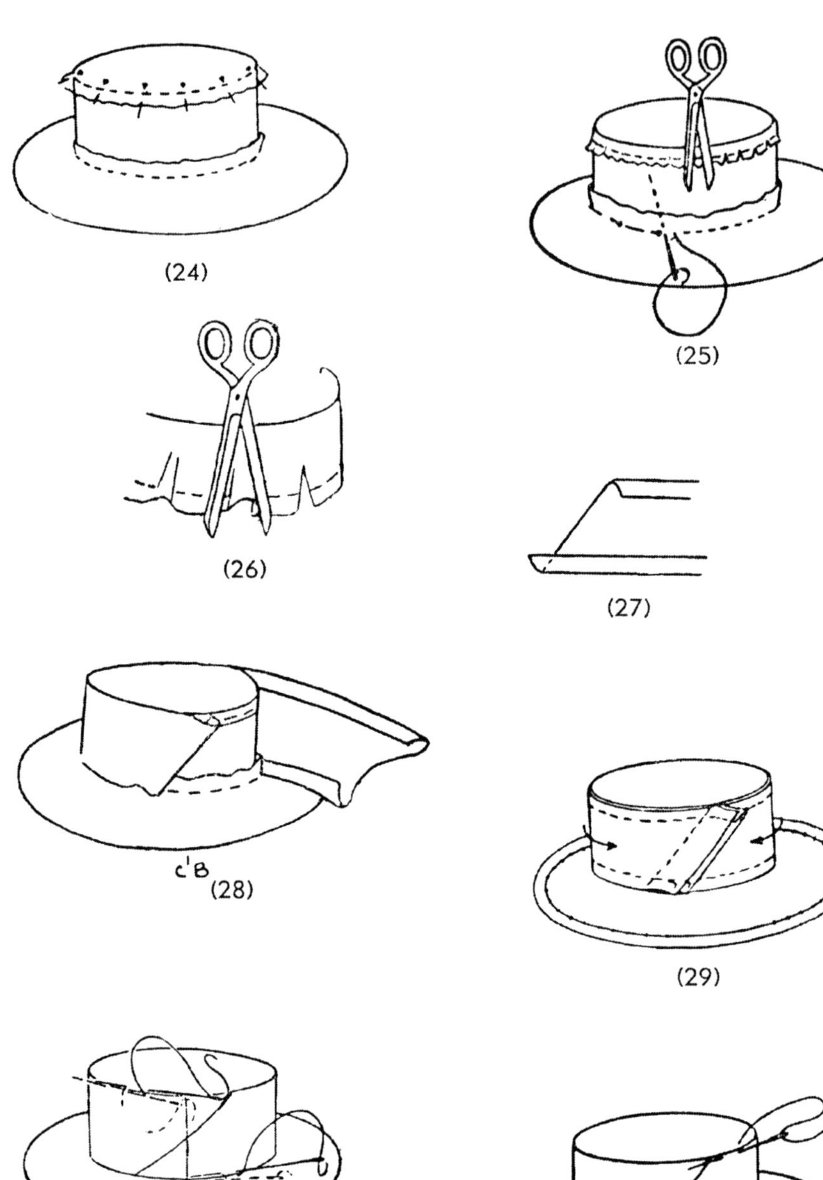

(24)
(25)
(26)
(27)
c'B
(28)
(29)
(30)
a
c
b
(31)

(24)

To continue the basic method of covering a frame: After Step 5, the tip is then covered. If the brim covering is bias at Center Front, tip must also be bias at Center Front. Match Center Front tip to Center Front crown frame tip. Also match Center Back and Sides. Stretch and pin.

(25)

Sew tip cover through crown side, down from the tip edge about 3/16". Use backstitch, or long and short backstitch. Snip off any bumps so that side crown covering will be smooth.

(26)

Close-up of cutting bumps or unevenness from turned-down circular edge.

(27)

Measure the width of side crown. Allow a generous ⅝" for each side and measure the circumference of side crown, allowing about 1". NOTE: As bias is stretched, it will become more narrow.

(28)

Stretch this bias length snugly around the side crown. Pin at back. (A bias seam.)

(29)

Remove from frame and sew the bias seam by machine. Trim seam to about ¼", open and press (Figure 42). Place again over side crown, top and bottom edges turned down and in, as shown in Step 28.

(30)

Adjust seam directly at Center Back. Check all markings of Center Back on frame, facing coverings, side crown and tip of frame, against tip and side crown coverings. Slipstitch top of side crown covering to tip, and bottom of side crown covering at Headsize to Headsize extension of brim covering.

(31)

"a" and "b" show Step 30. "c" is an alternative stitch, the stabbed invisible backstitch.

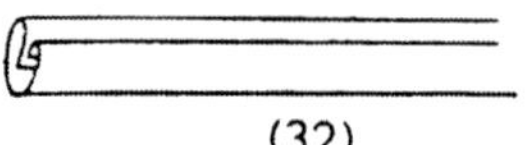

(32)

(33)

(34)

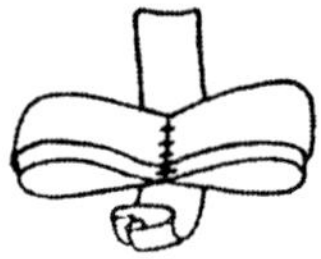

(35)

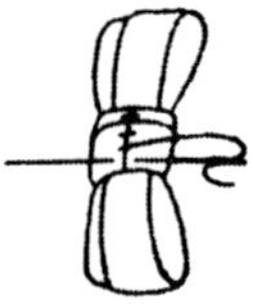

(36)

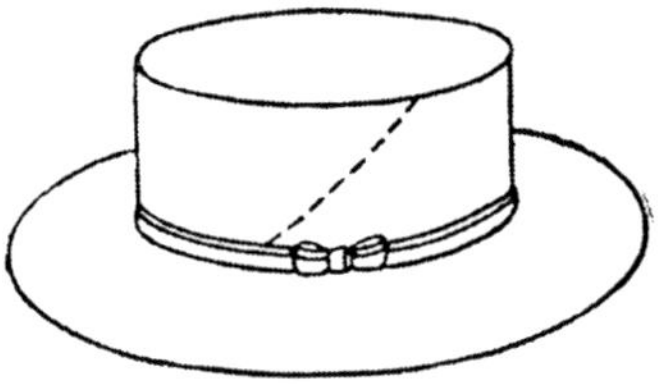

(37)

(38)

(39)

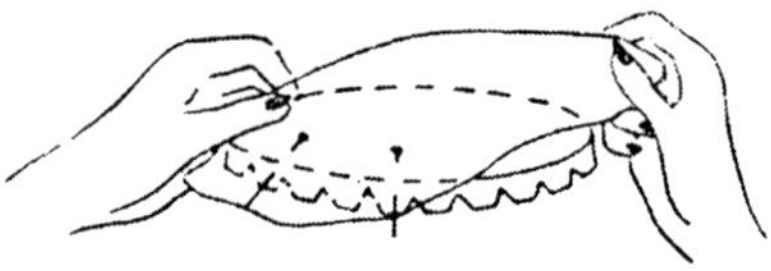

(40)

★ THE TAILORED BOW

(32)
This is a covering for the crown-turn at brim. Cut a band about 1 1/4" wide
—when folded it should be about 3/8" wide. **Stretch** this band around base of
side crown. Cut so that end touches end, but does not overlap. Remove and
overcast ends together. Replace at base of side crown. Since it is so snugly
stretched, it is not necessary to tack to hat.

(33)
From the same folded band, cut a length about 4" long. Fold as in accompanying figure.

(34)
Overcast two raw ends to middle of folded band.

(35)
Over this tailored bow, wrap a length of the same folded band around center,
stretch and cut with one end touching other.

(36)
Overcast. In this tailored bow, no ends overlap. Therefore, there is NO extra
bulk.

(37)
Place tailored bow over overcast seam of band at center back of side-crown
base. Tack bow to band, through covered frame.

(38)
See Figure 10, Turbans, for the drape. As an alternative, it can be used on
the side crown. But **stretch!**

(39)
See Figure 12 and 13, Headsize Bands. Headsize Band in Figure 39 is a band
about 2 1/4" wide. One side is folded over 1/2" and the other side 3/4". The
folded side lies inside hat, and smooth side against hair. Figure 39 sews into
hat on bottom, as pictured.

(40)
OR the sailor may be made and assembled by first covering the tip of frame.
Pin fabric to tip and sew to buckram tip at side, through tabs, using back-
stitch.

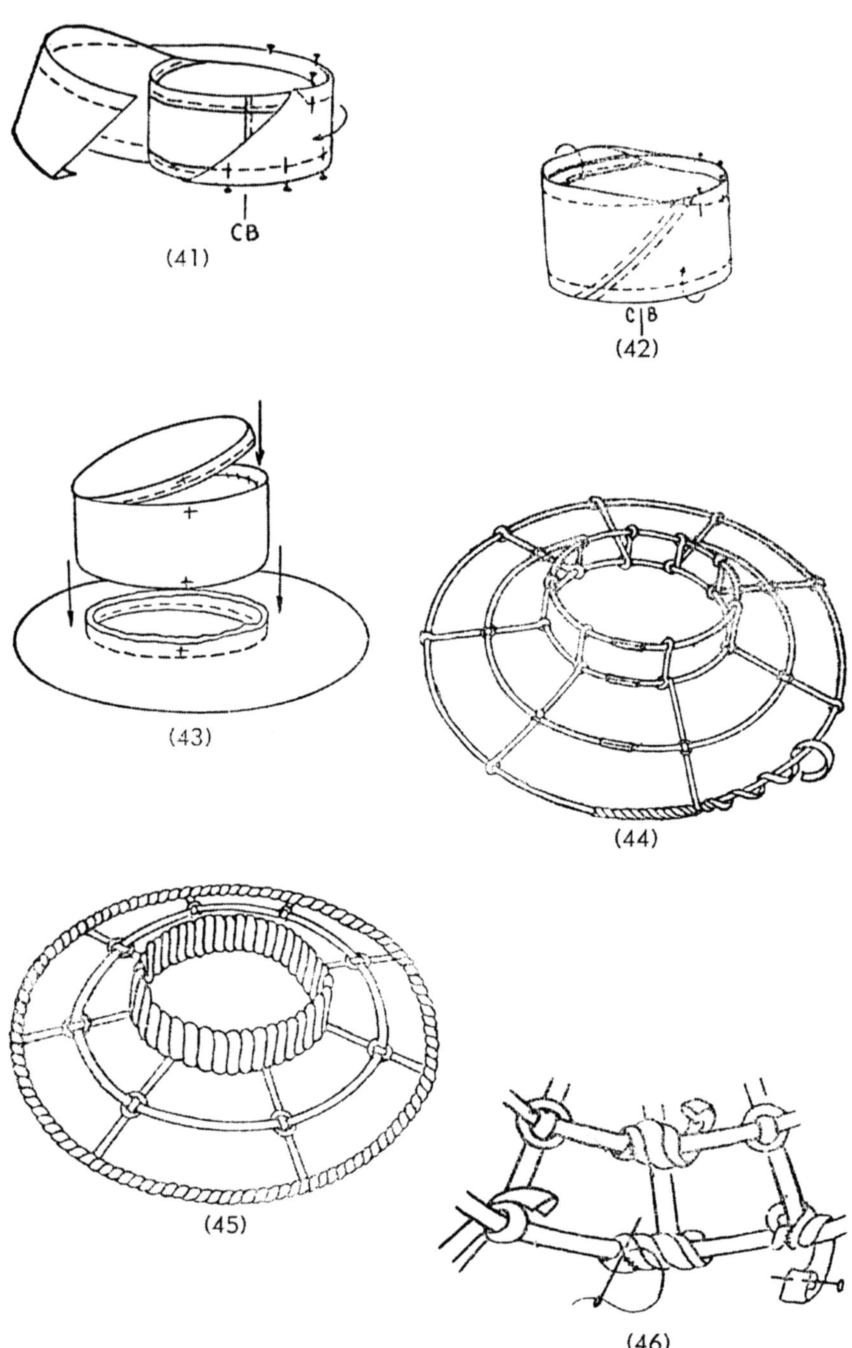

CB
(41)
C B
(42)
(43)
(44)
(45)
(46)

(41)

Note top and bottom bias crinoline coverings of side crown frame. Top is wired. The back seam of frame covering may be done by machine, as in Step 29, or one turned-under end laid over other and slipstitched.

(42)

Top edge of side crown covering is turned over and down into inside frame, and bottom edge of side crown covering is turned up and inside side crown. Pin. Sew with long, loose overcast stitches to crinoline bias bindings at top and bottom.

(43)

Set tip into side crown, slipstitch side crown to tip, crown over Headsize of covered brim. Slipstitch, or invisible backstitch.

★ COVERING THE WIRE FRAME

Keep wire frame light in appearance. If there is too much wrapping, it will appear heavy. Covered wire can be bought in two colors: black and white. To color the white, paint with colored ink, water colors, or dip into a water soluable dye bath. To color a steel wire, paint with enamel. Wrap intersections and edge only when necessary. Covering fabrics for wire frame generally are cotton or rayon nets, georgette, organdie, maline or any very transparent fabrics. Try wrapping flowers on frame, then cover this with thin film of net. Or cover frame with only flowers, by twisting two or three inches of stem from each flower. Fabrics like maline or net should be doubled when used as covering.

(44)

This figure shows Center Back of wire frame. Note direction of wrapping on outer wire edge. Wrapping should be same soft, thin fabric as covering. Fold covering as in Figure 47, or drape as in Figure 49.

(45)

If hat is to be crownless, the Headsize extension can be wrapped in the manner shown, or draped as in Figure 38.

(46)

This figure shows how joint wrappings are folded, started and finished. See how finishing end is tucked under intersection. Overcast finished end.

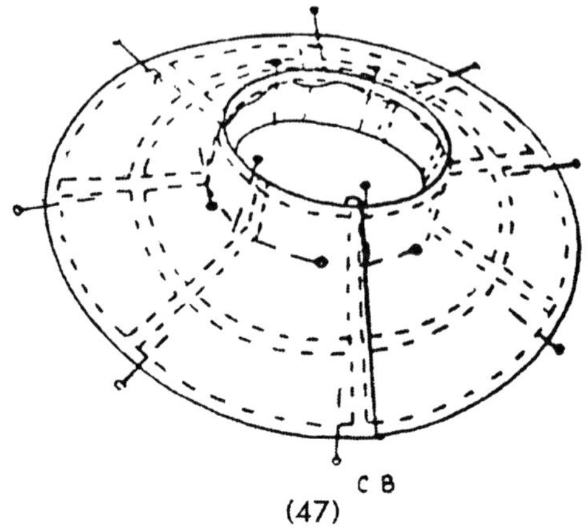

(47)

(48)
Refer to Figure 17, this Chapter. Also see Figure 28, PATTERNS.

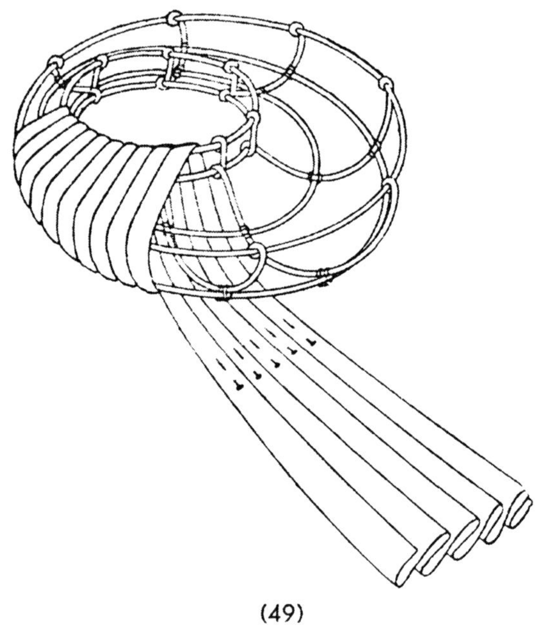

(49)

(47)

Fold the grain of net that stretches most. Stretch over a steel hoop, See Step 17. Remove from steel hoop and place over wire frame. OR block net over a block, if it is to be used on a rounded frame. See Step 19. Place folded swirled edge over edge of wire frame. Pull over wire frame at brim edge, turn under one end, pin at Back, and pin at Headsize. Sew Center Back Seam, using slipstitch. At Headsize, use long and short backstitch. Brim is now ready for crown.

(48)

Step 17 describes preparing a steel wire and stretching fabric over it. Try first painting this steel wire with enamel the same color as net or maline. Cut fabric and put in drawstring, as described in Figure 17. Do not remove drawstring, net or maline. Hold over steam and pull fullness to center. Lay Headsize pattern (Step 28, Patterns) on desired place. Trace around Headsize Pattern. Allow ⅝" inside line for Headsize upward extension. Before cutting on marked Headsize line, backstitch so it will hold its shape. Now cut inside the backstitched Headsize for ⅝" allowance. The brim is finished. **It has only a steel wire inside the fold.**

(49)

For another variation of covering a wire frame, start at Center Back, and wrap with folded strip. Finish at Center Back Headsize, so that it is invisible.

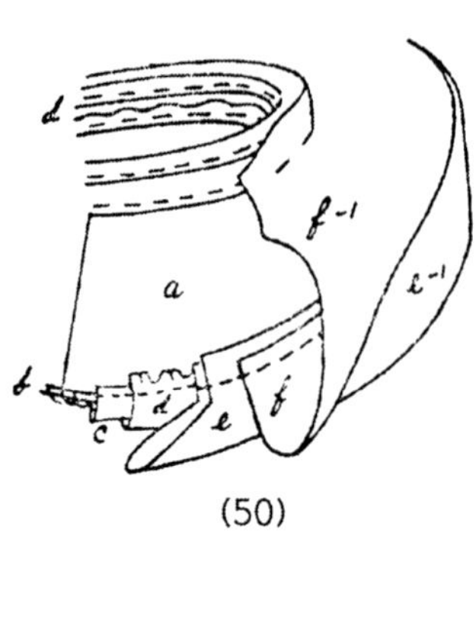

(50)

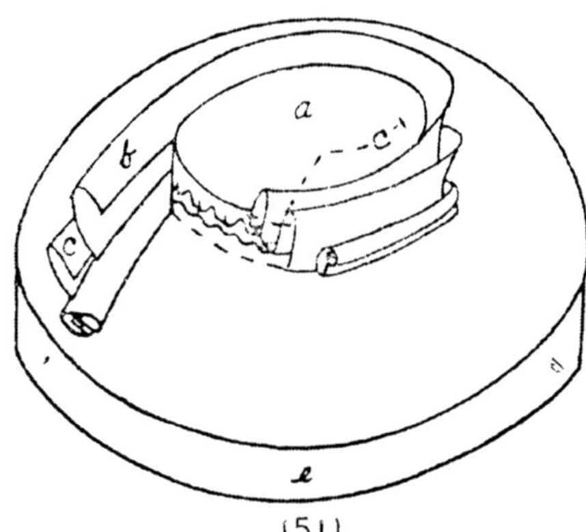

(51)

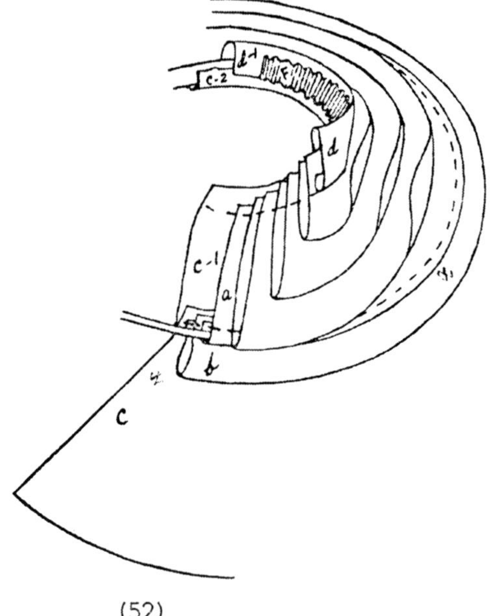

(52)

★ FLANGE HATS

A flange is a swirled fabric or ribbon. Swirl by using an iron, as in Headsize Ribbons and Bands, or over a steel wire, as in Figure 17, this section, or stretch one edge.

(50)

Frame "a" is wired "b" and wire covered, "c." Cover facing "d" as in Figures 3, 4, and 5, this section. "e" is folded bias cover fabric, not stretched. Measure and make bias seam on inside, at Center Back. OR fold end to inside, and use straight vertical seam in bias band "e." "f" is a bias length, the same width as "d." Swirl edge of "f." "d," "e" and "f" are all sewed at one time through brim at edge. Pull "d" under brim, "f" over top, and up on brim to Headsize "f-1." Bias band "e" hangs down. Sew through "d" and "f" at Headsize, using long and short backstitch. This is nice in fabric: all organdie, or just "e" in organdie, net, maline, etc. "d" and "f" may be cut from patterns with bias at Center Front and Center Back. If a flat brim there will be no seam at Center Back, if a flared brim there will be a seam at Center Back. Keep all Center Back seams consistent with thread grain —bias or straight. The edge of facing "f" can be turned under and slip-stitched to "e."

(51)

After Step 50 is finished, finish crown. If open crown, slip folded "b" over Headsize extension, and "c" against "b." Sew through bottom edge of "c-1" and through "b" and Headsize extension. Refold "c" to position and cover raw edge with small folded band. If crown tip is to be covered, prepare buckram tip, cover "a" and sew through bottom edge only of folded "b," and bottom edge only of "c-1." Note position of "e." Pull folded edges of "b" and "c" for a little flare. Finish Center Back seams consistent with "e."

(52)

This swirled-flange hat is done over a steel wire. A separate wire for "b," and the three top folded layers. The only frame is self-fabric (net, maline or organdie, etc.). "a" is cut from a circular pattern, and pinned over a pre-pared wire. "b" has been stretched over steel wire as shown, and pinned to underside of "a." "c" is a straight bias length, but swirled or cut from a pattern without a seam). With "a" on top, sew "a," "b" and 'c" at one time, near wire, using small backstitch. At Headsize, lay three prepared (over steel wire) flanges, pull "c" to "c-1" position, and sew through at Headsize. Fold bias band "d" desired height, and under at outside Headsize and over Headsize extension to "d-1." Cover "d-1" with Headsize Band, "f."

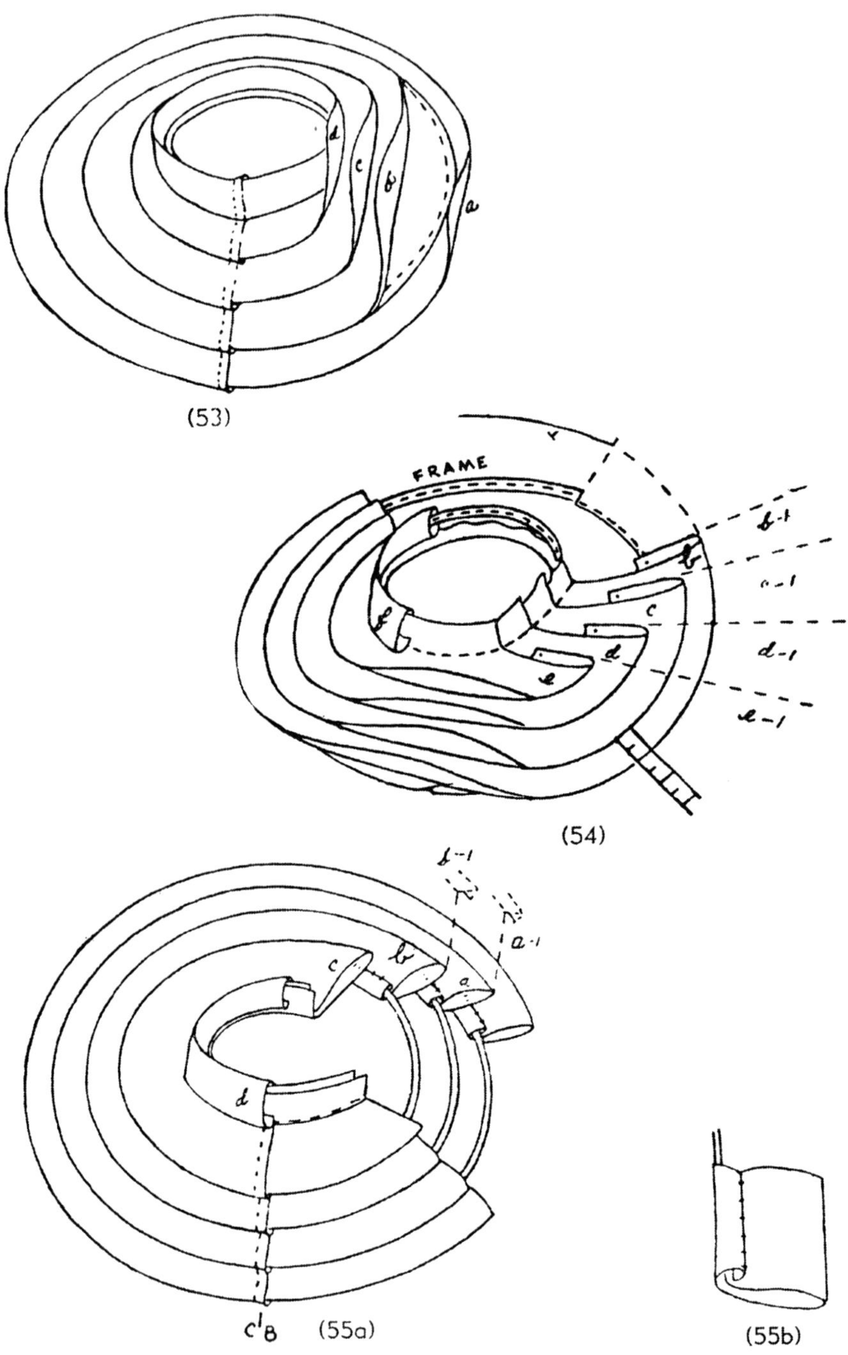

d
c
b
a
(53)
FRAME
b-1
a-1
c
d-1
e-1
d
e
f
(54)
b-1
a-1
c
b
a
d
c' B   (55a)
(55b)

(53)

Swirled fold "a" extends out. Swirled folds "b," "c" and "d" lie flat on brim. Note Center Back seams. The bias ends are turned under, slipstitched, or bias seams.

(54)

This flanged hat is done over a frame. Cut four bias bands. "b" allows for extension over brim, and width from Headsize band to folded edge. "c," "d" and "e" extend from Headsize Band to folded edge, plus allowance for turn-under. These should be swirled over separate steel wires, using drawstrings, as in Figure 17. Cut a bias length for underside with allowance for turn-up at Headsize, and allowance at outer-edge turn. This outer edge, pulled and stretched (or swirled over steel wire) is pinned on top brim, extending out. "b" is pinned on top in "b-1" position. Sew through "b-1" and underfacing. Lay "b-1" back in "b" position. Sew "c-1" through frame and fold to "c" position. Continue same with "d-1" and "e-1." Check width of "b" from edge to folded edge of "c," and folded edge of "c" to "d" and "d" to "e." Pin all at Headsize. Now take underfacing and pull to underside of Headsize. Sew through "b-c-d-e," and underfacing at Headsize bend, using long and short backstitches. Cover with folded "f," if hat is to be crownless.

(55a & b)

Stretch and swirl each bias fold over a steel wire. Fold first outer edge over a steel wire, as shown in 55-a. Open "a" and sew through "a" to first folded band, backstitch if catching turn-under and top fold. If completely through the outer fold use stab backstitch and sew very near wire. See 55-b. Do the same with "b" and "c," using steel wire. There is no frame. Study bias fold "d."

See Figures 37-44, Straw, for folded-bias brims.

Pattern Hats

There has never been a more comfortable hat than the beret, and there are so many, many variations of the basic beret that a flattering style can be found for any face. Everyone enjoys the beret—a hat that can go anywhere and everywhere at a moment's notice. At only a little more than a moment's notice you can whip up your own beret in the color you've been wanting, and the style that suits you.

Pattern hats are soft hats, with no wire. They do not cover a frame. Sometimes Pattern Hats are made from straw or felt bodies.

Straw cloth, skirt felt and many other types of fabric are ideal for Pattern Hats. If stiffening is needed, use a lining of a soft light weight fabric such as taffeta, French crepe, honeycomb, net, sized crepe, satin and others, or an interlining of cotton muslin, crinoline, taffeta, cotton felt or cotton flannel. The lining should be cut 1/8" to 1/4" smaller than the hat itself. Inter-linings may be sewed at the same time the hat is sewed. Lay in linings separately, seam to seam, and tack. Pattern hats are generally sewed from the inside. A sewing machine seam is strong and practical.

The variations of pattern hats as presented in the following chapter are sectional crowns, two-piece crowns, tip-and-side crown, soft brim without frame or wire, two-piece beret and sectional berets.

A section of a sectional crown is usually cut so that the straight thread grain runs up and down through the middle of the section. This way, the rounded edges of the section are on the bias and must be held in when sewing. The edges are therefore made to curve when the sewing is being done.

Basically, the beret is composed of two circles, but its possibilities are unlimited. The Headsize position is optional—and here again, the only limits are those of your own imagination.

If you want to take it easy—take your needle and thread, and make a Pattern Hat!

(1)
See Instructions.

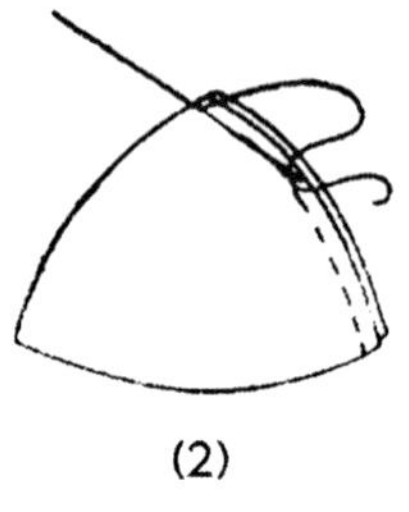

(2)

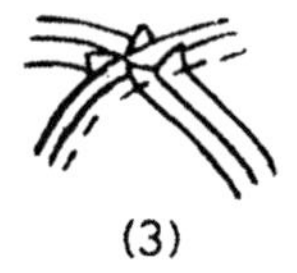

(3)

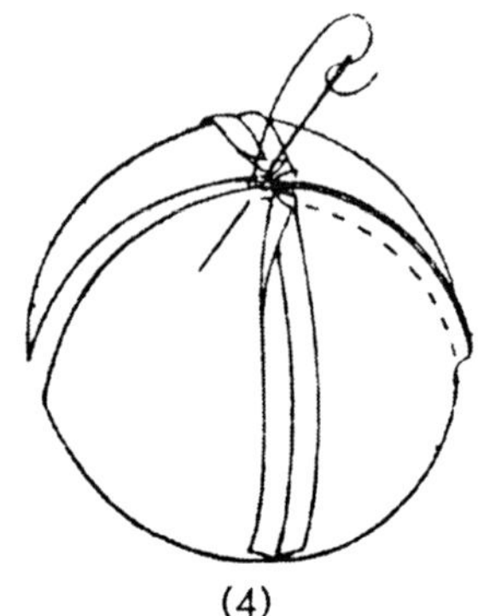

(4)

(5)
See Instructions.

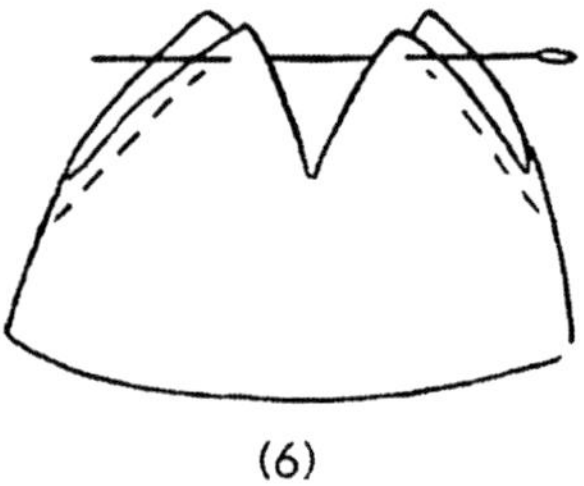

(6)

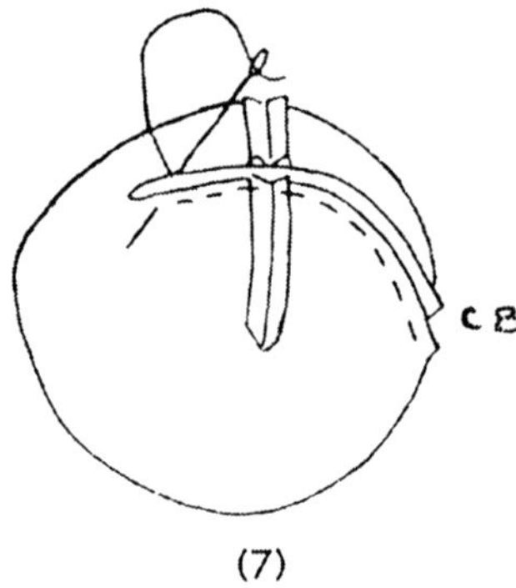

(7)

(8)
See Instructions.

(9)

(114)

Pattern Hats

THE SECTIONAL CROWN

(1)

See Figures 34-51, Patterns.

(2)

Each half of a sectional crown should be sewed together, then the two halves sewed together. These seams are on the bias, and should be held in adequately.

(3)

All the seams must come together at one point.

(4)

After each half has been sewed, pin the two halves together, making all four seams meet at one point. Sew.

(5)

See Figures 36 and 37, Patterns.

(6)

Place a needle through two adjoining Center Top points, pull together and sew the seam gradually to nothing down the side of the crown.

(7)

After both seams have been sewed, put each half side-to-side, as shown. Sew full length through Center Top at one time. Use running stitch or backstitch, although machine stitching is preferred.

(8)

See Figure 49, 50 and 51, Patterns.

(9)

Work on wooden block. Pin sections as in "a." After each section has been measured, sew each seam by machine, as in "b." After each seam has been sewed, place again on wooden block, open seams as in "c," and press over damp cloth. Or use a steam iron. Reverse it, and it is ready to be used as a crown or calot.

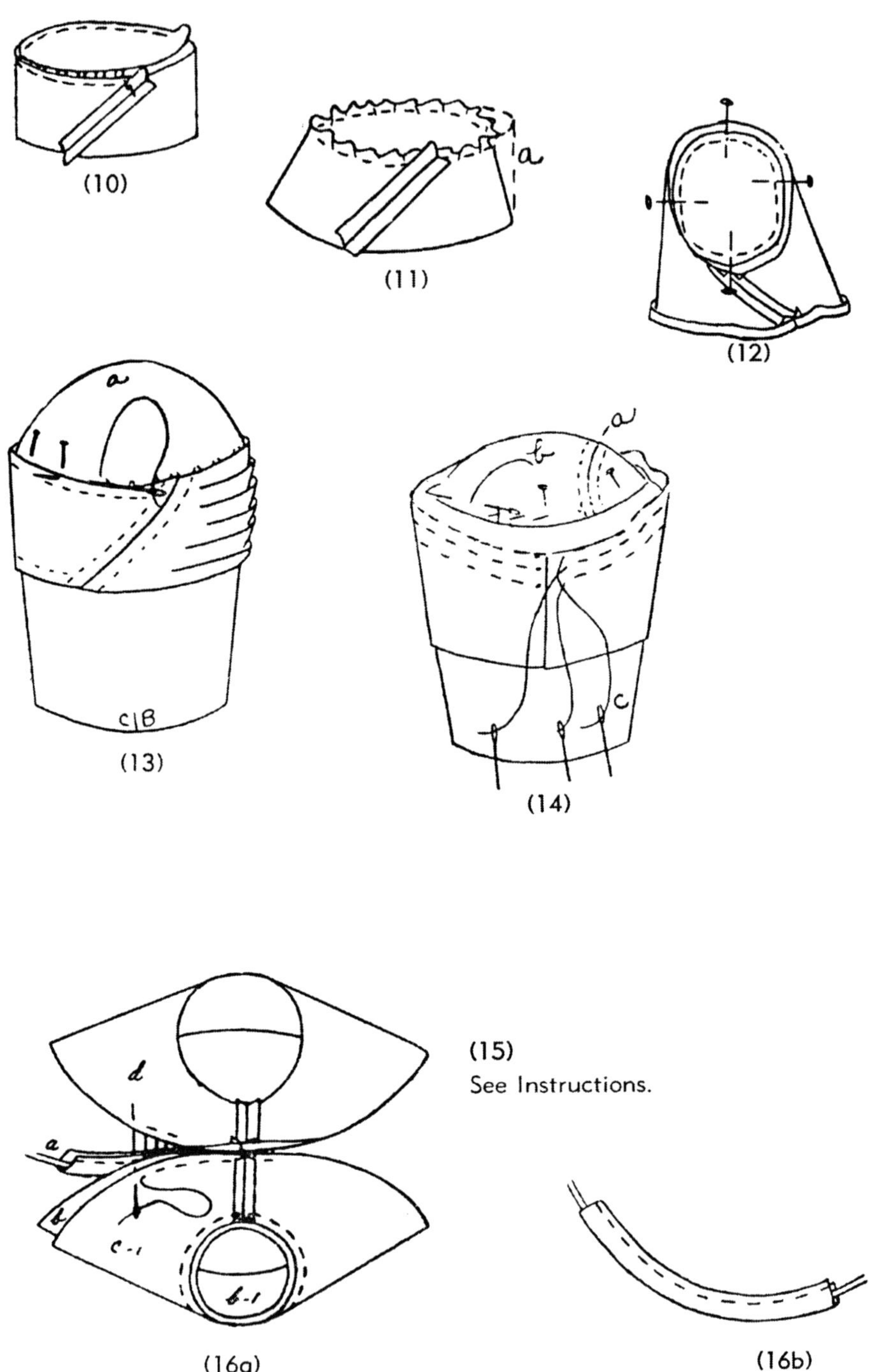

(10)
(11)
a
(12)
a
(13)
c|B
a
b
c
(14)
d
a
c-1
b-1
(16a)
(15)
See Instructions.
(16b)

(10)

A side crown may be cut on the straight thread or on the bias. Unless stretched at top or bottom, it will extend up straight. On a bias cut, make a bias seam. The tip is cut with the same circumference—round or oval from Center Back to Center Front, or from Right Side to Left Side. Or it may be oval on only one side. Pin and sew, as in Figure 10. If tip is larger, the side crown can be stretched at top to fit tip.

(11)

OR side crown may be stretched at bottom to make flare inward at tip, or drawn in with a drawstring—but NOT gathered—"a."

(12)

In the case of setting in a rather small tip in circumference, it is advisable to put in a drawstring (Figure 11) so that the difference between the Head-size and tip circumference can be adjusted. See pins.

(13)

OR the tip "a" can be blocked and the side crown folded against it from the outside, and slipstitched. OR the side crown can be pleated or folded— See Right Side. **Stretch!**

(14)

OR the tip can be sectional, as "a," or blocked plain, as "b," with side crown shirred, "c."

(15)

See Figures 44-47, Patterns. Sew four sides together, then fit, pin and sew in tip. Turn up Headsize for Headsize band, or can be used as a crown.

★ THE SOFT BRIM

(16a)

"c-1," "b" and "d" are cut from the same pattern, having a seam at Center Back. They can be cut flat without seams. The principle is: top and bottom coverings with an interlining. The seams are first sewed at Center Back. Right side of "d" is placed against the right side, and cover or outside "b" against "c-1" (muslin interfacing). Sew the three outside edges together, turn, press. "a" is cord or edging that can be inserted.

(16b)

Bias covered cord or wire.

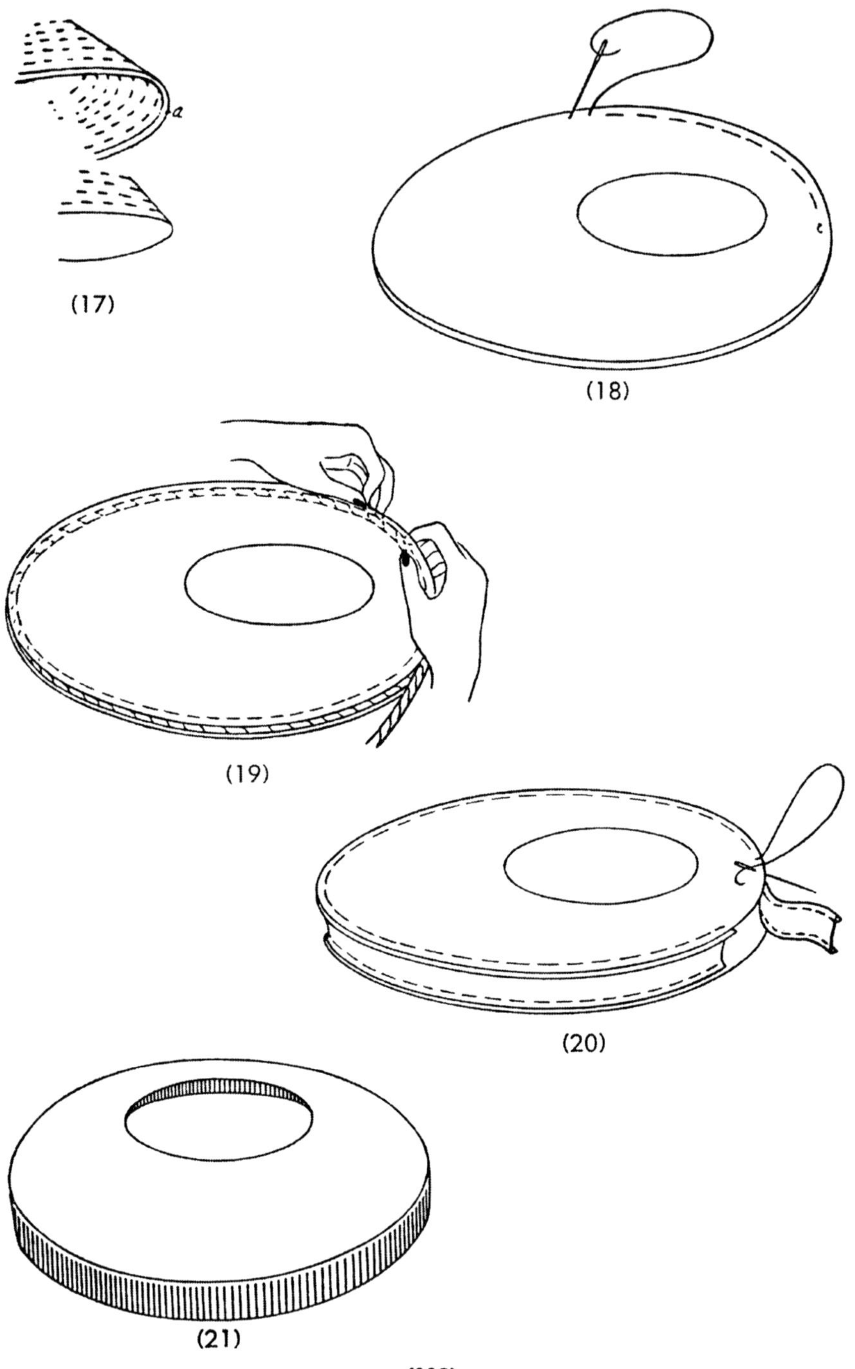

(17)

(18)

(19)

(20)

(21)

(118)

(17)

"a" is edging, as in Figure 16a. This brim may be left plain, or trimmed with a series of stitches. STITCHING gives body to a brim. If it is to be stitched by machine, **baste carefully** because interfacing and bottom cover slip out of place easily. Stitch either by hand or by machine. Stretch the headsize bias extension allowance until it stands up. This is a washable hat and perfect for summer wear.

erets

★ THE BASIC BERET

Berets may be blocked in felt or straw, or made from patterns.   This section is devoted to Pattern berets.   The basic beret is in two pieces, having the same circumference.   One has a Headsize cut into it.   Figure 53, Patterns. A beret can be one unit or used as a crown.

(18)

The simplest beret is in two flat pieces. The top disc, and the bottom with Headsize cut out. Both have same circumference. Sew outside with back-stitch or by machine. Press seam open and turn.

(19)

After seam of Figure 18 has been opened and pressed, a soft twisted-cotton cord or a wire can be laid inside the seam and overcast, for a stiffer edge. Turn to right side.

(20)

Between the two discs, insert a bias band, or straight thread-grain band. Seam at Center Back. Pin to top and bottom, and sew by machine, or backstitch. Open seams, press and turn to right side. Stitch on each side of the seam or cover seams with braid, etc.

(21)

OR insert a contrasting fabric between the two discs of fabric. . . .

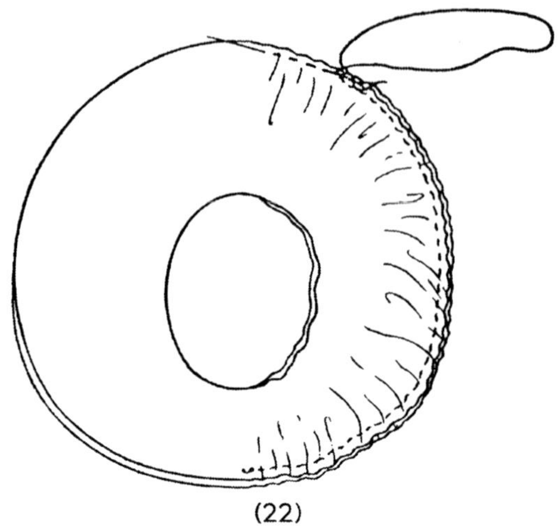

(22)

(23)
See Instructions.

(24)
See Instructions.

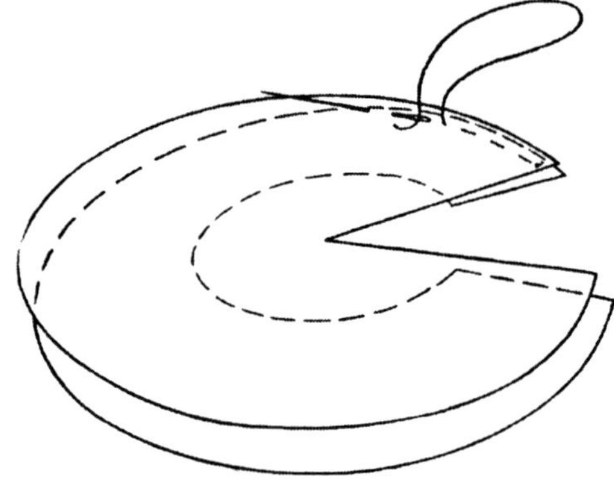

(25)

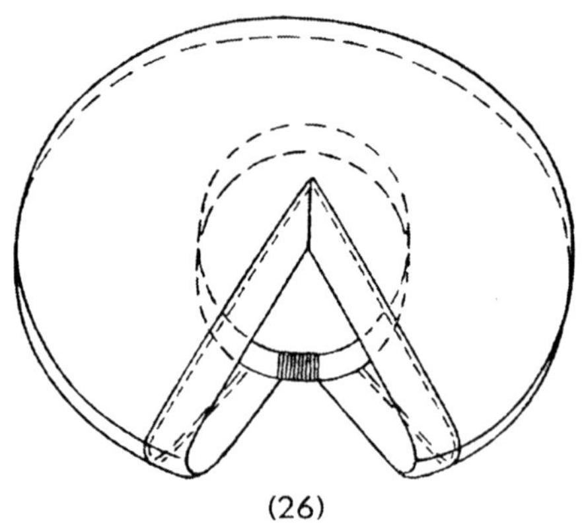

(26)

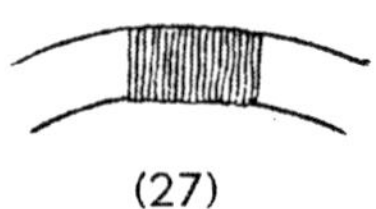

(27)

(22)

OR the edges may be gathered, or the top gathered to a smaller disc on Headsize side. OR, vice versa, the Headsize side gathered to a smaller circumference at the tip.

(23)

See Figures 54-56, Patterns. Figure 54 is assembled by sewing first top disc "a-b" to underpiece "c-d" at seam "a-b," separately. The next two "doughnuts" are sewed together at outside-edge circumference. This is four. Turn these to right side, and join each respectively, at Headsizes.

★ THE "PIE" BERET

(24)

Turn to Figures 43 and 60, Patterns. If these "V" edges are lapped, the beret tip will be peaked as in Figure 15, FRAMES.

(25)

Sew top and bottom discs together by machine, or backstitch.

(26)

Face the "V" at Center Back. Sew from right side and turn facing to inside. If it is to be lined, do not turn under edge of facing, especially if beret fabric is heavy, to avoid a bulky finish.

(27)

Elastic is sewed in at Center Back Headsize.

(28)
See Instructions.

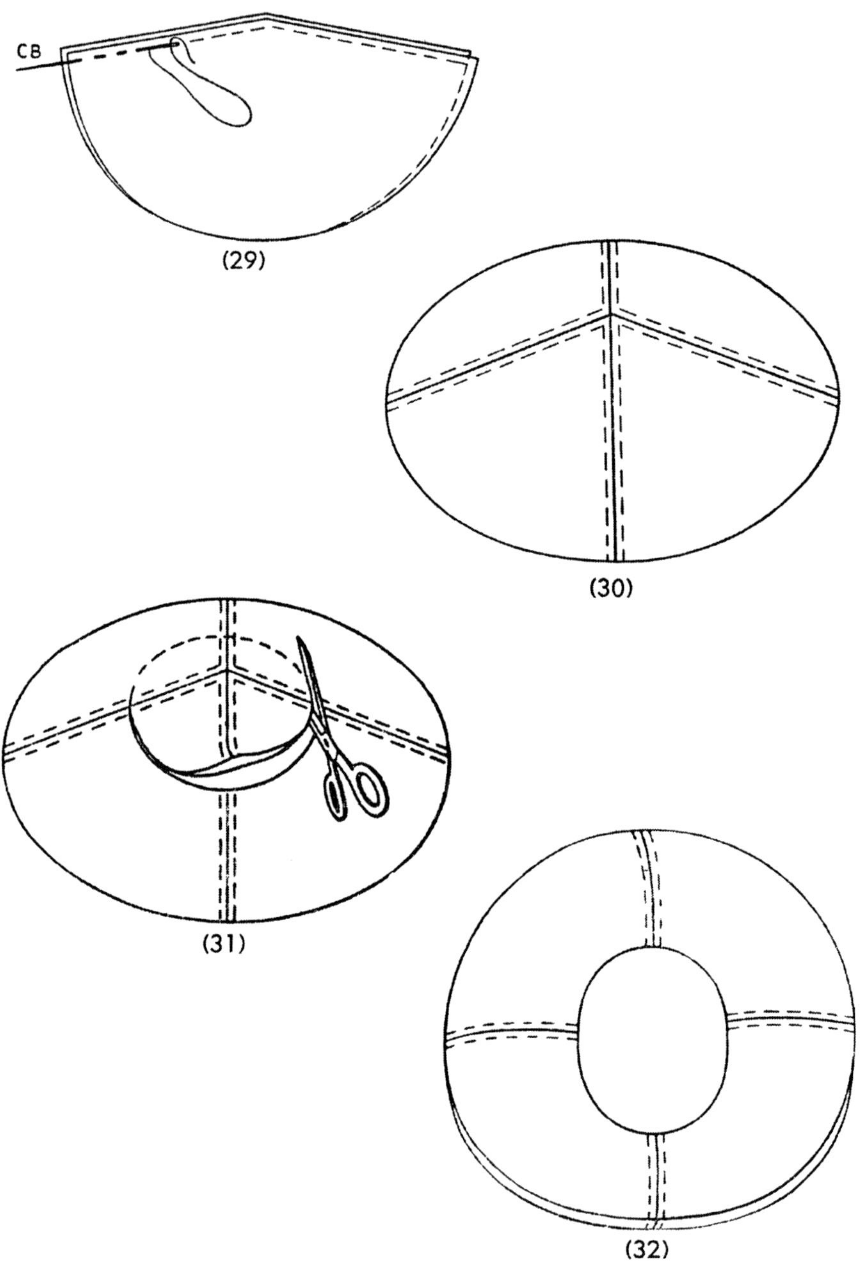

(29)

(30)

(31)

(32)

★ THE SECTIONAL BERET

(28)
Refer to Figures 57-66, Patterns.

(29)
A TWO-SECTIONAL beret is sewed across, from one edge to the other. For marking Headsize, see Steps 28 and 53, Patterns. The shaped-top beret can have a straight underside ,or the underside can be shaped with a straight top.

(30)
A FOUR-SECTIONAL beret is sewed together in halves, then the two halves are sewed together with one seam. Match seams at Center Top. Open seams, press, and turn to right side. If interlined, sew at same time. For decoration, each side of seam may be sewed by hand or machine on the right side.

(31)
Allow for turn-up at Headsize when cutting out the marked oval. Mark oval from Oval-Headsize pattern, or draft Headsize.

(32)
Headsize after oval is cut away.

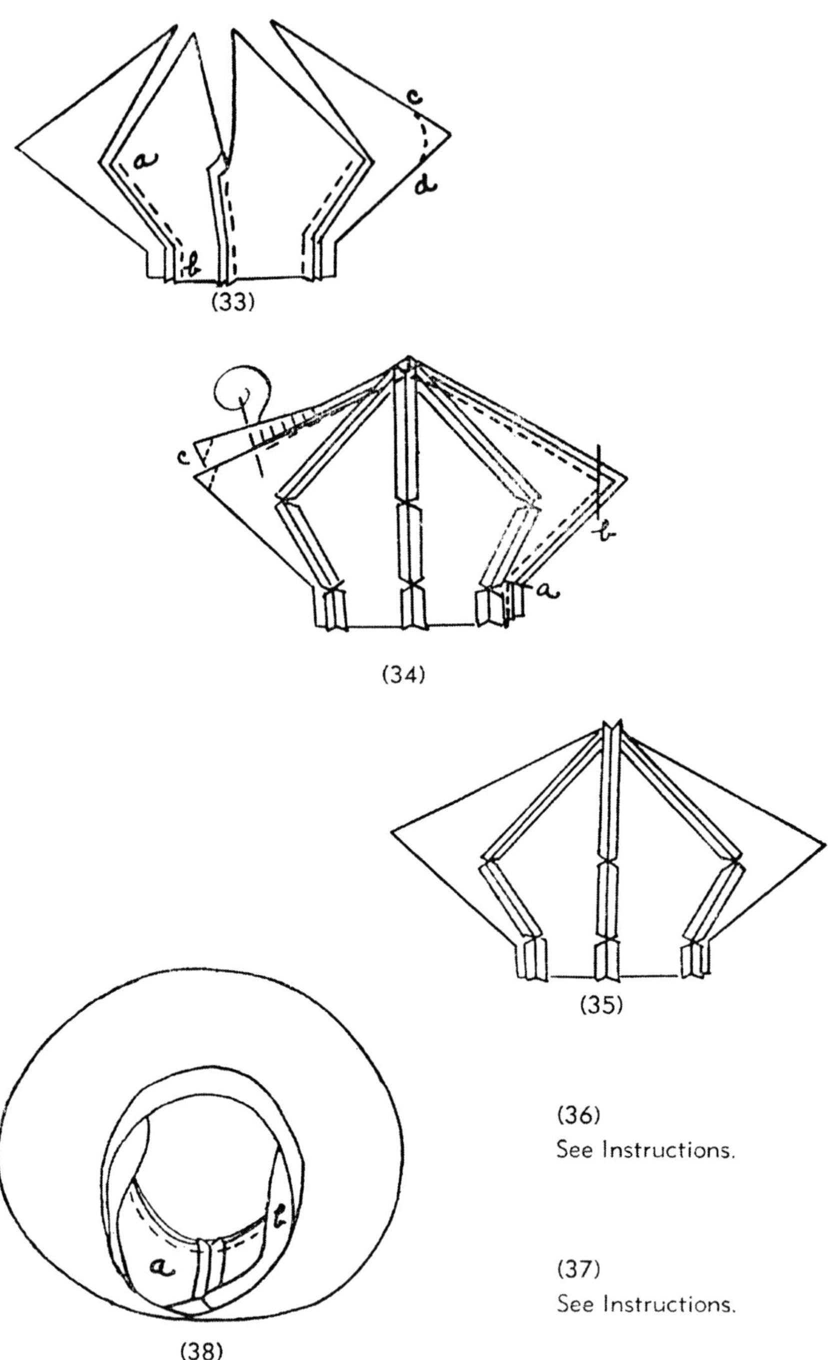

(33)

(34)

(35)

(36)
See Instructions.

(37)
See Instructions.

(38)

(33)

Sew sections from Headsize up to largest part of circumference for EIGHT-SECTIONAL beret, as "a-b." Or sew half the sections together and then join the two halves. The corners at "c-d" may be rounded when sewing.

(34)

After each half is finished, machine-sew the two halves together from Headsize on one side to Headsize on the other side. Snip off ends at "b" and snip at "a."

(35)

Open seams and press. Turn to right side.

(36)

See Figures 57-66, Patterns.

(37)

See Headsize Bands.

(38)

A straight thread or bias band "a," seam at Center Back, may be sewed at Headsize of beret. Extend the band down between ½" to 2", and turn up "b" into headsize to meet the seam. Overcast. Lay in Headsize Band of grosgrain ribbon.

Straw

The first robin may be the sign of spring to some people—but to a woman, it's the first straw hat that means winter is over! In this chapter of HAT TACTICS, you'll learn how to create your own Spring bonnet, and it's a pretty safe bet you won't want to stop with one. Remake, Restyle or Renovate old Straw! Presto! A whole wardrobe of glamorous hats for YOU —and By you!

Straw is woven in bodies, hoods, plaques, cloth and braid. REMEMBER— Straw is worked while WET when possible. Dry Straw is brittle and breaks easily when sewed dry. Work hair braids dry, press over a damp cloth, then iron with a warm iron. Hair braid seams are lapped, not turned under, and sewed with running stitch. WOVEN STRAW should be blocked.

STRAW CLOTH is a fabric with a straw-like finish. It is sold by the yard. DO NOT WET Straw Cloth, unless it is a fiber cloth. Instead, use this fabric for covering frames, making Pattern Hats and Draping.

Don't overlook the many possibilities of ribbon, metallic, silk or cotton braid and straw braid. Basically, they are all worked the same, except that ribbon, cotton or metallic braids should **not** be wet. Use a damp or dry cloth over them when pressing—but test a small piece first.

To RENOVATE an old straw hat and restore its shape, remove the trimming and veil. Brush well. Rub gently with a damp—NOT WET—soft cloth which has been dipped into warm sudsy water. Restore the original shape by using a press pillow. Steam and pat-press. ALLOW TO DRY WELL. If the color is satisfactory and unfaded, paint top surface with Straw Sizing. However, if you'd like another color, size the hat with a colored enamel. That's right—the same kind you'd use to paint a kitchen chair! Press the veil, allow to dry—then size. Re-trim. Press the ribbon and turn to wrong side, or replace with new ribbon. Why not try a different color?

To REMAKE and RESTYLE an old straw body or braid hat—strip it! Remove trimming, wiring, stitches—**everything.** If the hat is braid, take it completely apart and wash braid in lukewarm sudsy water, rinsing well. Clean cotton, metallic or silk braid or ribbon in a good commercial cleaning fluid. Straw may be dyed in a water soluable dye. While still wet, follow instructions in this chapter on Straw braid and bodies.

The possibilities for remaking Straw Cloth are limited. Clean in cleaning fluid and press with an iron or pat-press over steam. You can use Straw Cloth for making a Pattern Hat—but be sure to choose a smaller type hat than the original.

NOW . . . let's make the straw bonnet that'll make YOU the "most alluring in the Fashion Parade." . . . . .

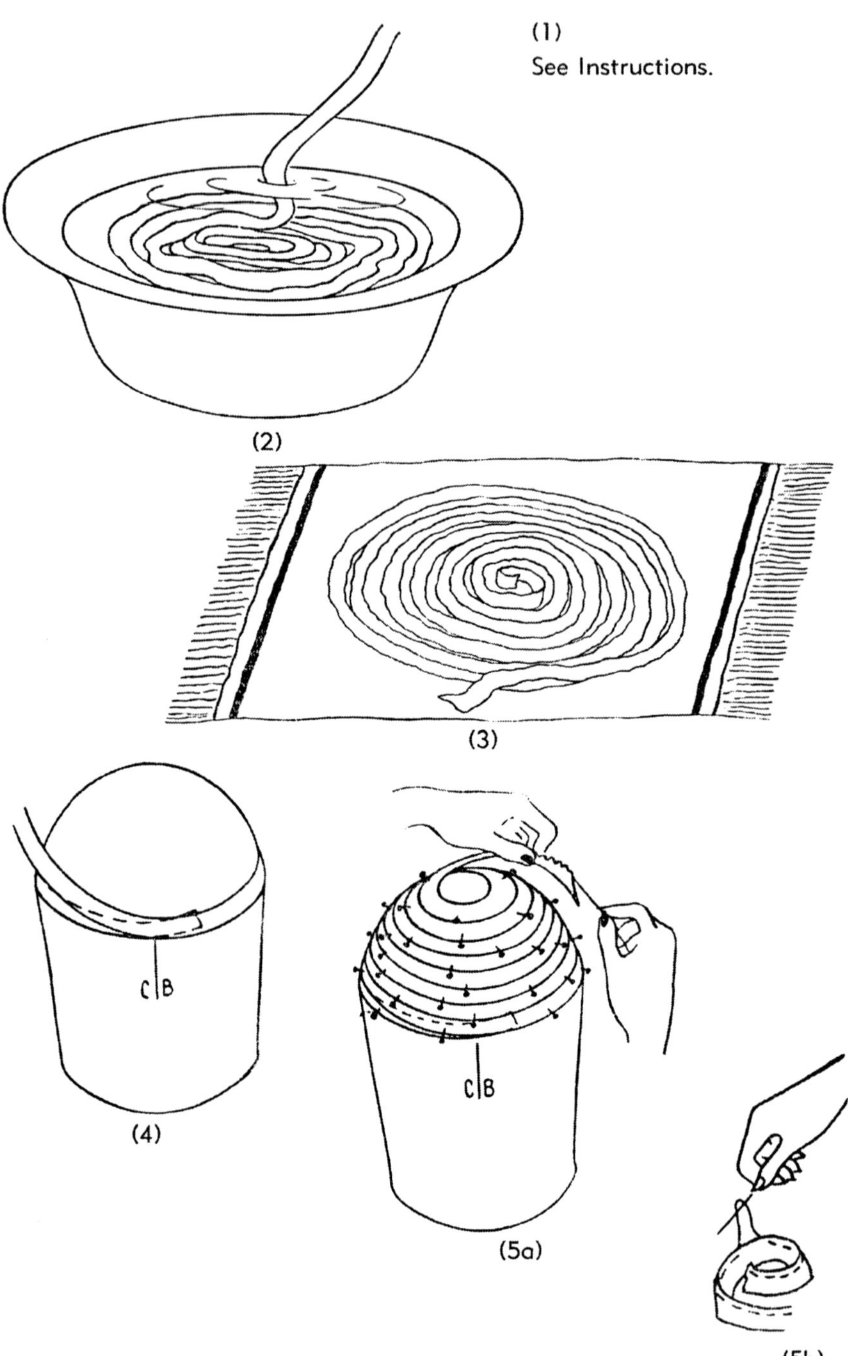
(1)
See Instructions.
(2)
(3)
C B
(4)
C B
(5a)
(5b)

S*traw*

★ BRAID

(1)

Refer to Figures 7-10, Measuring Head in Patterns.

(2)

Before wetting straw braid, cut a small piece and test in water, to be sure it will not shrink or dissolve.

(3)

Leave wet straw braid on towel as you work. Straw, when possible, should be sewed wet. Dry straw is brittle and easily broken.

★ BASIC CROWN

(4)

Starting a little to the right of Center Back, work from right to left. Pin, stretch and follow Headsize-depth line, which has been marked.

(5a & b)

One edge of straw must be stretched more than the other, to make it lay flat. (Most braid has a drawstring in one or both sides. Pull string to hold in one edge.) Continue pulling, pinning and lapping about ⅛", up to center Top. Some braids can be laid edge to edge. Sew with a running stitch, catching one edge to the other.

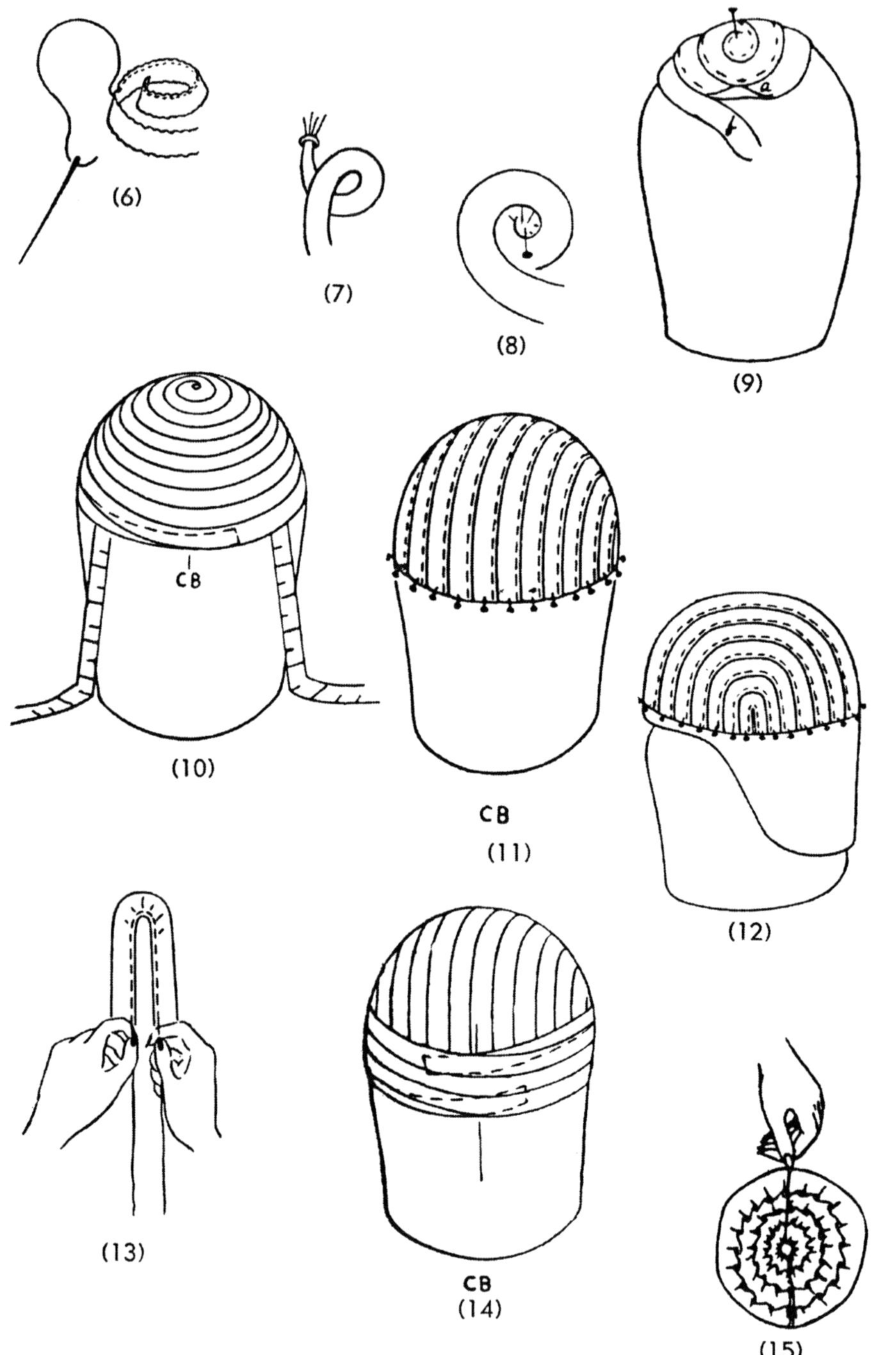

(6)
(7)
(8)
(9)
CB
(10)
CB
(11)
(12)
(13)
CB
(14)
(15)

(6)

If braid has no drawstring, put in one, using a running stitch.

(7)

Turn end under. If braid ravels, tie end.

(8)

After tip is arranged, pin and sew whole crown on the edges of the braid. See Figure 29.

(9)

OR the crown may be worked from tip down to Headsize if desired, with "b" under "a," or edge to edge.

(10)

Measure up from table on either side of head block to check depth. Depth should be equal at right and left sides of Center Back, also at right and left sides of Center Front.

★ OTHER SUGGESTIONS FOR BRAID OR RIBBON

(11)

Starting at Center Back, pin end of braid through Center Top to Center Front at marked Headsize line. Work down, completing one side, then work other side correspondingly. Sew on edge, using short backstitch. OR, pin edge to edge and sew with running stitch.

(12)

Side view of Figure 11.

(13)

Close-up of Figure 12. Pull drawstring of inside edge of braid, and lap edges, or edge to edge.

(14)

The tip of Figure 14 has been blocked like Figure 11 and a side crown has been added. Start side crown to right of Center Back, and work toward the left. When finished, tuck in remaining end. Sew.

(15)

When the top of Figure 15 is drawn up, it makes a round hole.

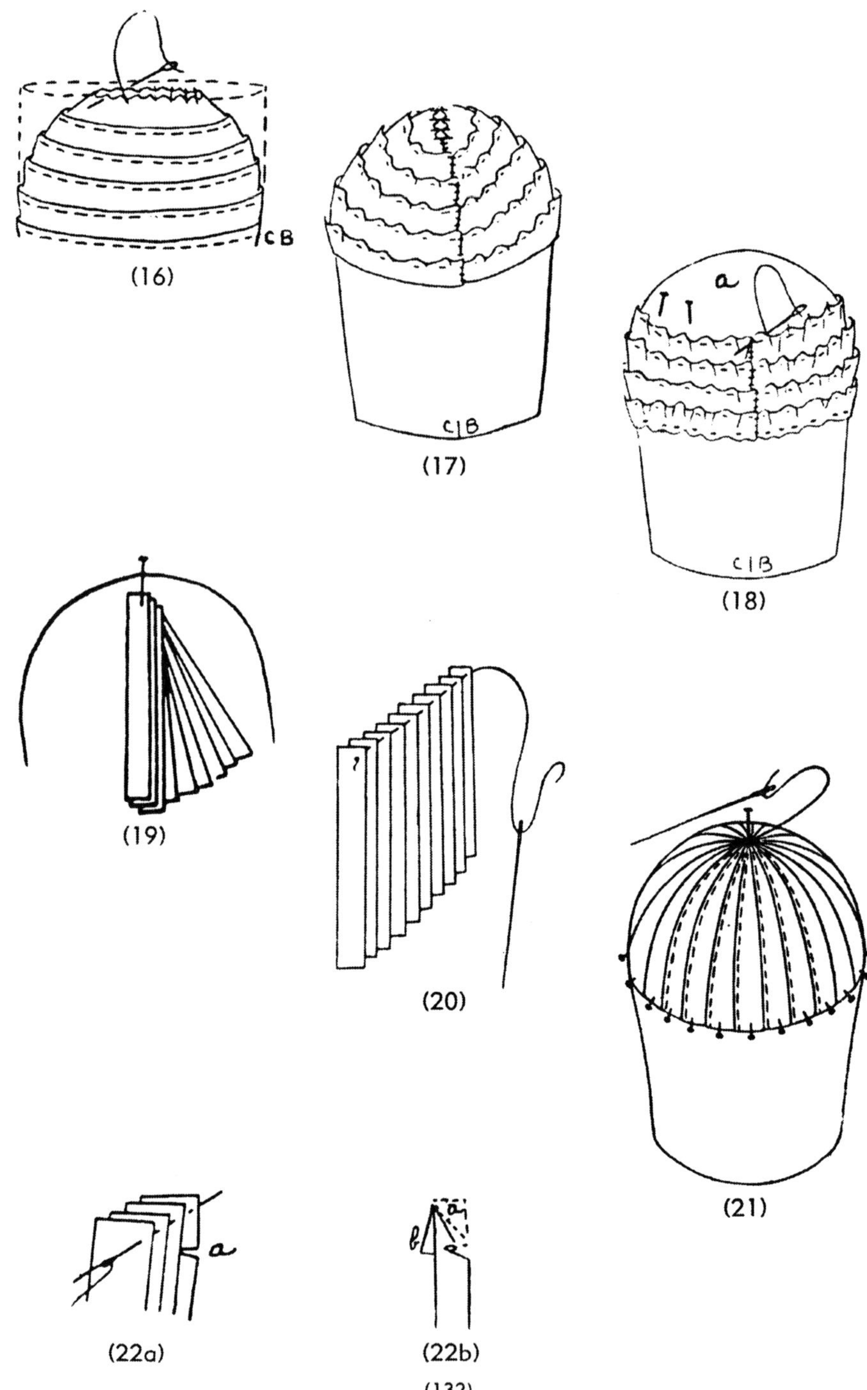
C B
(16)
C|B
(17)
a
C|B
(18)
(19)
(20)
(21)
a
(22a)
b a
(22b)
(132)

(16)

From the wrong side, fold at Center Front and Center Back, laying two halves together, and overcast the drawn-up tip.

(17)

Center Back of crown. NOTE the elongated tip seam. The braid or ribbon has been gathered on one edge.

(18)

The blocked tip "a," of matching or contrasting fabric, has been marked and cut, and the side crown of braid lays over tip. Sew to tip, using invisible backstitch.

(19)

Measure ribbon or braid length from Center Top to longest length at marked Headsize, and circumference for number of braid or ribbon lengths. Allow for ⅛" lap.

(20)

To one side, at right corner, run a strong thread. Pin again at Center Top, like Figure 19, and arrange at Headsize.

(21)

Pin ribbon or braid ends at Headsize. Lap at Headsize is ⅛", gradually increasing to Center Top. Sew on edge like Figure 29. Turn to wrong side and cut away bulky laps at Center Top. OR let these ends continue on outside of Center Top, and tie them like a tassel.

(22a & b)

"a" is a horizontal cut at edge of ribbon. The top "a" is turned under—"b" and the lower horizontal cut is also turned under. This simplifies the final lap, so that the lap will be uniform all around.

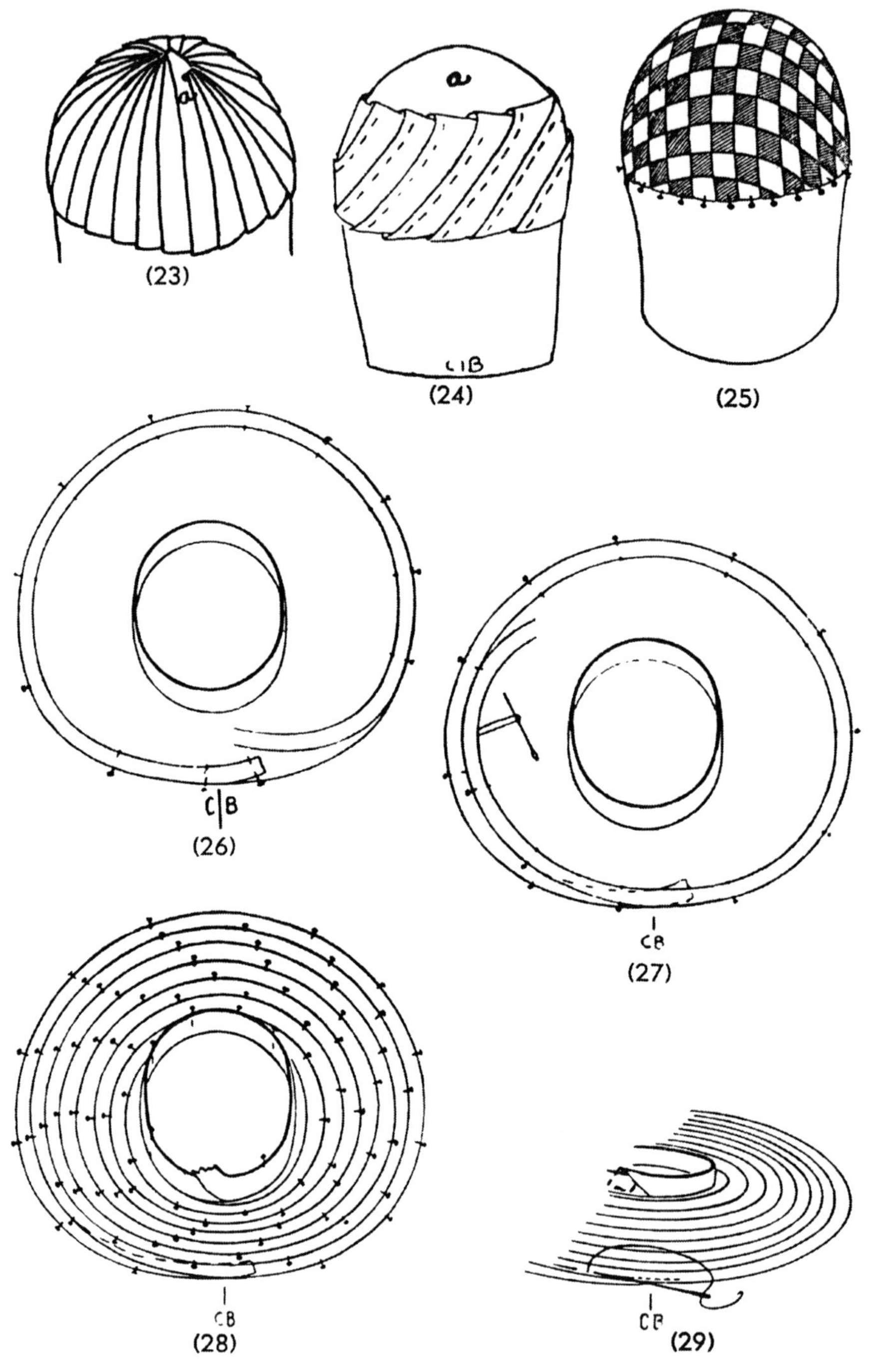

(23)
a
(24)
CB
a
(25)
C|B
(26)
CB
(27)
CB
(28)
CB
(29)

(23)

"a" shows Center Back of finished braid or ribbon.

(24)

Braid may be laid diagonally. Turn under top and bottom edges of side crown.
"a" may be plain tip or no tip.

(25)

The entire crown may be woven with ribbon.

★ BASIC BLOCKING . . . . BRAID OR RIBBON BRIM

(26)

Start braid 1" or 1½" to right of Center Back. Pin, pull and continue
around, working over a block or a drawing done on heavy cardboard or board.

(27)

Continue around, lapping just at the Center Back, and gradually decrease
lap to ⅛", or edge to edge.

(28)

Continue pulling (use drawstring if necessary), lapping and pinning, turn
straw up vertically at Headsize. Gradually taper up at Center Back.

(29)

Sew very near edge, using small backstitch. Edges can be machine stitched.
Hand sewing is softer.

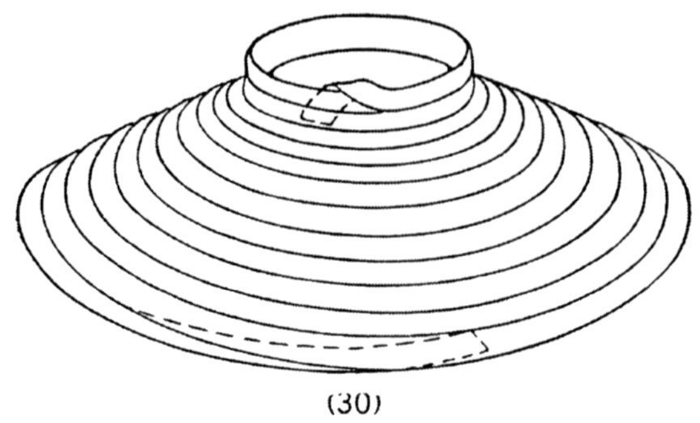

(30)

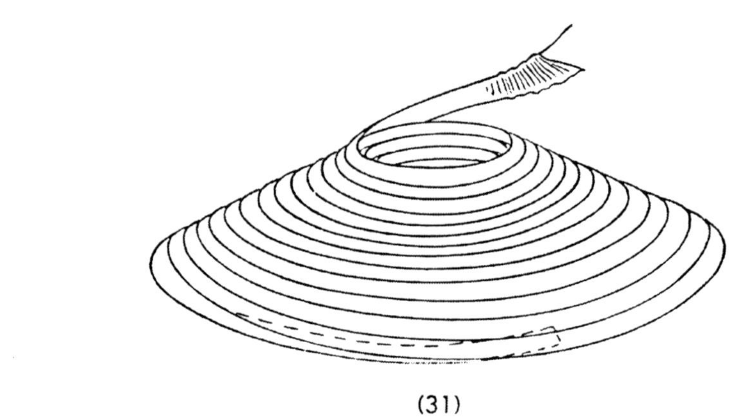

(31)

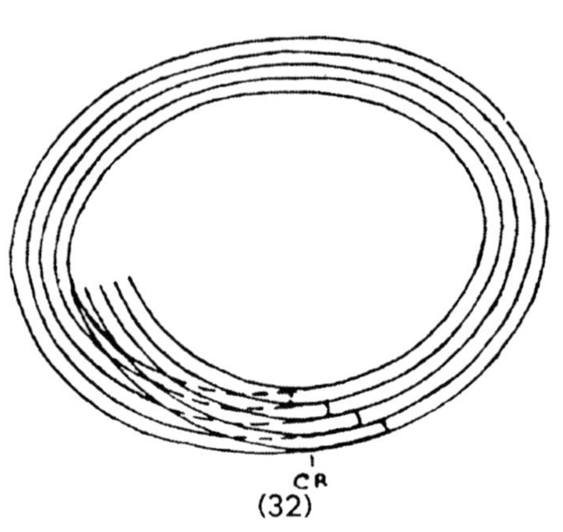

(32)

(30)

If brim is to have no crown, turn Headsize end to inside, wire at top from inside and add one braid of straw to cover wire. Buttonhole stitch wire at top, from inside. See Figure 34 for sewing extra braid of straw.

(31)

Continue lapping straw for a peaked one-piece brim and crown. See Figures 6-8, this section, for finishing crown.

(32)

Very narrow straw braid is often sewed together when bought from Millinery Supply Houses. Treat it in the same manner as one braid width, but shorten first ends and follow Steps 26 and 27.

(33)

After straw has been sewed and dried, or if hat is of thread braid or ribbon, put on block and press over a damp cloth. Or use steam iron.

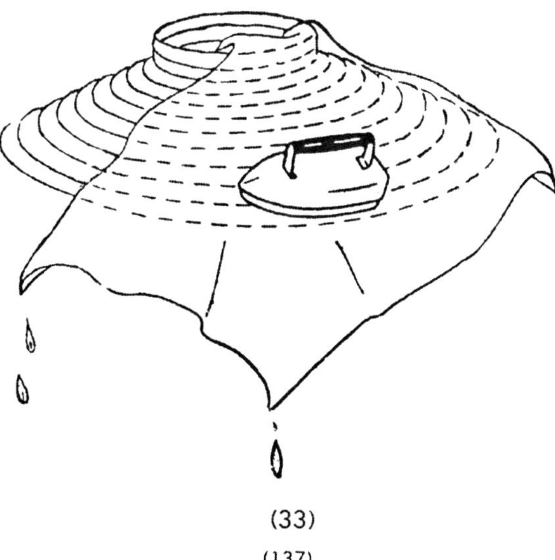

(33)

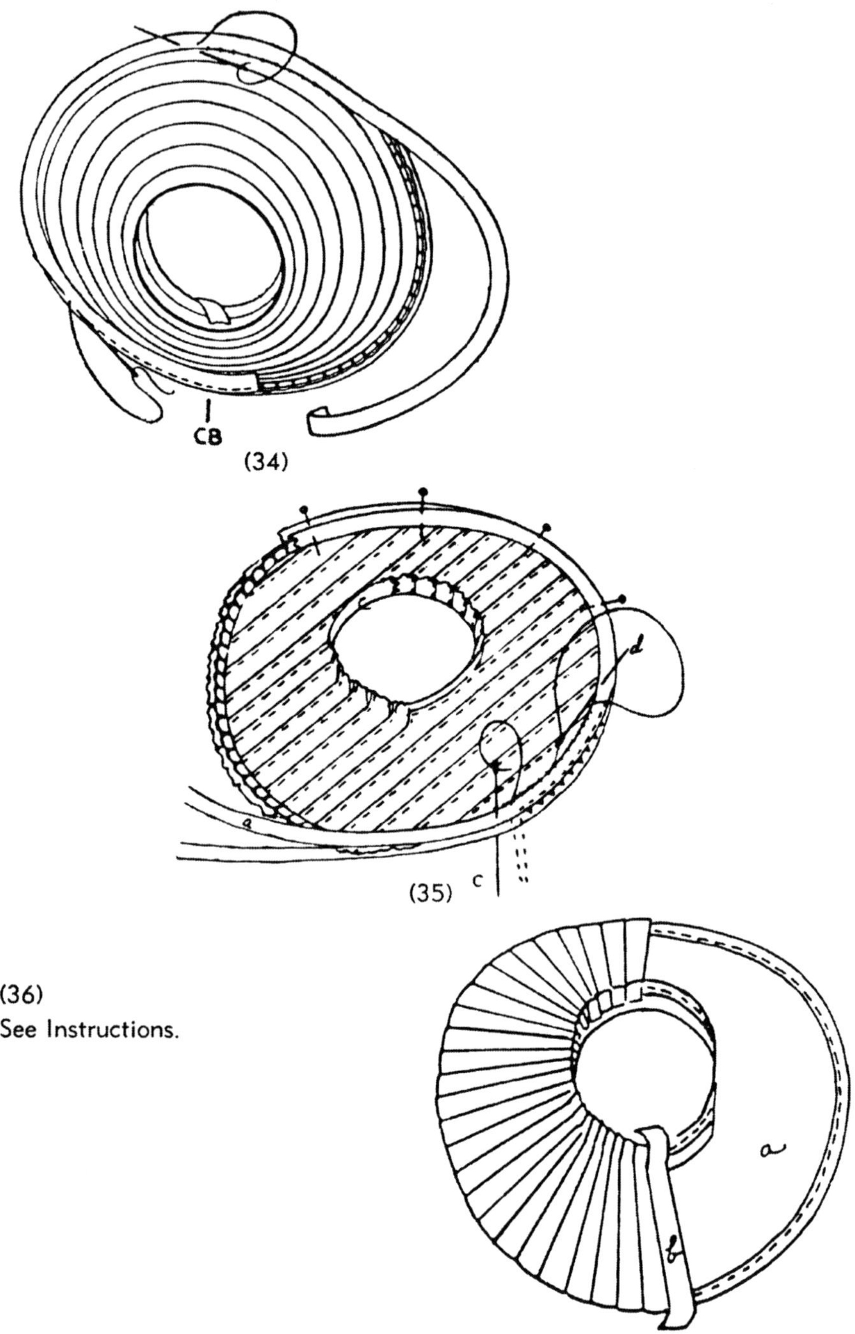

(36)
See Instructions.

(34)

After brim is pressed, on wrong side measure a wire and pin ¼" from edge. Sew with buttonhole stitch. Lay a swirled length of braid over the wire, turn under at Center Back. Sew to hat on inside edge of braid with invisible back-stitch. On outside edges use a small running backstitch, but stab it through. Sew crown to brim. **Be sure** straw is dry, then size.

★ OTHER EDGES AND BRIM FINISHES

(35)

Notice horizontal direction in which the braid was blocked. Try vertical direc-tion, diagonal, horizontal or sunburst. In the case of Figure 35, the edges are cut and raw, so must be covered. Sew wire close to edge on top. Prepare covering braids as in Figure 34 for both top and bottom edges of brim, each braid extending out over blocked straw edge ⅛", or a little more. Sew "d" with invisible backstitch, "c" with small stab-backstitch.

(36)

Finish selvage edge of straw like Felt, Figure 16. Or lay steel wire or pliable wire in fold and **don't sew edge to brim,** or **sew edge to brim** using the back-stitch. The edge of a ravelling straw must be turned twice like the hem of a dress, or the edge can be covered, Figures 19, 20, 21 and 22, Felt.

★ FRAMES COVERED OR DECORATED WITH BRAID

(37)

Cut strips of braid or ribbon, and over frame "a," start at Center Back Head-size and turn over edge, following contour of frame from Headsize over brim. Turn about ¼" or a little more to underside of brim—"b." Pin. Note lap at Headsize turn is greater than outside edge. Keep outside edge lap about ⅛". This crown is open. Tack at Headsize and Brim edge, or sew through frame with machine. Underside must be faced, see Covering Frames. Lay in Headsize Band. DON'T use bulky straw for this method.

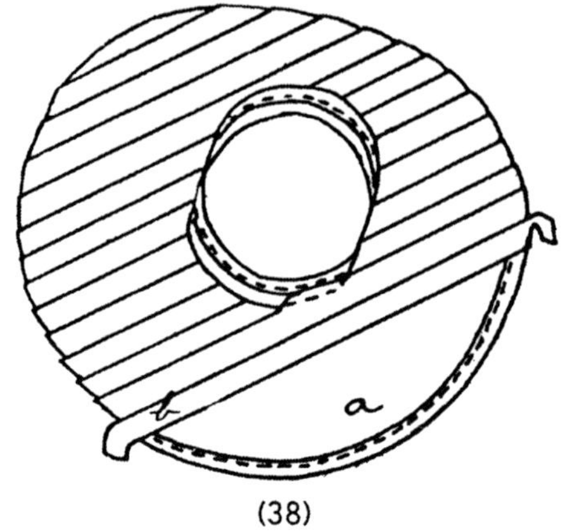

(38)

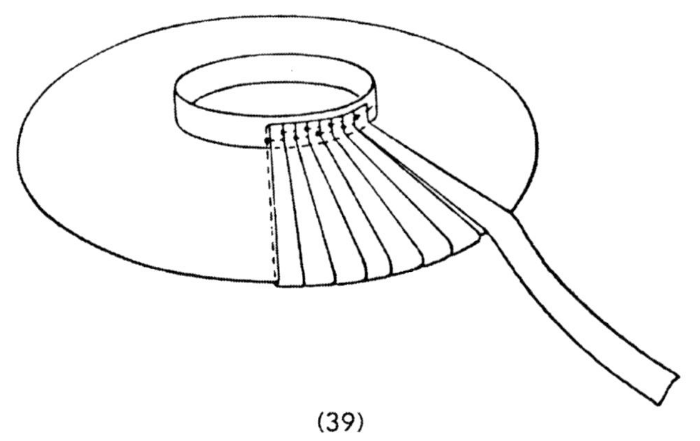

(39)

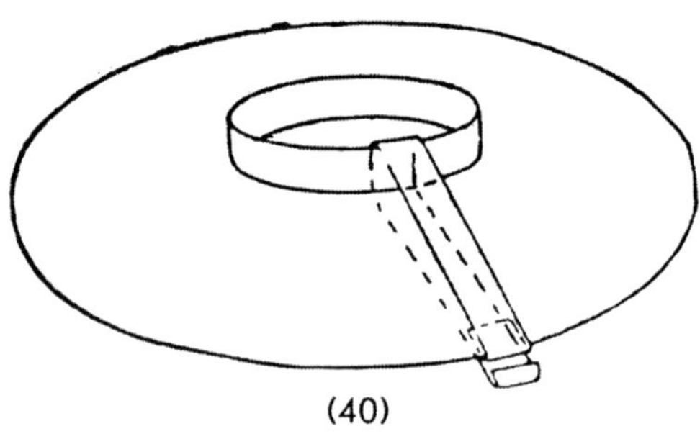

(40)

(38)

This principle is the same as described in Step 37, except the direction in covering is diagonal. Note braid or ribbon "b" is turned under, as in Step 37, and is faced to cover frame "a." Or face underside first and turn ends under on top frame "a." The other end of braid or ribbon "b" is cut off just at the edge of frame "a." A facing is necessary on the other side to cover frame "a." Use a bias strip, stretch and sew at edge on braid side then turn to underside of frame. Set a crown over the Headsize. This frame is to be covered at Headsize so it must be finished with a crown or covered with adequate trimming.

(39)

Shows strips of braid or ribbon cut twice the width of brim plus allowance. Starting at Center Back, pin at Headsize, turning under at brim edge and up into Headsize. Pin. Sew only at Headsize, and let ribbon or braid lay loose. (Optional.) This is very nice for velvet or grosgrain ribbon and should be covered with a crown.

(40)

This is the same principle in reverse of Step 39. To start, turn end under at Center Back brim edge. Pin. Pull gently through Headsize and across Headsize upward extension, to brim edge. Turn end inside just to edge, sew with slipstitch at edge only, or continue with Step 41. . . .

(41)

Start at Center Back in same manner as Step 40—but NOTICE how top of braid or ribbon is held in, or indented, at Headsize. Turn at brim, pin and cut end off at brim edge, leaving allowance of 1¼" or 2". Continue. . . .

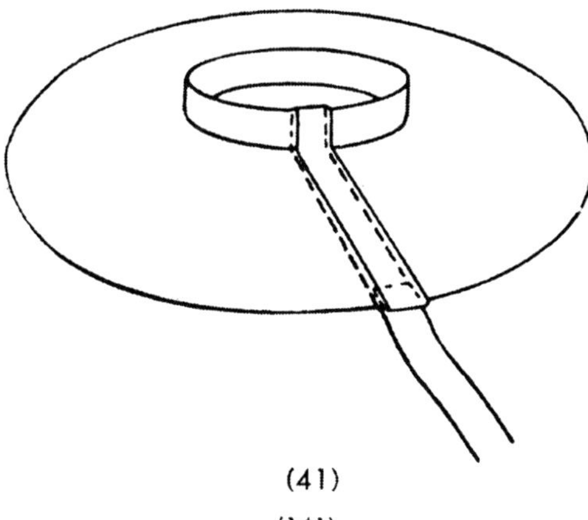

(41)

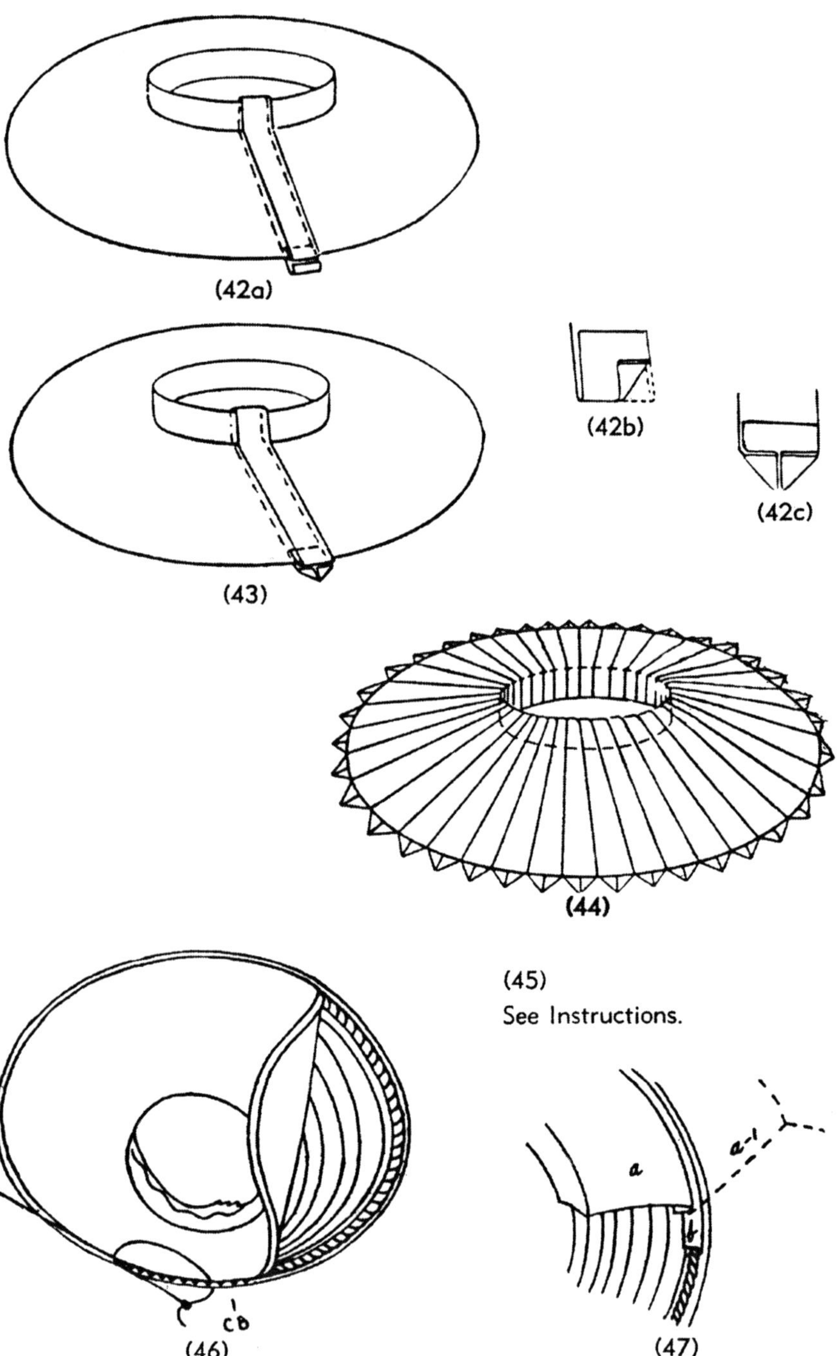

(42a)
(42b)
(42c)
(43)
(44)
(45)
See Instructions.
(46)
cb
a
a'
(47)

(42a, b & c)

Turn allowance end back. Experiment here, depending on width of braid or ribbon. Don't use too wide ribbon, as it is difficult to swirl and may be too bulky. For turning end, follow Figures "b" and "c." Pin, continue wrapping and pinning only at brim edge and Headsize indentation.

(43)

With length of end and size of turn decided, continue to wrap and drape, lapping at brim edge about ⅛". Braid or ribbon, grosgrain or velvet, are best suited to this principle.

(44)

After frame is draped, tack only at brim edge where each braid or ribbon is lapped at folded edges and Headsize indentation. Tack only where necessary.

★ FACING STRAW BODIES OR BRAID FRAMES

(45)

Refer to Figures 19-21, Covered Frames. Assume in this case the frame is straw, against which facing "a" has been glued, or "b" faced. The frame may be faced "b" on the convex side, or a separate straw shape over which "a" is faced and glued on the concave side.

(46)

Edge of straw brim must be selvage and wired, or raw edges must have wire inside turn-back fold as with Felt, Figure 16. Before facing, cut facing same as straw shape, allowing ½" turn-under at brim edge and at Headsize extension. Slipstitch at edge.

(47)

Turn swirled-bias facing "a-1" to "a" position. Or turn under pattern facing, on top at edge. For variation, an edge may be inserted, "b." See Figures 7 and 13 in the section on Covered Frames.

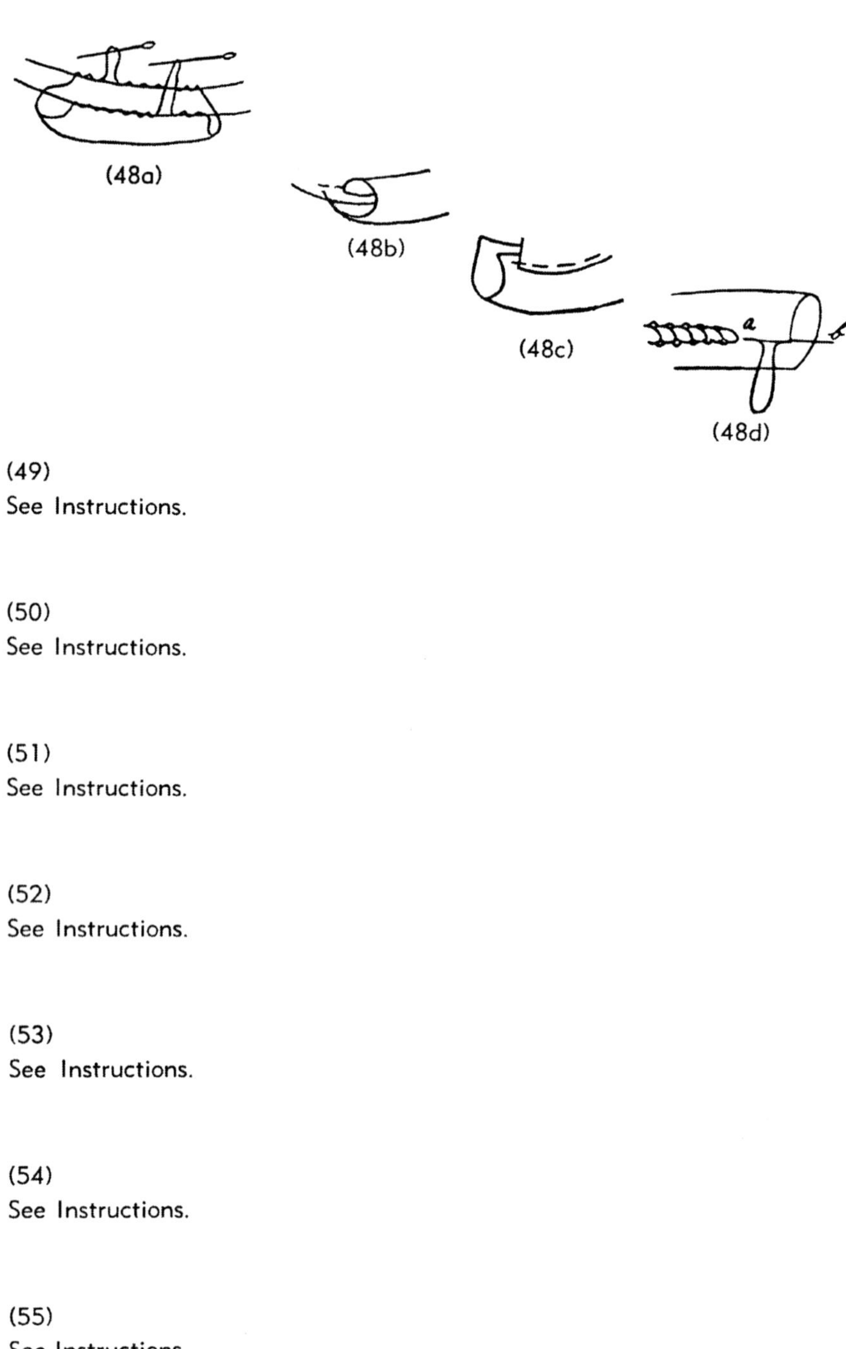

(49)
See Instructions.

(50)
See Instructions.

(51)
See Instructions.

(52)
See Instructions.

(53)
See Instructions.

(54)
See Instructions.

(55)
See Instructions.

(48a, b, c & d)

Pull drawstrings of a piece of woven braid, "48a." The center will cup and round out. Insert one edge between body-brim or braid-frame and fabric-facing, as in Figure 48b and 48c. Pull one edge only of braid, using draw-string "b" of Figure 48d. Insert as above, and on the top of braid "a," sew an additional smaller braid. Beads, etc., may be added.

Blocking Straw Bodies and Finishing Edges

★ THE CROWN

(49)
See Figure 1, Felt, for information on estimating the amount of material needed.

(50)
In blocking crown, if body is contrary and wiry and won't block to shape, tie below desired Headsize, Figure 5, Felt. Pull edge of crown down. Pin, and tie.

(51)
Follow Figures 9, 10 and 11, in the section on Felts if straw edge ravels easily on crown edge. Then leave an allowance and turn under, as in Figure 11. This edge needs no covering unless desired. If straw is closely woven, it can be cut on the desired Headsize mark. The crown sets down over the brim. This raw edge should be covered with a band or trimming.
For a straw calot or pillbox follow Figures 10 and 11, Felt, and add Head-size Band.

(52)
For other edge finishes, see Figures 19, 20 and 21, Felt.

★ THE BRIM
(53)
Sometimes hand blocking is all that is necessary in shaping a brim. In this case, consult Figure 2, Felt—Rolling Edge over Stuffed Roll.

(54)
To block straw brim, wet and follow Figures 13 and 14, Felt—although steam doesn't help much, because straw does not have as much elasticity as felt.

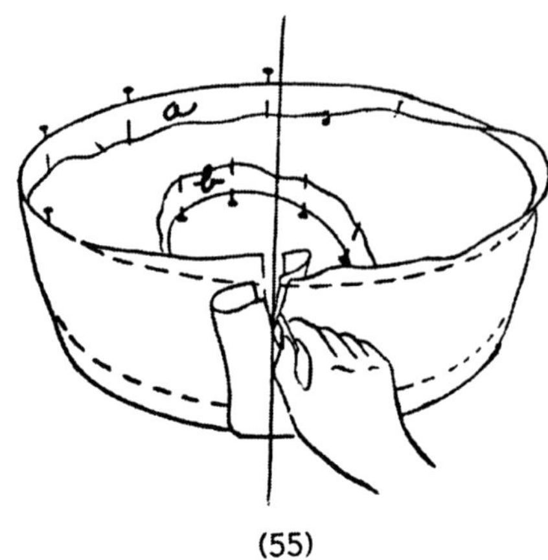

(55)

(56a)

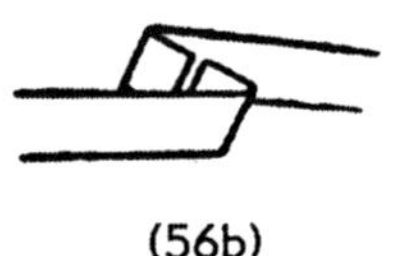

(56b)

(57)

(55)

If the selvage or outside edge is to be used and the brim to be blocked is too
large around, continue in the same manner, pinning outer edge of straw
to block. Start at Center Front and work to Center Back on one side, and then
from Center Front work the other side, pulling vertically and horizontally.
Lap at center Back. Stretch string vertically. Leave allowance for seam. Cut.
Finish edge hems as Figures 16, 19, 20, 21 and 22, Felt. See instruction 36.

★ STRAW BRIM SEAMS

(56a & b)

Cut away surplus at Center Back, as in Figure 55, and allow ¾". Mark each
end at Center Back. Crease each end—one over, one under, at mark—so that
the ends can hook together. See Figure 56-a. After the ends have been
creased on the marked lines, Figure 56-b, trim the ends shorter to about
3/16" or ¼". Hook the two together and sew on each side, using invisible
backstitch.

(57)

OR—after the back has been lapped, Figure 55, and cut straight, with allowance, turn this allowance to wrong side of brim and sew by machine if
practical, or use small backstitch. Cut and leave allowance as narrow as
possible for a small narrow turn-under seam. These ends are raw and will
ravel, so turn ends under as in Figure 57. Sew these edges to brim, using
invisible backstitch.
For brim edges: See this section, Covering Frames and Felt.

★ STRAW CLOTH

If straw cloth is real straw, or fiber cloth, it can be wet and blocked, or
worked over a wire—Figure 17, Covering Frames.
Generally straw cloth, when factory made, is used to cover frames, and as
draping fabric. See Covering Frames, and Figures 27-30, Turbans.
Straw cloth can be cut and made into Pattern Hats. If it has enough body a
lining is not necessary. If straw cloth is flimsy, use a lining such as taffeta,
honeycomb or French crepe (optional), with an interlining of crinoline. Cover
all hat pins, as in Figure 24, Felt.

To sharpen hat pins, pierce through sand paper.

Size straw braids and bodies after hat is assembled. **Be sure straw is dry before
sizing.** Allow plenty of time for drying. Then trim, and sew Headsize Band.

Felt

When you buy a hat, the word "Original" on the label adds enough to the price to make your budget shiver and gasp its last. The reason is obvious —but very few of us feel we can afford "Original" models. Oh—but YOU can! HAT TACTICS shows you how every new hat you wear can be a "YOU Original"! A lovely hat, made especially for no one else in the world but **you**—by the one person who knows best what you want to wear—is a real thrill. And it's a thrill you can have whenever you're in the mood.

This chapter of HAT TACTICS deals with Felt——a fabric you wear from nine to twelve months of the year.

To RENOVATE a felt hat which has lost its shape, remove the trimming and brush the felt well. Dampen a cloth with a good commercial-cleaning fluid and rub over the hat evenly, removing spots as you go. After cleaning a white felt, rub it with a cake of powdered milk of magnesia. To restore the shape, hold hat over a teakettle with a press pillow on the underside against the out-of-shape part. Steam. Steam softens the sizing in felt and makes it easy to shrink or stretch. Push in one direction with left hand against the out-of-shape part and pat-press with fingers of right hand. Allow to dry. Size from the inside, and lure (see Luring details in the following chapter) from the top in one direction on the brim, and in a circular motion on the crown.

To REMAKE and RESTYLE an old felt hat, remove all trimming, wire, stitches, Headsize Band—everything. WASH in lukewarm-sudsy water—rinse in lukewarm water. If the color has spotted, or you wish to change the color, dye in a water soluable dye. Rinse well and dye while still wet.

Skirt felt is worked dry. It can be washed and repressed when remaking. It is too thin to block, but can be blocked if reinforced on the back side with an additional layer of skirt felt, or a layer of hat felt.

A blocked felt, pattern felt, etc., can be stitched for interest and decoration.

Don't be afraid to experiment! Try making over one of your brother's or husband's old hats. (It's a **very** good idea to get his permission first!) Then follow blocking procedure and sewing, as described on the following pages. . . . so get your materials—all your creative ability—and let's start. . . . .

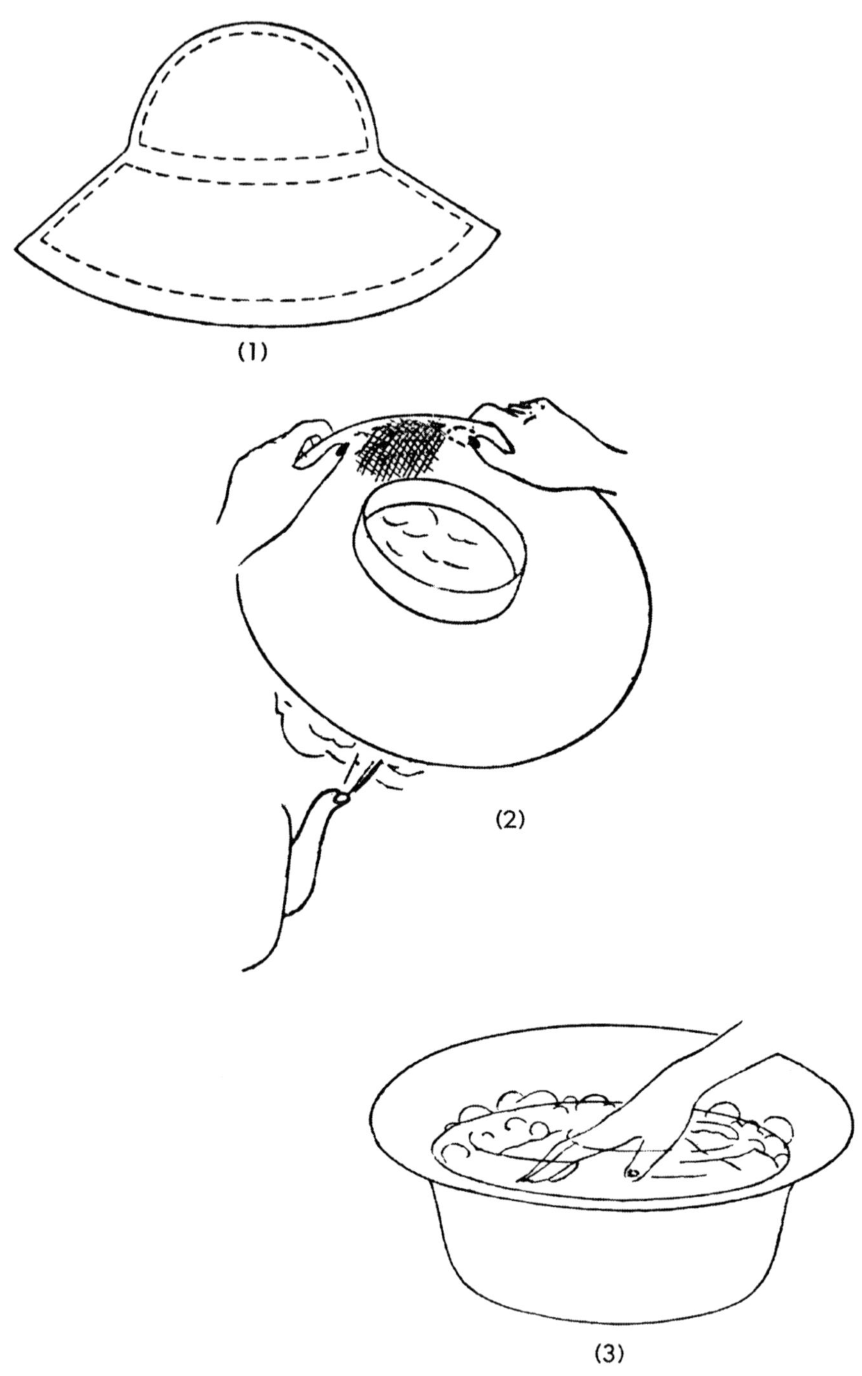

(1)

(2)

(3)

(150)

Felt

BLOCKING

Felt does not ravel, so there is no need to have extra allowances for turn-under.

Felt is available from millinery supply houses in all colors, and in fur or wool. Fur felt is much easier to work with and makes a nicer product. Large and medium bodies, hoods, plaques and length pieces or tubes called skirt felt, are the types of pieces available. The bodies are heavier in thickness and have a crown and brim shape. A hood is only a deep crown and a plaque is a flat disc. Skirt felt is used for pattern hats and draping, because it is soft, and thinner than bodies and hoods.

Refer to blocking, in sections on Straw and Frames. Also see Edge Finishes, in sections on Straw or Covering Frames.

(1)
Decide on Headsize depth. Hold felt body over crown block, and over brim block to estimate quantity of material necessary before starting to block. In the illustration, the dotted lines represent the Blocks.

(2)
Hand blocking is usually done with dry felt, when not much blocking is necessary. For a curved edge, over steam pull felt about one inch from edge with thumbs in an outward motion. Or iron edge over a stuffed roll of felt about 1″ in diameter and five or six inches long.

(3)
An **old felt** hat should be torn apart, all wire, trimming and stitching removed. Wash in soapy flakes, the same manner in which a sweater is washed. A new felt body or clean felt is wet only in lukewarm water. To absorb water, lay on an **old** towel. Sometimes dye will run and ruin a good towel.

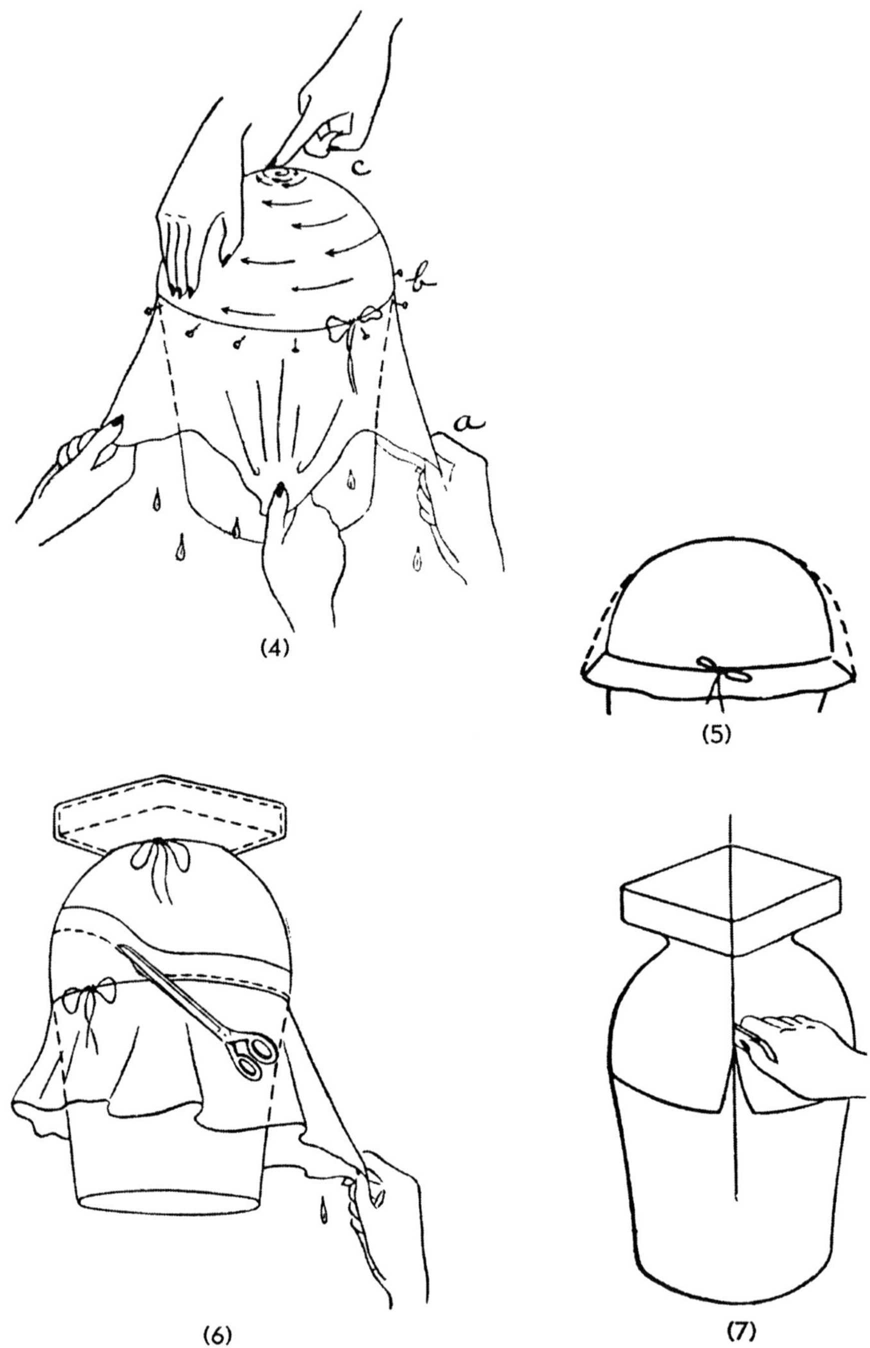

(152)

(4)

Then pull over either brim or crown to block. If over crown, first pull "a"
down well, and hold over steam as you work. Pin, and if necessary, tie a
string "b" around block below Headsize. Continue pulling and repin. Hold
over steam as you pull if it is difficult to stretch. When finished, start at
Center Top "c," and in a circular motion rub felt nap in one direction. Continue around. It will appear to have a thread grain.

(5)

String tied around the blocked felt helps hold felt in place when pulling out
surplus fullness, indicated by dotted lines.

(6)

Pull over block and tie. (See hand.) If block is an odd or unusual shape, a
string will help hold indentations in place. Mark the Headsize, and cut about
¾" below mark to allow for turn-up toward the inside.

(7)

It will be impossible to remove the shape when dry, without spoiling the
blocked felt. It is possible to buy collapsible wooden blocks but it will be
difficult to find the shape you have designed. So, to remove the felt, pin
a string at the top of the block to the felt at Center Back, and pull the
string down through the Center Back line. Cut straight, using a razor blade.

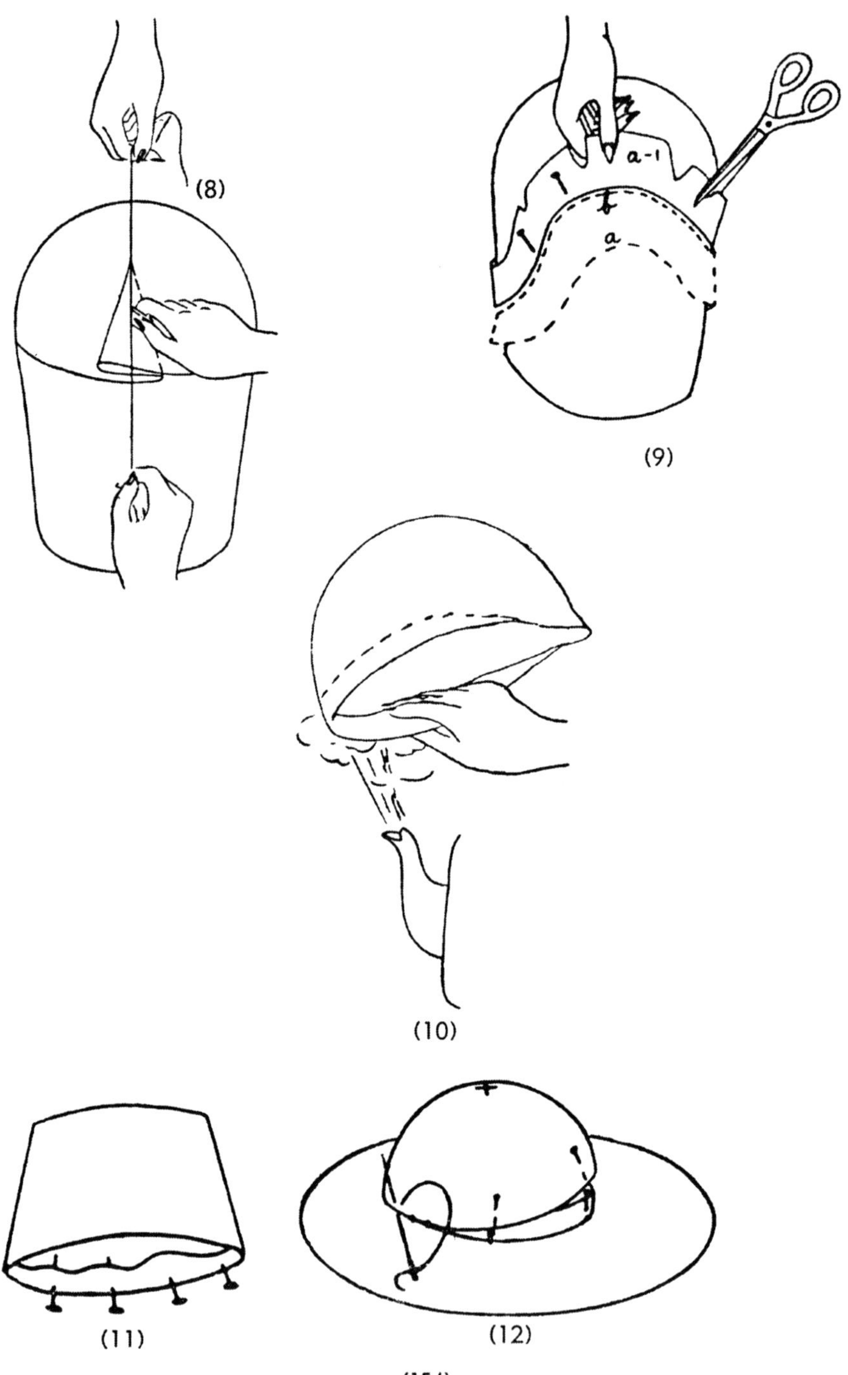

(154)

(8)

It is difficult sometimes, particularly in wool felt, to rid of surplus. Lap fullness and stretch string, starting at Center Top Back, through Center Back. Cut with a razor blade. Turn to wrong side, lay two right sides together and overcast.

(9)

Mark Headsize on right side with tailor's chalk. Pull bottom edge "a" up to "b," in "a-1" position. If felt doesn't stretch enough, snip. Remove, then trim off to ¾" from marked Headsize. Turn edge to inside on marked Headsize, and sew in Headsize Band.

★ CALOT, OR PILLBOX

(10)

Turning the ½" or ¾" allowance to the inside, press with fingers, after holding over steam.

(11)

Pin turned-up Headsize allowance. Add Headsize band.

★ CROWN AND BRIM

(12)

The edge of a felt crown used over a brim is cut off just on the marked Headsize depth. No allowance, and no turn to inside. Match Center Front, Center Back and sides of crown to Center Front, Center Back and sides of brim. Pin. Sew with invisible backstitch.

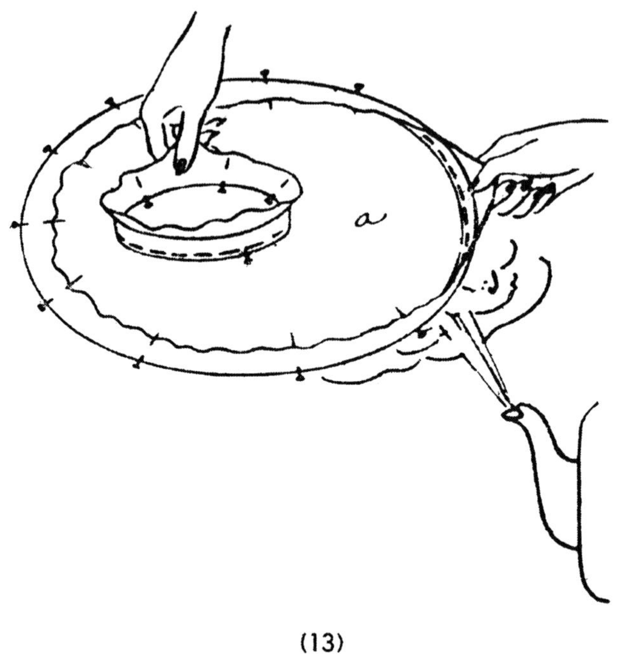

(13)

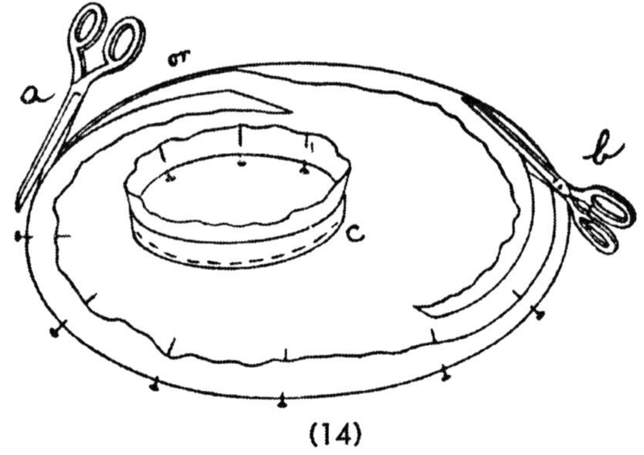

(14)

15
See Instructions.

★ BLOCKING THE BRIM

(13)

After the crown has been blocked, stretch remaining felt over Brim Block "a," pulling up at the Headsize. Pin and pull out and up at the outside edge. Pin. Steam, then pull, repin. This illustration shows hem blocked to the topside for an off-face hat. If worn forward, turn the hem to the underside. Rub nap in one direction, to appear as thread grain.

(14)

Allow about ¼" for hem allowance from turned edge. Cut evenly at "b." If a ribbon or covered edge is to be used, cut on the folded-over edge "a."

(15)

To block a strip of felt with seam at back, pull horizontally and vertically, and lap at back, as in Figure 55, Straw,—**no seam allowance.**

(16)

Lay wire in fold of felt, sew in with buttonhole stitch. Turn edge over wire, pin and sew with invisible backstitch. Trim headsize extension.

(17)

Check to see that nap of both crown and brim has been rubbed in the same direction. **Be sure it is dry.** Brush on sizing from inside crown in circular motion, and on wrong side of brim. See Figure 10, Blocks.

(18)

Figure 18 illustrates small press pillow which has had a small amount of thin oil (sewing machine oil is suggested) brushed on, and then held against a hot iron. Rub this heated-oiled pillow lightly in same circular motion over right side of felt. This is called LURING. For BURNISHED effect, paint right side in one direction with sizing or thinned-clear lacquer.

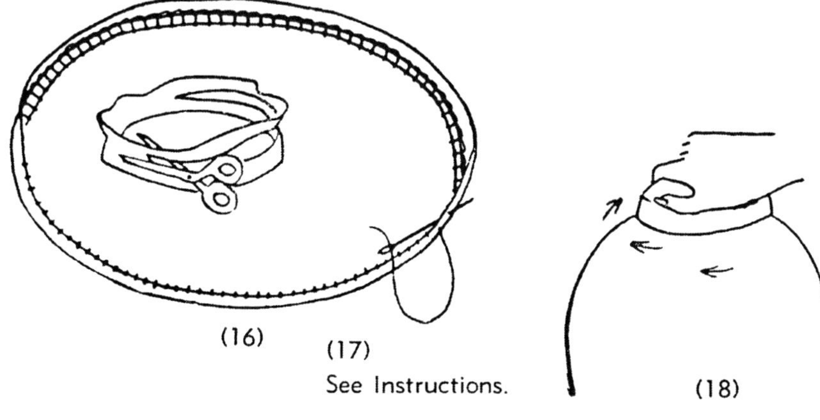

(16)

(17)

See Instructions.

(18)

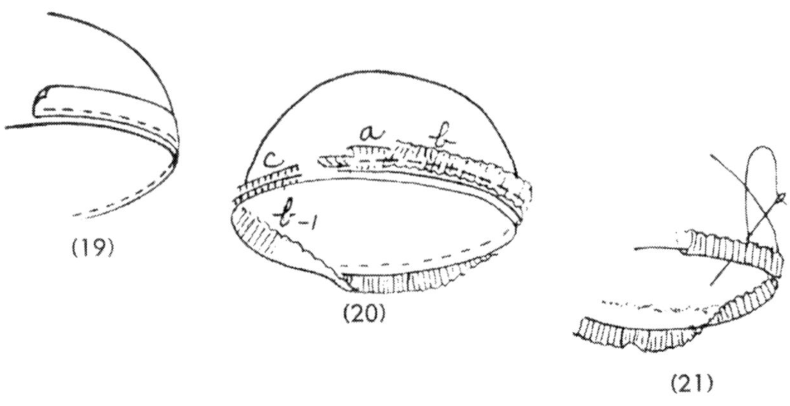

(19)

(20)

(21)

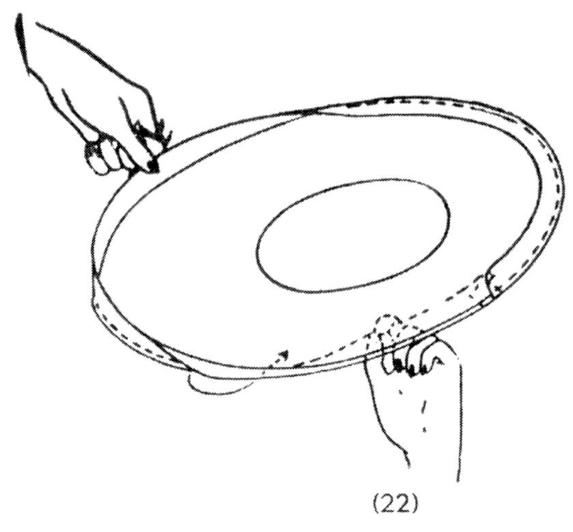

(22)

(23)
See Instructions.

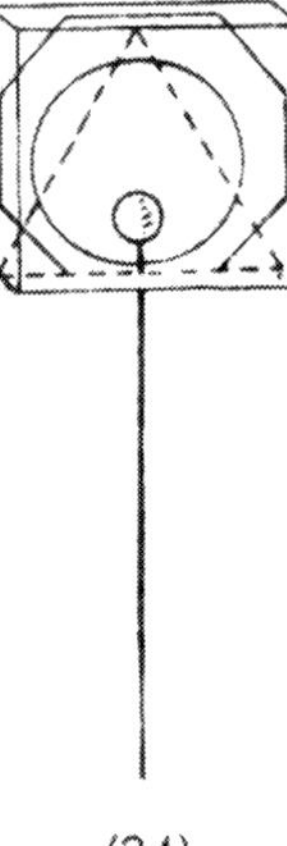

(24)

(25)
See Instructions.

★ OTHER EDGE FINISHES

The following figures can be used separately as calots or pillboxes, or as crowns over a brim.

(19)
On Headsize Edge, stretch and lay a grosgrain, satin or other ribbon. It may be necessary to swirl the ribbon if there is an irregular curve on the edge. Or use bias fabric. Pin and sew with small backstitch. Turn to inside, overcast. See Figure 7, Headsize Bands.

(20)
Fold ribbon about 1" wide, "a" and lay fold up, with both selvage edges at edge of felt. Lay "b" over folded ribbon. Sew these three edges through felt, using backstitch. Turn "b" over edge, as in "b-1." The finished edge appears as "c." It is optional to insert a cord in fold "a."

(21)
Fold a ribbon, swirl and lay over edge at Headsize. Pin and sew through both edges and felt edge, using invisible backstitch, sewing from the right side. Sew in Headsize band.

(22)
This edge is consistent with Figure 19. First swirl the ribbon. Start at Center Back, turn first edge back, continue around edge and lap loose edge over folded end. Sew less than 1⁄4" and more than 1⁄8" from edge. Use backstitch. Turn to other side. Sew ribbon edge to felt, using invisible backstitch, or leave loose. Bias flanges are often left loose in brim edges. Wired edge is optional.

(23)
For various edge finishings, refer to Straw, and Covered Frames.

(24)
Cover all your hatpins.

★ SKIRT FELT

(25)
For skirt felt refer to Pattern Hats, and Turbans. Skirt felt is worked DRY.

Turbans

There may have been a time when a Turban was known only as something an Arab wore on the sands of the Sahara. But since women discovered how exotic a Turban can be—how comfortable and adaptable—those days are gone forever!

You can drape a Turban in a jiffy, using almost any material you can think of. Wool for winter, sheers for summer, elegance for evening, the same gay print as your spring dress—the Turban is not only an all-year-round hat, it's an around-the-clock stand-by, too!

Before starting your Turban, decide on the style you will create. Know your head depth and the contour of Headsize edge.

The Turban Principle is: the foundation first, then draping over it. The Turban is always built on a foundation.

Foundation materials may be crinoline, French crepe, organdie, net, any thin, stiff or sized material, or just a headsize band.

The width of a draping fold depends on the weight of the fabric. If it is thin like georgette, the strip is cut wider. If it is heavy like satin or velvet, cut it much narrower.

REMEMBER that a Turban must appear light. **Don't over-sew,** and DON'T OVER-TACK. DON'T IRON—but pat-press.

After you understand the principle of Turbans, draping becomes a matter of creation. Here's where you can let your imagination go as far as it will.

If you've never fancied yourself as a designer, you may be pleasantly surprised. And if you've sometimes thought you'd like to try designing—here's your chance!

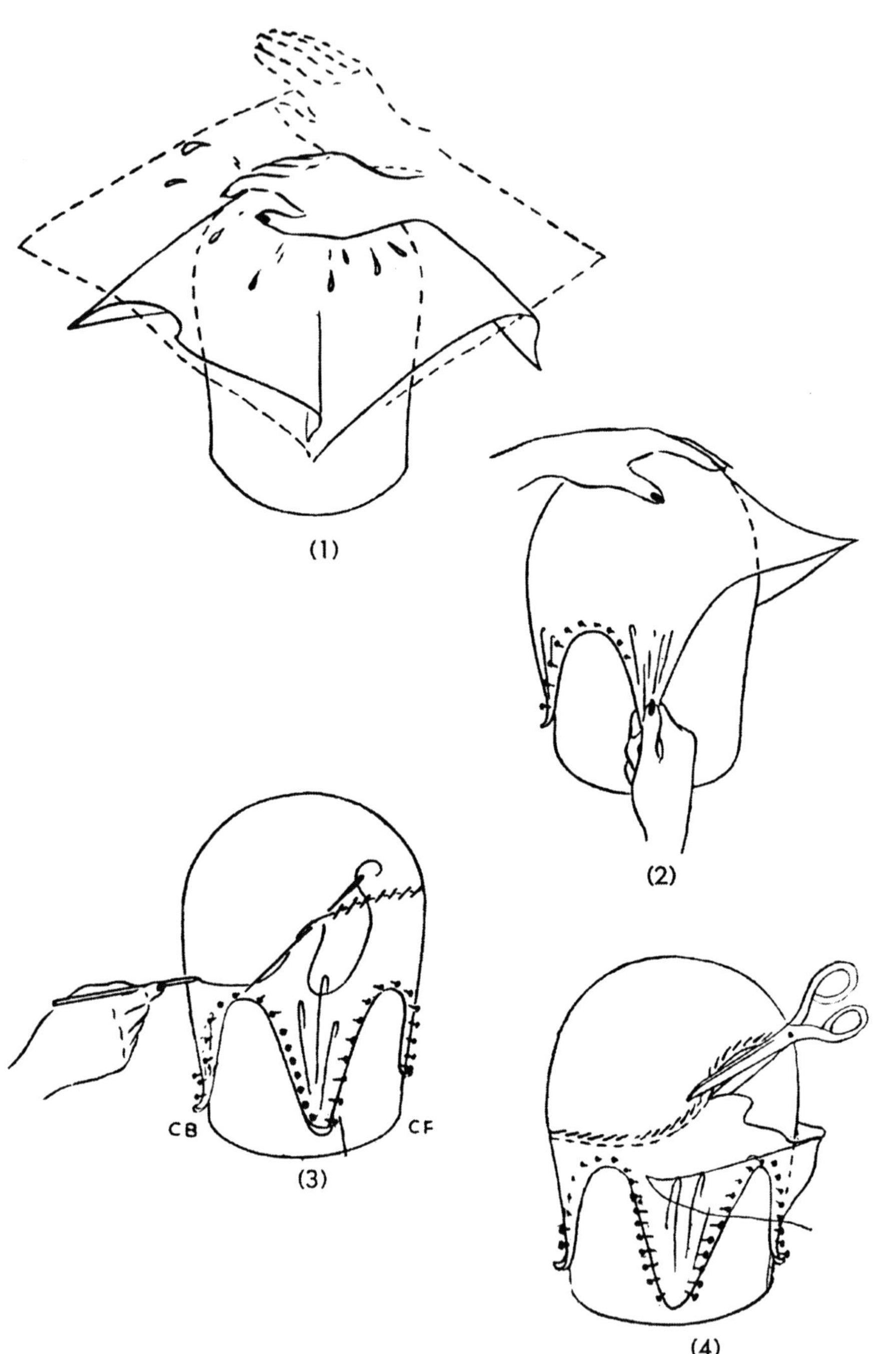

(1)
(2)
C B
C F
(3)
(4)

Turbans

★ PREPARING FOUNDATION

(1)

WET a 20-inch square of crinoline, and with corners at Center Front, Center Back, Right Side and Left Side, place on headblock.

(2)

Pull corners down, pin and tie with string. See Figure 4, Felts. Pin and allow to dry.

(3)

After foundation is dry, mark head depth on crinoline. Loosen partially from headblock and overcast-stitch the line. KEEP EDGE FROM STRETCHING!

(4)
Cut crinoline foundation, just below overcast stitches.

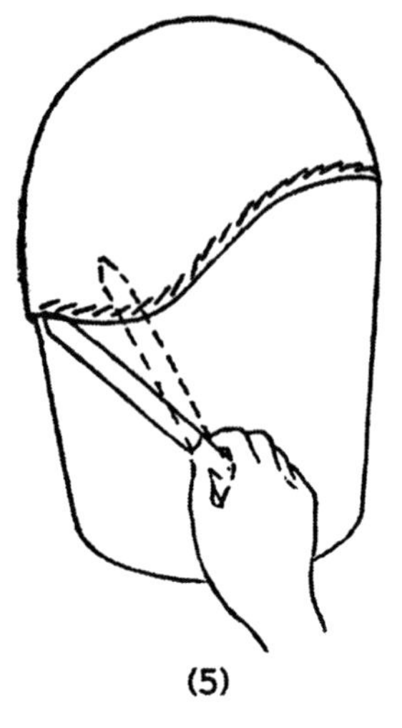

(5)

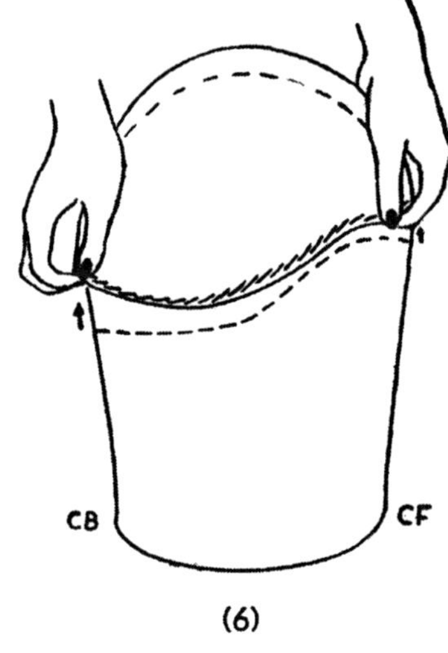

(6)

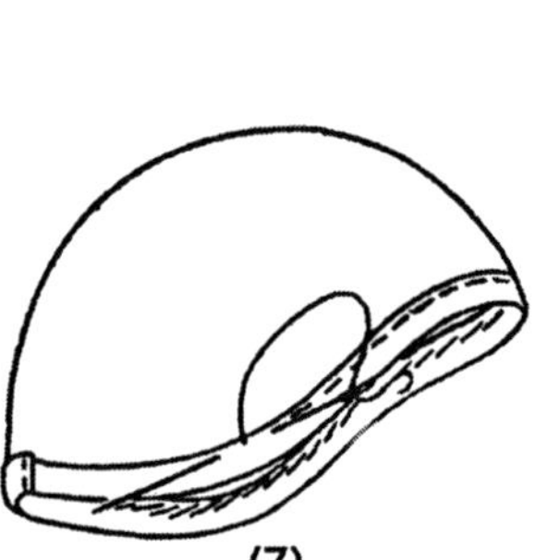

(7)

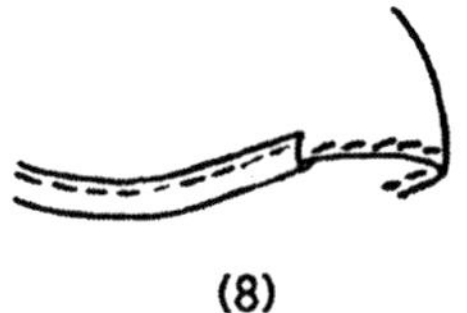

(8)

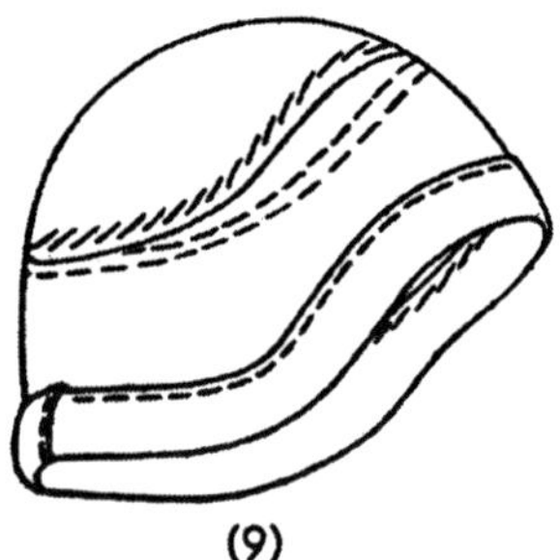

(9)

(164)

(5)

Use a pliable flat steel stay to loosen from headblock. . . .

(6)

OR—remove by turning wrong side out: "skin the rabbit"!

(7)

See Figures 1 and 2, Frames, for cutting bias-crinoline covering. Cut crinoline covering about 1'' or ¾'' wide, and fold lengthwise at Center, stretch
and swirl.

(8)

Slip folded bias crinoline over edge of foundation. Backstitch. NOTE: Overlap at Center Back is not turned under.

(9)

Stretch piece of covering over headblock with bias at Center Front. Steam.
Let dry, then remove to foundation. Overcast stitch the edge to foundation.

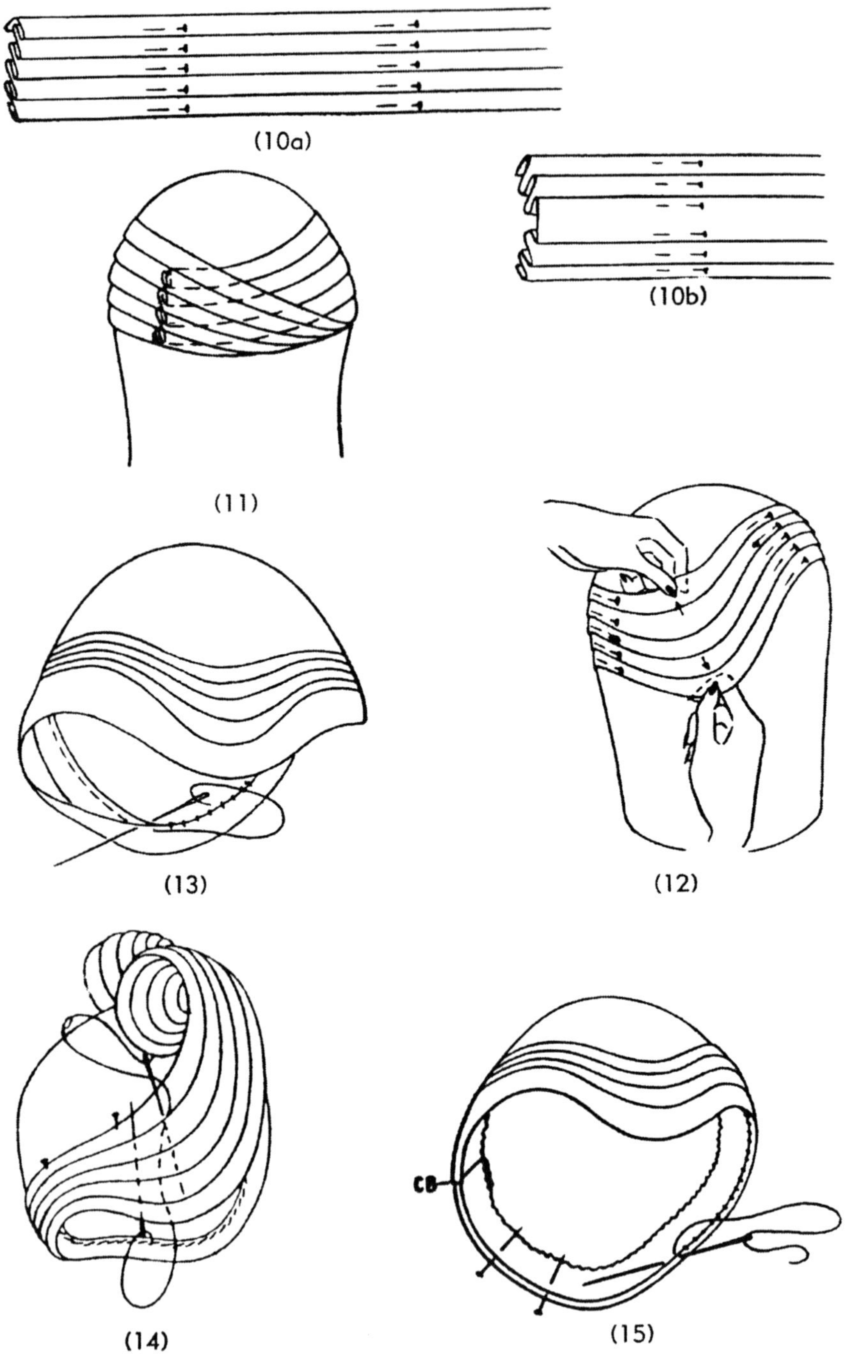

(10a)
(10b)
(11)
(12)
(13)
(14)
(15)
CB

★ DRAPING WITH ONE FOLDED BIAS STRIP

(10 a & b)
Prepare a bias or off-bias strip, folding in pleats or tucks (about ½" deep).
Pin the length at regular intervals. Note the directions of folding.

(11)
Fasten at edge of foundation, and start draping 1½" to 2¼" to left side of
Center Back. Stretch and drape. Pin. Remaining end overlaps first end at
Center Back, and tucks under foundation.

(12)
Adjust folds to desired width.

(13)
Bottom edge should be turned under foundation and overcast, catching raw
edge of bias crinoline, to raw edge of draping fabric.

(14)
Tack folded-bias fabric inside the folds ONLY where necessary—no more.
Remove pins, pat-press.

(15)
Before laying in Headsize Band, place foundation again on headblock and
mark on block around edge. Remove foundation and drape Headsize Band
above mark. Lay in Headsize Band, pinning. See Figures 9, 10 and 11, Headsize Bands. Sew Headsize Band with invisible backstitch.

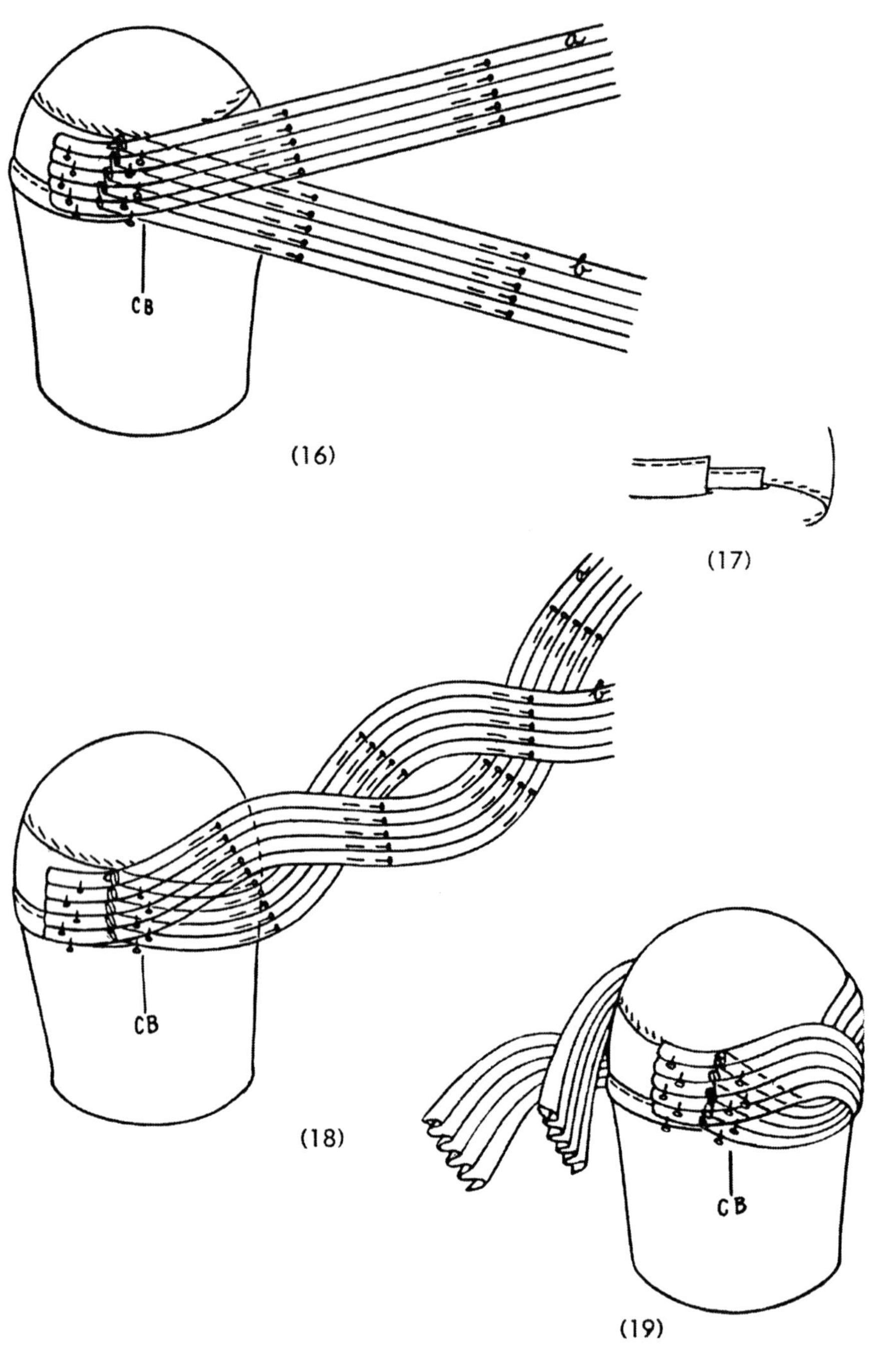

CB
(16)
(17)
CB
(18)
CB
(19)

★ DRAPING WITH TWO FOLDED BIAS STRIPS

(16)
NOTE distance each end is pinned to the left of Center Back. Note also the
tip position. "a" is pinned over "b."

(17)
If the TWISTED STRIPS are to lie on the outside and not turn under at
Headsize, the crinoline edge must be covered. Over the crinoline bias edge,
put a wider folded bias strip of draping fabric—about 2" wide.

(18)
Twist the two folded strips, stretch by pulling. Pin and adjust.

(19)
Illustration shows adjusted strips.

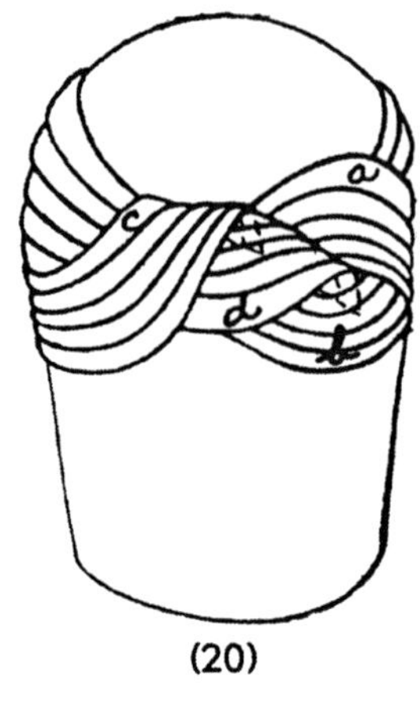

(20)

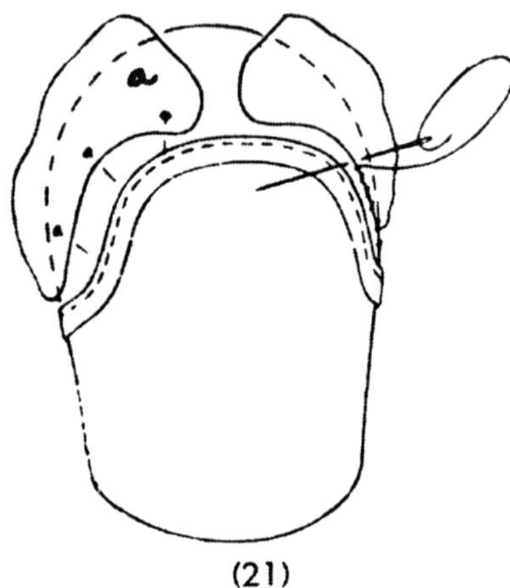

(21)

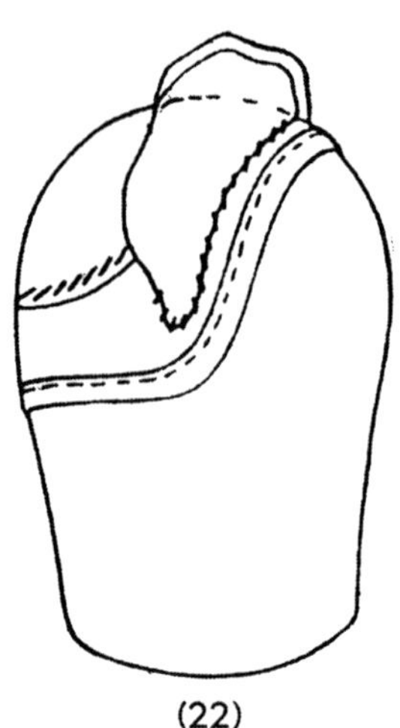

(22)

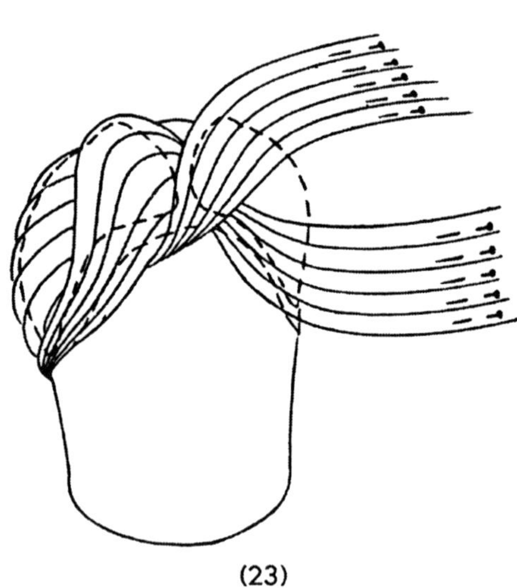

(23)

(20)

Center Back looks as though ends are continuous. "a" and "b" are starting ends. "c" is tucked over "d"—and "d" tucks into "b" to finish. Tack and pat-press.

★ DRAPING OVER PADDING

(21)

Pin cotton pads "a" to foundation and overcast.

(22)

Illustration shows folded bias crinoline binding over edge, tip and cotton pads.

(23)

Drape over padding. Stretch, pin and adjust.

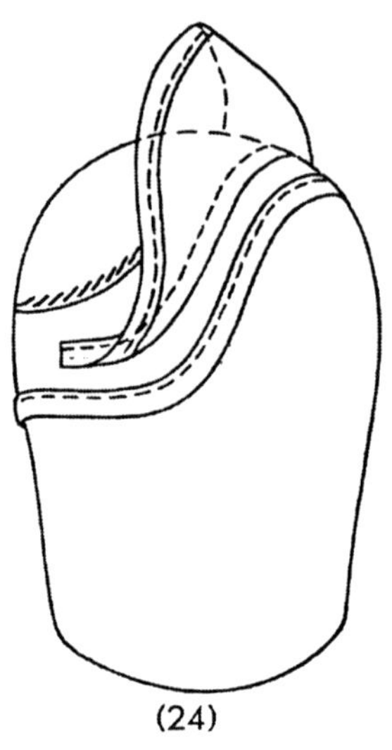

(24)

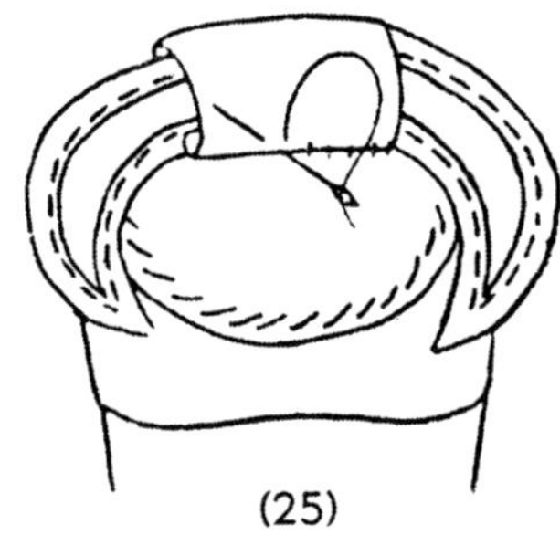

(25)

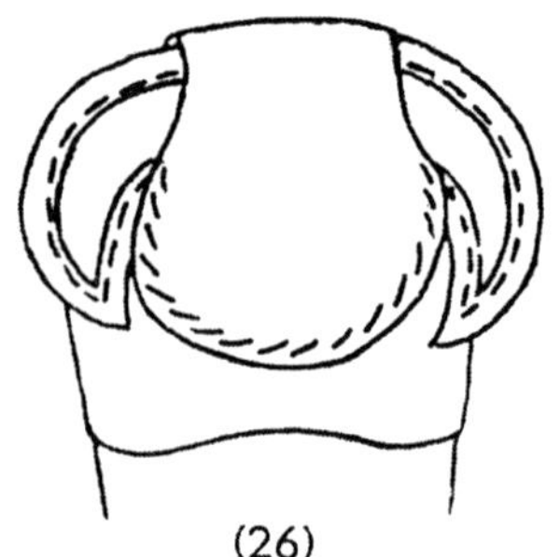

(26)

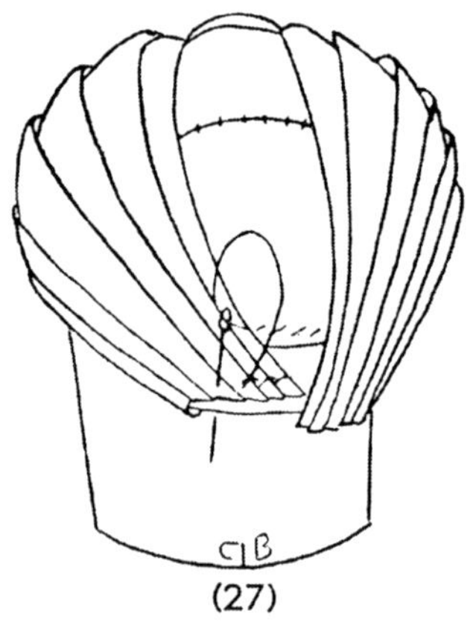

(27)

★ DRAPING OVER BUCKRAM OR CRINOLINE FRAME

(24)

Illustration shows bias-crinoline-covered edges of foundation, tip, and finished-blocked crinoline or buckram-partial brim sewed to foundation with back-stitches.

(25)

Sew on tip and any other under part, according to draping requirements. In other words, **where there is no draping, the part must be covered.**

(26)

Tip is cut in one piece, covering tip foundation and front and back of brim.

(27)

OR pin folded strip at Center Back, drape over front, stretch, pin and adjust. Bottom edge of cover strip turns under foundation. Sew beginning end, lap finishing end over first end, and tuck under foundation.

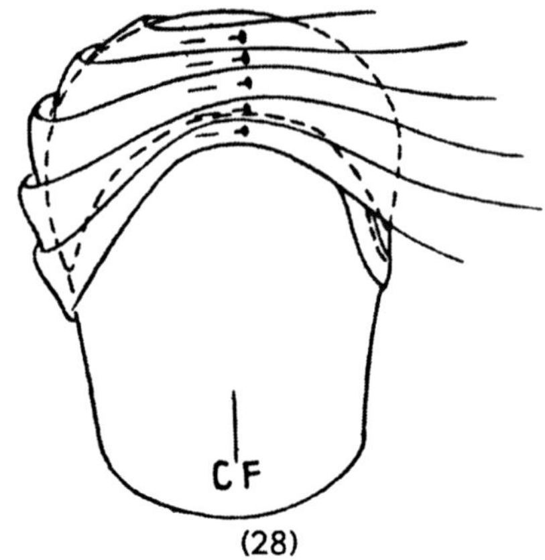

(28)

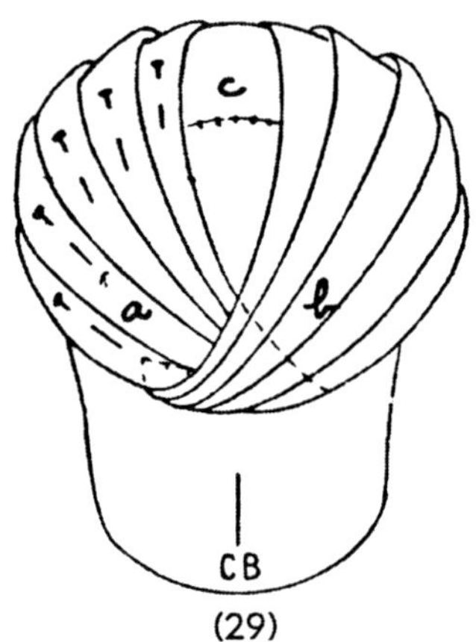

(29)

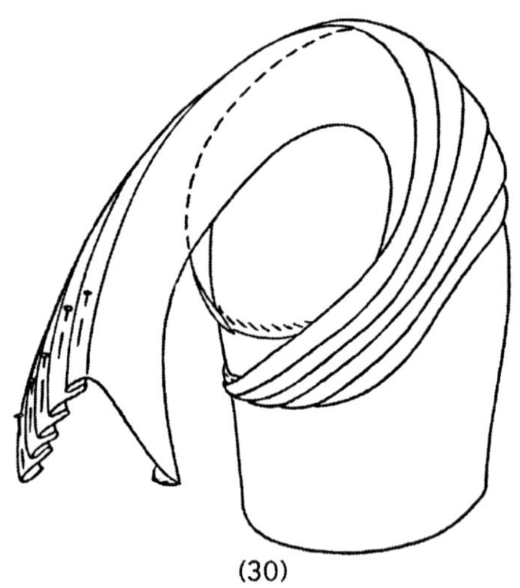

(30)

(174)

(28)

Front view of Figure 27. Tucks turn upward.

(29)

Finished back. ''a'' is pinned, strip draped and sewed. See Figure 27. ''b''
laps over and under foundation. ''c'' is tip. Lay in Headsize Band.

(30)

OR the folded bias strip may begin at Center Back and cover both front and
back of buckram brim, with the edges turned under. This strip should first
be blocked over a similar shape.

Trimming

Although the ideal face is oval, most of us find we are not gifted with this perfection, and we range from short to long, round to square, triangular to inverted triangular, diamond to heart shaped. To determine the shape of your own face, sit before your mirror, **close one eye,** and with your lipstick or eyebrow pencil, trace your reflection **on the glass** from the hairline. Then proceed to draw from your headline, which is the top of your head. Usually, we judge the shape of a face by the portion framed by the hairline. Now you can cover your tracing with tissue paper, and accurately record exactly in which category of face-shapes your face belongs. However, once you have decided on the shape of your face, you can correct irregularities, and make your own face-shape seem more symmetrical through optical illusions. These illusions or tricks can be achieved artfully by clever coiffures, careful make-up, and of course, with the hat that is RIGHT for YOU.

Now, the basic hat, while it must have fundamentally pleasing lines, good balance, elegant proportion and subtle rhythm, also requires a CENTER OF INTEREST or TRIMMING. Consider your untrimmed hat as a basic melody, and let the decoration be the counterpoint to enhance the harmony. All eyes will be riveted on your CENTER OF INTEREST, so take care that you first choose a becoming shape for your hat, then marry it to the perfect trimming, and you'll have a lovely unit. Of course, the ornament also must be well balanced and in proportion, because an unfortunate choice of trimming can spoil an otherwise perfect head-dress.

Hats are perhaps the most emotional garment in a woman's wardrobe, and remember, your hat will awaken emotion in your admiring observer, too. Silhouette and direction, shape and material, texture and color, size and placement of decoration can, and do, provoke definite feelings. For instance, a large hat may be dreamy and romantic; it may be flaring and restlessly exciting. And a small hat crushed close to your head, cuddled on your curls, may be youthful and chic, provocative and frivolous. Irregular shapes can be eccentric or exotic. A tailored hat can be austere, demure or dashing. There is simply no limit to the moods you can create.

As in any of the other arts, you can convey an illusion of motion or a static impression by the direction you choose to tilt your head-dress, and the manner in which you fasten the trimming. If you place your hat exactly vertically or horizontally, the effect is starkly severe, with little movement. A diagonal angle introduces motion, and immediately creates a more lively impression. Perhaps you wish you were taller? You can add inches to your height by using a vertical ornament to sweep the eye upward. Would you like to make your face seem longer? Simply place your decoration high on your basic bonnet, and you'll be surprised at the result. If you wish to cut down height, a horizontal arrangement of trimming will produce this desired illusion, and if you fasten it low on your hat, you can reduce the length of your face, and shorten height.

Of course, shape of ornament is important too. Large round flowers or globular ornament suggests opulent elegance. Small circular shapes sparkle with youthful effervescence. The most feminine shape is the soft oval, while the spiral form is alive with graceful movement, exciting in its ever-changing views. Eyes will be attracted at the convergence of lines and contrasting shapes and shades, so let's consider briefly what you can do with color.

Did you know light tones appear to advance, or come forward, and dark tones recede, or give depth? Then, too, color is divided into two main cate-gories, warm and cool. In the first group are the tawny shades——yellows, oranges and reds with their intermediaries. These are considered stimulating, and provide good mental resistance against dreary weather. The cool colors range through blues, greens and violets, and many women feel crisp in these restful shades even on the hottest day. You can see there is more psychology to color than meets the eye.

Veiling is one of the most popular among trimmings. Fine misty veiling, net and maline are all delightfully soft and filmy. They are so feminine, and you will be delighted with their flattery. Coarse veiling is more sleek and tailored, but equally dramatic in its place. You can swirl a straight veil by pulling one of the straight edges over a circular form or pattern. Gather the other edge, then pull the gathered edge to where you want it, iron with a damp cloth or steam iron, and size.

You can do tricks with flowers too. If you wear them perpendicularly at the front of your hat, they seem pert. If you decide not to use them this season, don't throw them away——tie a thread around the blossoms to hold the shape and store them. Should they look limp and tired, restore them by rubbing a small amount of thinned gelatine (which has been brought JUST TO A BOIL) very lightly from inside the petals. Use your thumb and fingers to shape when necessary.

Feathers may be renovated also by rinsing them gently in a good com-mercial cleaning fluid. If you need a feather of a different color——don't buy a new one——dye your old ones. It's fun and so easy. Mix oil paints in a small container like a teacup with a little cleaning fluid to make a smooth paste. Then add and mix thoroughly a bath of cleaning fluid, and submerge the **cleaned** feathers. Presto——New Trimming! Drooping ostrich plumes can be curled to new life by pulling each separate feather against the dull side of scissors.

Whatever type of trimming you decide to use should depend on your own face and figure, your personality, and, of course, the type of hat with which you are working. Decoration is so versatile; it may match the basic hat, or it may be in complete contrast. Don't oversew your trimming. Make it look light and airy. When using a flower tie-tack it lightly with strong milli-nery thread. Let it appear to grow there.

Experiment by copying hats you've admired in windows and fashion magazines. Study well-dressed women carefully. It won't be long before your imagination and skill will create the perfect hat for you!

GLOSSARY

BIAS SEAM—A seam sewed on the straight thread of bias cut fabric, but lays on a diagonal slant . . .

BLOCK—A wooden, or hardened form over which blocking is done . . .

BLOCKING—Molding a fabric to a wooden or hardened form . . .

CB—Center Back, CF—Center Front, CT—Center Top . . .

DRAFTING—Drawing patterns with compass and ruler . . .

DRAPING—Copying or designing by laying tissue paper or fabric directly on the hat. See Patterns . . .

FLANGE—A swirled or straight fabric to be attached to the hat . . .

FOUNDATION—The underpart of the hat. A turban is draped over a foundation . . .

GORE—Of triangular shape . . .

HEADBLOCK—A wooden head, shaped or unshaped—can be bought in sizes 21, 21½, 22, 22½, and 23 . . .

HEADSIZE—The inches around the head where the base of the hat rests.

HEADSIZE BAND—Ribbon or flange sewed to inside headsize of hat . . .

HEADSIZE BEND OR TURN—Right angle turn of side-crown to brim . . .

LS—Left Side . . .

LURING—Pressing the nap of felt in one direction, then rubbing lightly in the same direction with a small press pillow (small amount of thin oil has been applied to the press pillow then held against a hot iron) . . .

OFF-BIAS—Not true bias . . .

PAT-PRESS—Pressing by use of steam, and patting with fingers . . .

PRESS PILLOW — Small stuffed pillow (about 3″ x 3″, round or square) . . .

RS—Right Side . . .

SIDE CROWN—Upright portion of crown . .

SIZING—A liquid which fills and stiffens material. Prepared sizing can be bought from Millinery Supply Houses. To harden Blocks use prepared heavy sizing, "U BLOCK IT" or shellac, clear varnish, clear lacquer, or enamel. Gelatine brought to a boil and diluted is an excellent straw sizing. Press after gelatine sizing has dried. Clear lacquer may be used as sizing if properly diluted. Use a thinner. Straw sizing is very thin, and Felt sizing is slightly heavier . . .

STRAIGHT THREAD GRAIN—With the straight thread . . .

STRAIGHT SEAM—Sewed on thread grain or on bias . . .

SWIRL—To twist or whirl as applied to a ribbon, braid or flange.

TABS—A flap or tag (cut at headsize for extension) . . .

THREAD GRAIN—In the direction of the threads, vertical or horizontal . . .

TIP—The top of a hat, especially in Sailors and Turbans . . .

TRUE BIAS—Intersection of vertical and horizontal threads—diagonal to the texture . . .

UNDERFACING—Facing placed on the underside . . .

WIRE FASTENER—A small round metal split tube which holds two ends of wire together . . .